DARE TO DREAM

Published by Brolga Publishing Pty Ltd
ABN 46 063 962 443
PO Box 12544
A'Beckett St
Melbourne, VIC, 8006
Australia

Email the publisher: markzocchi@brolgapublishing.com.au
Email the author: peter_clif@bigpond.com

National Library of Australia
Cataloguing-in-Publication data
        Dare to dream / Peter Cliff.
        9781925367041 (paperback)
        Subjects: Motivation in adult education.
                Adult education students--Australia--Biography.
        920.710994

Printed in Australia
Cover design & typesetting by Wanissa Somsuphangsri

BE PUBLISHED

Publish through a successful publisher. National distribution, Macmillan
& International distribution to the United Kingdom, North America.
Sales Representation to South East Asia
Email: markzocchi@brolgapublishing.com.au

DARE TO
DREAM

PETER CLIFF

To my mother
Jean Stuart Graham Dawson

AN INSPIRATION

Never say "no" to a dreamer.

Peter Cliff's life story proves anyone can achieve, despite formidable hurdles early in life.

A nagging inner voice, after being told "anything is possible if you work for it," changed his life.

The voice kept telling him, as he worked through a succession of low-prospect jobs, that he should be doing something more challenging. He set his sights on becoming a doctor. Forget the fact he had not qualified for university study.

Doggedly sticking to a daunting work and study regime, he got to university and was diverted to a dentistry course.

Lack of money was a problem but Peter married and raised a family, finding innovative ways to fund his studies, including driving taxis, doing agricultural contracting work, running businesses and as a mature-age student achieving his goal of dental practices in country areas.

With the help of his former wife and their two sons, he ran a dairy farm and cattle stud and later a successful lavender farm where he developed harvesting and distilling equipment eventually bought to life through visits to historic sites in Europe and the US. More recently he has spent time doing voluntary charity dentistry work in Papua New Guinea.

His insights from these trips are compelling.

In short, Peter's life story is an inspiration.

Ed Featherston
Former senior journalist with The Herald and Weekly Times

CHAPTER 1
STAN

We were excited. Our father was coming home from the war. My brother Bruce, 18 months, and me, a 3 year old, clung to the front gate of our home in Newport. Dad came into view wearing his uniform and carrying a large drawstring kitbag over his shoulder. He seemed pleased to see us although I was to learn later he had been drinking heavily. So began the saga that changed our blissful domestic life to one of watchful fear.

My grandfather, Emanuel Cliff, and my grandmother Anne, immigrated to Australia from Bradford, England, in 1920 with their children, Stanley, 9, and Majorie, 6. For three years Emanuel ran a small bakery in Kongwak Gippsland after which he moved to Williamstown before returning to England in 1927. Within a year, he returned to Australia and bought his own business, a rundown bakery in a dilapidated weatherboard building in Williamstown. Stanley, as a boy of 16, began work as assistant clerk in a law office but later became an apprentice to his father. Emanuel replaced the wooden bakery with a substantial double story brick building. The expansion was helped by a small legacy from his wife Anne's family, the Thornton's of Bradford, England. The shop provided an outlet for his popular pastry products and the bread was delivered in a horse and cart.

1938, Stan was 27. After a brief courtship, he became engaged to Jean Graham, the only daughter of Anne Graham, a divorcee who had a dressmaking business in Spotswood. Anne was a controlling advocate for the engagement of Jean into the Cliff family because of the Cliff success. Jean married Stanley Cliff in Scotts Church Melbourne on the 18th March, 1939. At 18 and still far from certain about her feelings for him, Jean was a reluctant bride, coerced to marry 27 year old Stanley by her mother.

Following a subdued honeymoon to Healsville, Stan and Jean moved into the pleasant painted weatherboard house owned by Emanuel in Oxford Street, Newport. Stan continued working in the bakery, a bike ride away.

January 1941 was not a propitious time to be born. The Second World War had begun and although my arrival was welcomed by my mother, my father did not share her joy. I was accorded the status of the 'The Bastard'. This unwarranted slur on my mother was without foundation - my arrival was simply inconvenient to him.

Unfortunately, prior to my birth, the relationship between Stan and his father had deteriorated after a huge argument the result of which saw my mother and her 'Bastard' being told to stay away from the bakery. Stan's response was to join the army without consultation with Jean. It was war time and his movements in the army were vague and unknown beyond references to Brisbane. The anonymity suited Stan for he kept little contact with Mum throughout his service apart from a brief period of leave when he relieved his father who had fallen in the bakery and broken a leg. This was allowed because the bakery was considered an essential wartime service. On my grandfather's recovery, Stan returned to his army assignment in Brisbane.

The argument between Stan and his father after the marriage evidently arose from lies told by Stan to his father. He suggested that in some way suggested that Mum had stolen cash from the business along with some missing work clothes. The very idea was enough to alienate the Cliffs who consequently only provided minimal support or co-operation to Mum. They were yet to realise that Stan was a habitual liar and the more probable suspect for the irregularity. The office lady, Jean Simmons, who was in a position to know, later maintained the allegation was baseless and cowardly of Stan, who to avoid accepting blame, joined the army.

In 1944, Stan was discharged from the army. He returned to buy the bakery business from Emanuel who had retired to a large bush block in Tecoma, next to the Ferny

Creek in the Dandenong Ranges. We moved into the house vacated by my grandparents. Arguments between my parents began. Stan would yell loudly and insist on radical changes to the business. Mum, wishing to be cautious, preferred a 'wait and see' approach to which Stan responded by dramatically locking the desk and denying her access to the details of the business. He was going to show everyone how clever he was.

The bakery ceased making cake and pastry products. The shop verandah was removed and the interior space incorporated into the house. Thus a lucrative trade was forfeited in favour of expanding bread supply. By 1947, the number of bread carts had grown from two to six with as many drivers. To accommodate the bread carts, a large shed was built with undercover access to the bakery. To fund the expansion and provide for the additional staff, Stan borrowed money from the flour mills in addition to the debt owed to his father for the business. Consequently, although busy, profitability was marginal.

I recall being terrified by the savagery of the arguments that sometimes became violent. The abuse, which for me had the quality of loud incessant roaring, became indelibly etched in my memory. A common theme of my father's tirades was that I was not his son and he frequently referred both directly and indirectly to me as the 'useless fucking bastard'. It was my earliest persistent memory and it confused and upset me. I found it impossible to do anything to please him. He found fault with everything my mother or I did, and yet, to others he maintained an effusive friendliness.

The loud roaring would begin with accusation and progressively became threatening, sometimes followed by thuds and cries of pain. Mum or I were the recipients. I had no idea why. I was frightened, isolated and unable to trust him.

Fortunately, Dad worked long hours.

When especially busy, Grandfather Cliff would appear to assist and stay the night. He always greeted us warmly but found it difficult to engage in conversation because he was deaf. He spoke with a broad accent and his manner was courteous and engaging. Below wispy eyebrows his brown eyes twinkled with pleasure. I felt close to him and wished fervently he would straighten out his son. Emanuel was more than capable of doing so but he remained unaware and disbelieving of his son's behavior. This gentle successful man neither drank alcohol nor used foul language. He had attained what he wanted by hard work and perseverance.

In 1946, I started primary school at the North Williamstown State School. Like all kids then, I walked unsupervised to school. I enjoyed the walk because it enlarged my experience of the world. Overhead were formations of military aircraft still flying about. I became adept at identifying Spitfires, Wirraways, Beauforts, Catalinas and other military areoplanes. On the roads were a fascinating variety of early model cars, motor bikes and many horse drawn vehicles.

The atmosphere of the time was uncertain with the emerging issues of the post war period. Some families had lost loved ones and were struggling with the consequences. Many men had been wounded and were now finding it difficult to readjust in society. There were many hotels in Williamstown all doing a roaring trade. The Prince Albert Hotel was on the corner of Albert Street, only yards from the bakery. On Saturdays the bookies and helpers would huddle in doorways and the lanes, ever watchful for police who seemed reluctant to find them. Some food and clothing items still required coupons to buy and many building materials were in short supply. Even our teachers were older since the younger people had been required for the war effort. An air of optimism and hope was building. There was a release of energy as the country confronted a future that needed more of every resource, especially of its people.

The school day started with an assembly presided over by the principal. The National Anthem was sung and announcements were made before we marched off accompanied by boys playing the drums to our classes. In all my primary school classes there were at least forty children and order was maintained by recourse to the strap when necessary. I had great difficulty with the need to be quiet and received frequent reminders of the teacher's prowess with their chosen instrument. It was not only the male teachers who used the strap. A few of the women could 'lay it on' as well. The head mistress, Miss Haminow, the harridan from hell, berated children and parents alike.

We played a variety of marble games, each with a different name, like 'Bunny Hole' or 'Big Ring'. We collected football cards and invented other games that served to identify who the leaders were and how we each fitted into the order of things. After school, we dawdled along, soaking up the myriad details of the changing world around us. There were few cars and the streets seemed wide and largely vacant.

Most people used bikes for transport. Women commonly rode a bike with a basket on the front and a child in a seat behind. Men rode to work or to the hotel. We rode our bikes to explore and discover a variety of factories and projects going on in Williamstown. The whole suburb was our extended backyard.

In contrast to the industrial noise of the working week, Sundays were deathly quiet. It meant checking the horses and later attending church. Occasionally we would visit a family friend or a relative in the afternoon.

In the home there was an anticipatory tension as to when the next outburst of abuse would occur. Misdemeanors, real or imagined, resulted in a torrent of abuse and occasionally a punch or two with a promise of more to come. I was by now a severe asthmatic and missing school on a regular basis. It was a struggle to breathe for long periods. The more severe episodes required injections of adrenaline by a visiting nurse who, despite my attempt to hide, always found me. I still recall days of being confined to bed in a darkened room. There was speculation as to whether the asthma was caused by privet hedges, the pine trees in the Williamstown gardens, horse manure or stress.

In my father's absence, the home was peaceful. Mum could relax and be herself. Although not able to show affection easily, she was calm. My entreaties for her to sing opera would be met with a high-pitched tuneless 'Hark Hark the Lark' which we both thought was hilarious. Attractive and blessed with a lively sense of humour, she was popular with the staff and customers. I suspect this was another source of annoyance to my father.

The family was closely involved with the Methodist Church in John Street a few blocks away. My brother Bruce and I attended Sunday school for years before becoming members of the junior Order of Knights. In fact, our limited social life revolved around our church and the Masonic Lodge.

Stan, like his father, was an avid member of the Masonic Lodge, which served to highlight the hypocrisy of his ranting about other races, Catholics, communists and us. Stan was an enigma – a handsome man with dark hair and brown eyes, about five feet eight inches tall, and of medium build. When dressed for his lodge nights, he was the picture of a successful businessman ready and able to fraternise with anybody. He possessed a lovely tenor voice and sang regularly as a member of the Grand Lodge Choir. Unfortunately, when meeting people, he adopted an exaggerated friendliness. I found this embarrassing and hypocritical as it was a completer contrast to his behavior in private. The foulmouthed, sneering bully given to bragging about his ability to fight was reserved for his wife and oldest child. Looking back, I was unconsciously engaged in a futile effort to win my dad's approval and affection. The implicit anxiety of constantly failing to do so was, I suspect, the driving force of my asthma and defiant attitude to his authority.

The routine of working in the bakery was relentless and interesting. I was given many tasks, each year of growing complexity, thus increasing my usefulness. I ran errands to the harness maker or bank, opened flour bags and removed the tickets and string. I stacked wood, picked up horse manure and swept the yards and cart shed. Domestic jobs included polishing brass taps, dusting, table laying and dish washing. Everyone was busy so the work ethic was ingrained in us from the outset.

Stan was proud of his horses. They were rarely unfit for work. Many customers were fond of the horses and would greet them with tit bits from the garden. Almost everyone knew their delivery horse by name. The drivers loved their horses and would give them treats they brought from home. I suspect the drivers shared a friendly familiar companionship with the horses and their customers that later generations could only dream about.

My father spent most of his time working in the bakery. He came in at meal times but was unconcerned with the dynamics of the family and certainly had no time for what I was doing. Sadly, I cannot recall ever having a constructive conversation with him. I was at the periphery of his concerns and there to perform tasks, but beyond that, of no intrinsic value. This afforded me a remarkable freedom. After chores, I was free to play or extend my knowledge of Williamstown.

I often rode my bike to visit the docks, the wheat stacks, the beach, the rifle range, the abattoirs and the Newport Railway Workshops. I have vivid memories of the steam engines, perhaps 20 or more, all quietly dozing after a day's work – all just waiting for my mates and me to climb into and imagine we were the drivers. The guards had a different view and one day I was almost caught. It was all part of the fun. We also knew which fruit trees were ripe throughout Williamstown. The game was called 'Raiding fruit'. We would ride our bikes up back lanes and help ourselves to the fruit by climbing over fences and onto garage roofs. To be caught or threatened simply encouraged us.

At school, children I knew contracted a disease called polio. It was spoken about with dread as it caused paralysis and was sometimes fatal. When my school friend Sidney Sutton died from the disease I was deeply disturbed. How could this pleasant, well dressed gentle boy who bothered no-one just die? Apparently he had simply not woken up one morning. It was my first encounter with death. I would miss Sidney Sutton.

Listening to the serials on the radio after dinner was a regular part of our day. My favourites were, 'The Air Adventures of Biggles', 'Gould League of Bird Watchers', and 'Ovalteen Club'. Reading when I went to bed was encouraged and became a habit that has endured for life. My frequent periods of illness, mainly asthma, and the hundreds of boils I experienced meant I was often confined to bed, sometimes with the blinds drawn. I discovered the beauty of books and associated them with the peace of isolation. The periods of illness cut heavily into my time at school, as noted in my school reports. It was made worse by Stan's growing habit of keeping me home to help him deliver bread whenever a bread carter was unable to work.

To begin with, I thought this would be good fun - until his foul temper and indifference to me had him laughing. I was frightened of the dogs that bailed me up when I entered a property to deliver bread. Being small, and having no experience with dogs, this was a big problem but he insisted I deliver the bread anyway. I would often have to run and catch up with him because he kept moving on into the next street or beyond. He was unmoved by the occasional dog bites I received.

Each year, our church used to celebrate the Sunday School Anniversary. The children of the church would sit on raised benches at one end of the hall facing the adult congregation. On one occasion, the visiting minister was well into a story when he paused and asked the seated children if anyone knew where Jesus Christ lives. My brother Bruce put up his hand. 'Yes, the little boy up the back,' the minister said. 'Where does Jesus Christ live?' Bruce replied, 'Next to my father's horse paddock!' The congregation broke up with laughter and the poor minister, a visitor, was the only person who didn't understand why.

I enjoyed my involvement with the church, apart from the boring admonitions of the minister about the many sins that might befall us, or the repetitive hymns that droned on and on. Some sins, from my limited experience, held a tantalising attraction and would need to be tested. The Church Boys Club was run by Mr. Keith Miller who donated a lot of time to making us into decent citizens. At first it was gymnastics and ball games one night a week after which we graduated to the Junior Order of Knights with its rituals, secret codes and regalia.

Bruce and I had been adopted as 'helpers' by two of the longest serving 'carters' (our name for the drivers of the horse drawn carts). Bruce was adopted by Bert Harris, whose horse was Jack, an ex trotter while I was the favourite of George Neil, who drove Tiny, a 17.5 hand ex-hunter. George called me 'Picolo Pete' and treated me to a ride on the cart with him at every opportunity. I was very fond and proud of Tiny. He was so big even George, who was six feet tall, had difficulty putting Tiny's headstall on. One day when I was about nine, Tiny was kicked in the shoulder by another horse and had to be put down.

I remember his execution clearly. The man put the captive bolt to Tiny's lovely head and tapped it with a small hammer. 'Pop.' It was done. His lifeless body was hauled by a winch into the truck and it departed. But my memory of that day did not. Some images are never forgotten.

CHAPTER 2
WINDS OF CHANGE

By the late 1940's, Stan was grooming Bruce and I with the notion that we would be selling the bakery and moving to a farm. He was increasingly debilitated with abscesses and suffering from what he called 'flour on the lung'. He assured us we would get a pony and painted a picture of an idyllic life in the country that surpassed our wildest dreams. Our occasional family visits to the grandparents in Tecoma and my brief holidays there also reinforced my love of the bush. The drive swept gently up through the tall trees into the garage next to the small white weatherboard painted house. Inside, the smell of kerosene and candles was strong for at first electricity was not connected. The dining table had an ornate lamp in the middle that gave off a soft yellow light which cast shadows

in the room. These shadows were enlivened by the flickering of the fire as it warmed the room and added to the charm. My grandfather would greet us warmly and although finding conversation was difficult due to his deafness, he would engage us by playing cribbage, a game he loved.

Another joy was going for the milk. We would walk about a mile further up a track through the bush behind the house to a small property where, if we were early enough, we would see the man milk his cow by hand. When finished, he would fill my tin billy with milk. The pungent smell of the cow and her warm frothy milk was unforgettable.

The sights, the sounds, the smells – the bush was a magical other world. The fact it was always raining only added to the charm. On our many walks in the forest, we were on the alert for a glimpse of the lyre birds and wombats that inhabited the bush. Although eighteen months younger than me, my brother Bruce was similarly enchanted. We were more than ready to believe that life in the country would be wonderful.

Naturally, we were on Dad's side to go farming. Mum remained unimpressed. She knew this was a recipe for failure. Stan was in fact trying to avoid the reality that although the bakery appeared to be a raging success, he had expanded the business too rapidly and borrowed money from the flour mills. He had no strategy for its survival.

There were many subtle pressures at work in the community

at this time. People were becoming more prosperous. An increasing number had cars and shopping habits were changing. Plastic goods were coming onto the market and food and clothing, rationed throughout the war, became available. Larger bread companies like Tip Top appeared, sometimes funded by the flour mills that bought up the smaller bakeries and stopped home delivery to reduce cost. The advent of sliced bread and the saving of distribution costs allowed the consolidated bakeries to undercut prices. The demise of the small bakery business was inevitable.

One day my father was talking to the owner of the local garage, Mr. Carpenter. Stan told him that as a commando during the war he had parachuted from a low flying aircraft into New Guinea. I piped in suggesting that can't be true as it was not what he had told Uncle Bill. My father was furious and hurried me away before punching into my arms and head. I was at a loss to understand what I had done wrong. I had long detected inconsistencies in his exaggerated stories but this was direct proof of his telling lies. His war records which were released to my mother following his death in 1999, revealed he had never seen action or served beyond Brisbane.

A friend of my father, Hec Neil, owned a stable yard in Newport. Behind the high paling fence was a long stable with a loft above which contained the horse feed for about ten or more big draught horses. I was fascinated by this collection because of the size of the horses which were even bigger than ours. On one occasion I was allowed to go up into the loft. The atmosphere was quaint and dusty. The smell of horses, feed, sweat and manure was pungent and for me, somewhat addictive. I was in awe of that restless horsepower. Each horse in a dray was able to pull a ton or more at a trot for quite a distance. And besides, Hec owned a farm at Rockbank.

Hec invited my father and me to visit his farm. I felt fortunate to be included. Unlike the bush of my dreams, this was sheep country – open and almost treeless. There was an ancient house, the remains of a primitive tractor, a shearing shed and sheep yards. The true purpose of our visit was revealed after rounding up a flock of sheep. I was put to work catching lambs that I dragged to the waiting Hec, who castrated the males with a pocket knife and an emasculator before cutting

their tails off. I had to admit to wondering if it hurt. Hec said it didn't unless you nicked yourself with the knife.

A new dimension was introduced into my life when my grandmother, Anne, took Bruce and me to see the film 'The Wizard of Oz'. I had seen many films with my mother but this was different. I fell in love with Dorothy. I had never seen such an exquisitely beautiful girl before. My life had been about boy's things. Even Margaret Freath, my good friend in Princes Street around the next corner, had been accepted in our games as another boy. This new emotion would have to be factored into my limited life experience. Dorothy's voice, her femininity, her beauty – it was overwhelming.

In 1951 the Cliff Quality Bakery business was sold to a bigger baking group in Footscray. It had become a victim of the consolidation process that was irrevocably eroding the old way of life. I returned from school to find the horses and the carts gone, and the bakery empty of all machinery. Stan had sold the business but retained the freehold. I was sad that this pulsating business had been terminated without ceremony of any kind. There had been no time to say goodbye to the men or horses who had been part of my life since I was a 3 year old. I was openly resentful. How could such a busy business disappear overnight? The extended infrastructure of my life was gone, the familiar faces, the friendly greetings and a sense of being an important essential service to a grateful community gone. The bread carts, which carried the logo 'Cliff's Quality Bread' would no longer feature on the streets of Williamstown. The empty bakery was a silent reminder to me of our once important link to the bigger world.

Mum began work for the Tutt Bryant Company in Spotswood which sold and serviced earthmoving equipment where the West Gate Freeway now crosses Melbourne Road. For a time, family life approached what I had imagined was 'normal.'. Stan seemed to be relieved and happy in his new position as a trades assistant at the Naval Dockyards. The arguments were fewer, perhaps because he was relieved to be employed and unlike my relationship with him in the bakery where I was constantly berated, I was now invisible. This suited us both.

In 1951, Stan bought a new grey Wolsley 6/80 car. Mum bought a Hoover washing machine and a Frigidair refrigerator replaced the ice chest. Things were looking up – despite the arguments about whether or not to buy a farm. Mum maintained that buying a farm would be a disaster given my father's lack of experience and aptitude. Although an excellent baker, he was not a handyman.

The purchase of the car was an exciting milestone in our lives. The car had to be ordered some time before delivery. In the meantime the driving lessons began. There were endless discussions about how to start the car on a hill and how to park by reversing into the curb. To a generation who had never driven a car before, it was rocket science. Stan failed his first test for his driving license which was humiliating because Mum obtained hers the first time.

Cars were a big topic at school as many families were buying one. We knew the horsepower of each make and argued endlessly about the virtues and deficiencies of them all. My friend Geoffrey Dean defended his father's choice of a Ford Pilot V8 while others chose Standard Vanguards, Vauxhalls, Ford Prefects, and the ugliest of all, the Mayflower, which looked like a motorised coffin.

The Methodist Church announced a new initiative where children from country regions could reciprocate holidays with those in the city. It began for us when a lad, Max Major, came to stay and we all went to a church run camp for boys at Ocean Grove. We had a great time swimming, walking, playing games and enjoying the organised entertainment each night. Max and I became firm friends. He stayed on in our home after the camp, enjoying the sights and sounds of Williamstown, and further inflamed our passion for the country by telling us tales of his life on their family dairy farm at Leitchville on the Murray River.

Sometime later, our family was invited to stay with the Majors on their dairy farm. During a school holiday we drove up to the farm on Gunbower Island. We were introduced to Ernie and Dorrie Major, who immediately overwhelmed us with their generous hospitality. We were enchanted. They had a pony that we rode in turn until it was exhausted and we were made by the parents to give it a rest. The milking of the cows and the feeding of their pigs fascinated us beyond words – this was the life Bruce and I wanted. Uncle Ernie, as he had become, shot and butchered a pig while we were there, so our passion for country living rose even higher. This informal meeting of the two families was the beginning of a lifetime association between us. Dorrie Major befriended my mother that week, intuitively realising that my father was a threat to her. Max and I became lifetime friends.

My mates and I became keen fishermen for a time. We fished on the Gellibrand Pier using pilchards for bait. Although we only caught an occasional flathead or puffer-fish, we were kept occupied by watching the loading and unloading of the ships. For a few days in 1951 we were rewarded by watching a consignment of R-class British steam engines being unloaded and placed on the rails for removal to the Newport Railway Workshops.

I soon started school

at Footscray Junior Technical School on Ballarat Road. The school was attended by more than 1000 boys, all destined to be tradesmen if the teacher's efforts prevailed. There were many rough kids and corporal punishment was used to enforce the boundaries. There were the usual bullies to be stood up to. It was survival of the fittest, a language well understood in a post war environment. We received instruction in wood work, metal work, clay modeling, solid geometry, music, mathematics and English. I still recall Basil Cronin teaching us a song called 'Travelling the King's Highway', which seemed distinctly unlikely to me. In retrospect, I am amazed how much of this education I managed to absorb and feel it is about time our present community recognised the value of technical school teaching, particularly if provided to the right students soon enough.

Our physical education teacher was Mr. Croft - an ex-soldier not to be trifled with. One day while talking to a group of us, an apprentice, a big young chap with a surly countenance, was giving him cheek. He was called over by Mr. Croft and told to watch his mouth. The young man gave some smart arse reply, to which Mr. Croft responded with a punch that knocked him out. Unperturbed, our teacher went on talking to us as though nothing had happened while the apprentice lay in front of us. We understood. It is the only language some fellows learn by and often lasts a lifetime. We listened attentively.

My childhood so far had been a time of chores and interesting involvement with the routines of the bakery, occasional holidays with my grandparents, school, church activities, and a remarkable freedom to explore Williamstown. In the home, things had improved. There were fewer episodes of verbal and physical assault but the relationship with my father remained the same. I was wary of him, embarrassed by his behavior with others and despaired of ever pleasing him. The boys I played with were familiar with his language and abuse. I was not afraid of him and that seemed to infuriate him. I refused to cry when he hit me. Almost every confrontation in private resulted in belittling criticism if not of me then of my mother or someone else. The incident of his lying to Mr. Carpenter and others about his war experiences served to erode any sense of respect I might have had for him. These were not isolated incidents. He would regale people with his bragging and exaggerated stories, seeming to have no regard for the truth or his own veracity.

Late one afternoon, as the pubs closed, he was on the footpath in front of the house with my mother. I was further away in front of the butcher's on the corner of Albert Street. My father called, 'Come on, you useless fucking bastard, get a move on or I'll give you a fucking hiding.' A man who had just left the hotel and walking past said, 'That's no way to talk to the boy. Pick on someone your own size.' Stan told him to

mind his own business so the man ran toward him, whereupon Stan shot through the side gate and locked it. The man had a few words with Mum, who was grateful for the intervention. So was I. That man was the only person I ever saw tackle him directly.

Mum and I went to the movies regularly. We each had a keen sense of humour and found a lot to laugh at. She seemed to regard me like a brother or the man about the house. This was understandable perhaps because she was an only child and frequently expressed her regret at not having siblings. Mum's intention was to have a large family. Intelligent, articulate and possessing a quiet determination, she insisted on good manners and frequently stated she had no intention of creating a problem for some other woman. Her boys, she said, were going to be self sufficient around the house. Beyond that, she was remarkably tolerant of where I was or what I was doing, seeming to believe I could look after myself. It was not entirely my choice. In many ways I was accorded the freedom of a young adult without the luxury of being a child.

In August, three years after the birth of my youngest brother, Ross Stuart, my sister Pamela was born. This was very exciting as Pam was the only girl in our generation of the Cliff family. Mum was pleased she had attained the family she wanted.

We soon sold the bakery and house. Stan began the search for a farm with a visit to Albury and Yarrawonga after which he turned to Alexandria where a property there became the subject of heated discussion. A little later, having inspected farms at Ripplebrook and Glen Forbes in Gippsland, it was announced he bought the 150 acre dairy farm at Glen Forbes, on the railway line to Wonthaggi. We would take possession at Easter.

An irony was to occur in the 1960s when No 2 Albert Street Williamstown, the former Cliff bakery, became the Williamstown Little Theatre. I can think of no better way to enshrine the scene of the Cliff family post war life. Structurally, in 2015, it is largely unchanged from its former life.

CHAPTER 3
GLEN FORBES

It was Easter 1954. We could hardly contain ourselves as the car made its way out of the suburbs onto the South Gippsland Highway toward Wonthaggi. Skirting around Western Port Bay, we passed the fishing village of Tooradin, crossed the drains of Koo Wee Rup and went on to Grantville. We searched intently for the 63 mile post that would mark our turn to the east, away from Corinella. Mum's stifled tears were the only dampener but we had little sympathy for her. Our childish self interest prevailed.

To my inexperienced eye, this was heaven. The country was unbelievably beautiful. The house was perched a few hundred feet above the Bass flats overlooking Western Port Bay with both Phillip Island and French Island clearly visible in the distance. Behind the house, and rising very steeply was a large hill while over the road was another, if anything even steeper. Alarm bells would have rung a distinct warning to any adult with experience of farming but Mum's wail on entering the house was the only detractor from our awe. Her premonition of doom was compounded by the rudimentary weatherboard house that consisted of three bedrooms, a bathroom, a kitchen and two living rooms. Only one room was lined with unpainted three-ply cladding. The rest sported at least one wall where bare noggins served as shelves.

In the kitchen was a traditional wood stove. The water supply was provided by two 1000 gallon tanks beside the kitchen, another on the bathroom, and a smaller one with a tap outside. To her credit, Mum's tears stopped and she was soon directing the furniture to its chosen position. Bruce and I were more interested in the dairy and the old shed in a grove of oak trees that served as the hay shed, workshop, and storage for the heavy horse harness we found. I was instantly addicted to the sights and smells.

The inventory of the farm included 25 cows, one bull, two draft horses, a black kelpie dog called Prince, a two-furrow hillside disk plough, a six by four foot horse drawn sled and a rusted unusable horse drawn mower. Electricity was connected to the house but there was none to the dairy or the shedding. The simple bush timber dairy had six wooden head bails and a three unit 'Eclipse' milking machine driven by a vertical 3HP petrol Bamford engine. Hot water was provided by an old wood fired copper in the wash room. Only part of the yard was concrete – the rest was mud.

Only our extreme naivety could have allowed the optimism Bruce and I felt. God only knows what Stan was feeling. Mum somehow managed to put the house into working order. Stan seemed bewildered and uncertain where to start or what to do. For some time he made no attempt to milk the cows. I had just turned 13, Bruce was 11, Ross was 4 and Pamela 2. Naturally, our efforts would seem inept to an experienced farmer. By default, I got the milking machine going and with little difficulty solved the problems of milking. Mum had made it clear from the outset she was not going to work on the farm – she would be fully occupied with the children and maintaining the home.

The most immediate and vexatious of our tasks, apart from milking, was to maintain a supply of cut wood for the house and the dairy. To obtain sufficient wood it was necessary to drag fallen trees and limbs off the farm to a site near the house where it could be cut up with a hand saw and axe. To do this I would need the horses. Taking two bridles, I set out to catch the two draught horses quietly grazing in the paddock above the house. The previous owner had told us their names were Tess and Jess.

This was the beginning of my love of working farm horses. Luckily for me these horses were used to working hard and did not waste energy. They would stand where you put them and would work together when driven properly. I put their collars on, then the metal hames. By tying a short rope between their bridles and long reins to the outside of the bridles, they could be driven as a pair. I was able to drive them forward into place between the chain traces laid out in front of the wooden sledge. Once the traces were attached to the hooks on the hames we are ready to go. With a gentle flick of the reins and a click of the tongue we were off, gliding softly and silently across the grass behind the two gentle giants

Our daily routine evolved from necessity. I would get up before 6 a.m. to bring the cows in for milking. To begin, it was a task I really enjoyed. The first job was to light a fire under the copper in the dairy, our only source of hot water. We had arrived in autumn so at that early hour the hills were enshrouded with mist while the flats were invisible in the fog until later in the morning. The hills were so steep the cows would drift to the gullies out of the wind or lie down among the tussocks and bracken ferns that covered a great deal of the farm. The gentle breeze coming from the ocean in the south west was laced with the moist earth smell. I was truly enchanted as I strode along looking for the cows hiding either in the ferns somewhere on the hill or in the sheltered valley behind the Glen Forbes store. It was mystical and eerie to come across them quietly chewing their cud and exhaling their pungent breath in the mist of this beautiful place. It seemed a shame to disturb them. The sight of Prince with me would cause them to stand. Then, like most mammals after a nap, they would perform a luxurious stretch followed by a dump and a pee. Once yarded, I let six cows into the bails and tied a leg rope on each before washing their mud-encrusted udders.

The next step was starting the engine which meant filling the fuel tank, then closing the choke before swinging the crank handle as fast as possible. With luck and repetition, it was notoriously obstinate, it started. Put the plug in to the vacuum pump, assemble the milk releaser and arrange the washed-out milk cans under the cooler to catch the milk. During the milking it was necessary to keep checking the filling of the milk cans and to change them when full. On completion of the milking, the full cans were taken to the milk stand on the roadside. A full can contained 120lb of milk so the effort required was considerable for a thirteen year old boy.

Tying leg ropes could be a hazardous business. Our ropes were usually made from plaited baling twine and were fixed to the post against the cows inside leg. The free end was picked up, brought to the side where the operator stood close into the cow using his leg to move the cows leg back before leaning down and placing a half hitch on the cow's leg above the hock. Simple enough if the cow is cooperative, but difficult if the cow is kicking with intent and perhaps having a crap at the same time. When annoyed or upset cows are prone to crap and pee obsessively with no regard for your person.

Toward the end of milking, Bruce would appear and take over. He would wash the machines and clean the dairy while I changed and had breakfast in time to catch the school bus at ten past eight. Bruce attended the local state school so he had a little more time before walking about a mile down the disused road that passed through the property. The Watson sisters, Pam and Mary, from their farm further up the old road, would appear on their old pony Whisky and perhaps accompany Bruce if he was on time. The girls rode behind each other in all weathers sitting on a folded chaff bag. A regular amusing sight arose when they had to pass through the old slip rail gate across the old road below our dairy. Whisky, for unknown reasons, would lie down and refuse to get up again until, with much vocal encouragement and some rib kicking by the girls, he was persuaded to resume the walk. I was a little apprehensive about going to the Wonthaggi Technical School because I didn't know if the bus would stop as I stood by the side of the road, but it did, thus becoming the first of my many journeys to Wonthaggi. It was a drive through country unsurpassed for beauty at all times of year. The rolling hills gradually descending from the high to the low as they neared the sea. The ocean can be seen from Kilcunda to Wilson's Promontory from different vantage points along the road. Every day it was different because the colours changed with the weather, seasons and farming practices. I quickly learned the names of every farmer on the 14 mile ride and took an intense interest in every change each farm made. This was the best part of going to school as far as I was concerned.

On my first day my teacher was attempting to teach us a song 'Drink To Me Only With Thine Eyes' which he sang with a high, thin, reedy voice. I thought it was impossibly funny and began to take him off. He caught me – and he was furious. All the kids were laughing. I received two cuts in my first hour at the Wonthaggi Technical School. My previous schooling at Footscray had taught me many bad habits and exposed me to tricks he said were not going to be tolerated in Wonthaggi. In retrospect, I was a disturbed and rebellious boy. I saw no point in being there - I was needed at home.

There was a steady rhythm to running the farm and it could have been pleasant had we'd had some adult help. Stan was preoccupied with inconsequential things like pulling out the boobyalla trees that formed a wind break behind the house. Although they had grown to about 30 feet high and provided useful shelter to the house, Stan was determined to pull them out. He tied a rope around the branches about seven feet from the ground and attached the other end to the tow bar of the Wolsley. After starting the car, he would take off until the limit of the rope was reached and the boobyalla tree was bent like a fishing rod. This lifted the rear wheels of the car off the ground before springing back. Stan was beside himself with fury. He repeated the exercise over and over, eventually realising he had to take smaller pieces. We all kept clear because the task somehow become personal. Stan was determined to remove these trees. The vision I have of him going off his head is excruciatingly funny; a crazy ridiculous farce. The car suffered badly from this and other similar forms of abuse.

Stan began working for the Bass Shire so he left at 7 a.m. and returned after 6 p.m. Consequently, there was not a lot of time left to work on the farm. However, his attempts to milk cows on the weekend were short lived because the cows, accustomed by now to a gentle approach, were totally uncooperative for a man who yelled and used force as if their irritability was a personal matter. He could be merciless, on occasion thrashing them with the back of the shovel. As the excrement in the shed grew steadily deeper, the threats escalated until the ordeal was over. Perhaps it was a deliberate ploy, an excuse not to milk cows. In any case, for some time he rarely returned to the shed. Even Prince would run under the house and refuse to come out when Stan called him. Prince, we realised, was an impeccable judge of character. 'Prince you bastard, come here, you fucking mongrel, come here! I swear I'll shoot the bastard.' His voice topped 100 decibels, his eyes wide and his body shaking with rage while the veins in his neck pulsed madly and spittle hurled from his mouth. No one spoke. Prince wisely crouched under the house, eyes just visible in the gloom. He wouldn't budge. Stan would swing around looking for someone else to direct his anger at before loudly threatening to shoot the 'useless fucking dog' that would not work.

It was the same script he used when speaking to me. When he turned on you, as he did without warning, his face would be contorted by the full force of his rage and you got the hell out of there. Sometimes, he would simply throw a tool or whatever was at hand. I recall seeing him throw a claw hammer at Ross in this way. Stan had long established his prowess at throwing things but Bruce and I were nimble and luckily dodged many a missile.

Tensions in the home were reaching new heights. Stan's wages were inadequate to meet the loans and the cost of living. We were now accumulating a large debt with the local store.

Ron and Ivy Yann owned the Glen Forbes store, the focal point of the community. They delivered the mail, manned the telephone exchange, sold petrol and provided a full grocery service almost all on credit. At night the store was a meeting place for the exchange of gossip and where many practical jokes had their origin. It was the nerve centre of Glen Forbes for both Ivy and Ron extended not only credit and good will, but provided an organisational function that held this tight knit community together. Of course, running the manual exchange made them a party to all the local drama.

The sense of community was unbelievably strong. In a short time even Mum began to appreciate the support and generosity of these people. She quickly became involved with the other mothers whose kids attended the school and also joined the Country Women's Association (CWA). Mum began supplementing income by providing a hairdressing service to the ladies of the district. This furthered her sense of involvement in local affairs and the contact was essential to her because we only had the one car and Stan drove it to work each day.

Stan was increasingly violent. The frequency and volume of abuse to mum and me was increasing. We were without witnesses because our closest neighbour was at least 500 metres away on the flat land below. As his loss of control over the farm increased, Stan's need to blame others escalated. Mum was blamed because we were in debt. I was blamed for everything else.

In June the cows started calving. When a calf was removed from the cow we had to feed it in addition to milking the mother. Gradually the milking herd grew in size, but one cow died of milk fever because we were unprepared. Experienced dairy farmers keep a supply of calcium solutions on hand and an injection kit for milk fever so that when a cow has the symptoms, the injection can be given promptly. Delay or failure to treat the animal can quickly lead to death. At that time we were ignorant of the problem and had nothing to treat the animal with.

Calves too died, some simply too weak to survive while others developed scours, or diarrhea exacerbated by infection. Poor Bruce had the job of feeding the calves but with no sheds, adult guidance on procedure or experience, progressively, most died. Stan became incandescent with rage over that and of course, it was our fault. Bruce's teacher even informed Mum that when the children in his class were asked to write about their hobbies, Bruce wrote a pathetic tale titled 'My Hobby Is Killing Calves'. Although we laughed, in fact it was a serious reflection of Bruce's feeling of helplessness. He was only 11. It is no joke to be feeding calves in sometimes bitterly cold wet conditions without a raincoat, shelter, hot water, a clean environment, experience, electrolytes or antibacterial drugs.

That summer we assisted a neighbor, Cecil Eden, to harvest

his hay. We were remunerated with hay for our farm but not before we had learned a great deal about harvesting. Stan lent our draft horse to pull the hay sweep while I was given the task of removing and stacking the bales as they came out of the stationary baler. Cecil forked the hay into the baler while his father Bill threaded the wire and tied the knots as the bales progressed through the bale chamber. On a hot day the dust created envelopes everything, which can be hell for those with allergies.

From our first day on the farm, my father, who had previously been a hard worker, became strangely more distant and lazy, perhaps confused and unable to cope with the practicalities of the farm. Outwardly, he maintained the façade of a friendly caring man in charge of his affairs and one who knew all that was needed to be a successful farmer. The reality was he alone had bought the farm and arranged the finances but had denied Mum any knowledge of what he had done. The bills arrived but were left unpaid. By the end of the first year we owed the Glen Forbes store more than £500. This was a huge debt, with little prospect of us paying it, and it was not our only one.

Although I was thirteen and helped by Bruce, I was running the farm by default. Without cash or the opportunity to shop elsewhere, we lived on the meat, groceries and produce delivered and supplied on credit. Mum and I seemed to be the only ones concerned about the increasing debt and inability to pay. I was concerned and ashamed because the milking and running of the farm had become my responsibility and I could see no prospect of improvement.

Dairy farm income was seasonal. It rose gradually from nothing during autumn to a maximum during spring and early summer before declining again. Our facilities were inadequate and worn out, the fences were poor to nonexistent and we had few tools. Stan had no idea of how to farm. In short, the farm was unviable – and remains so to this day. Our poverty was visible: we were unable to replace leaking rubber boots, there were no torches and our largely secondhand clothing was inappropriate for the work required.

My asthma attacks become more frequent and debilitating and were only alleviated by taking a large dose of pseudoephedrine, a bitter white substance that caused my heart to pound furiously but miraculously relieved the breathing. The asthma caused me to wheeze loudly and I struggled for breath for long periods which were painful, exhausting and frightening. The worry for the family, the insoluble debts, the abuse, the violence and the recurring practical problems of the farm were making me deeply unhappy. According to my father, it was my fault.

By this time, Stan was coming home from work after drinking but generally not drunk. He would find cause to accuse either Mum or me of insurrection, first with outrageous abuse and vile language and then invite me to fight him. The familiar routine began with berating me and then turning on mum who would attempt to defend me, or conversely mum and then me. By then Stan would be in an irrational frenzy and punch her with his fists so I would attack him until we would somehow wrestle our way out of the house into the yard and make our escape. I became so concerned about my role in all this I began planning to run away. The little children were terrified by the fighting and would stand helplessly pleading for Stan to stop. Mum was beside herself. It seemed to me it would be better for all if I were to leave. I was almost 14 and I thought I would get a job somewhere, anywhere.

CHAPTER 4
RUNAWAY

One Sunday night I packed a small bag before going to bed. At about three in the morning I rose and left the house. It was a cold, still night with a little cloud cover. There was just enough moonlight to allow a view of the road when my eyes adjusted to the dark. I walked down the familiar gravel road to the store, crossed the wooden bridge over the Bass River, past the butter factory beyond which the road wound for about three miles through the dense undeveloped bush to the highway. The only noise was the scrunch of my footsteps on the loose gravel road and the occasional thump of a wallaby crossing the road or moving in the scrub. On reaching the highway I began trying to hitch a ride from one of the few vehicles at that hour. Eventually, a large truck stopped. The driver was on his way to Melbourne. He seemed amused when I said I was looking for work but he agreed to drop me off in the city. I intended to catch a train to distant relatives, the Johnsons who lived in Pascoe Vale, I had been there a number of times and knew the way well enough.

There was great consternation on my arrival, especially since the Johnsons had no idea of my coming. They were getting ready to go to work but anxiously changed their plans and began to question me. They said I could stay for a few days but persuaded me they had to let my parents know where I was since I had left without notice. My mother and father set out that day and arrived relieved and embarrassed about my intrusion into the relative's lives. The aunt and uncle, I am sure, had a suspicion things were not right in our family. Now Stan was concerned. He apologised and promised to be better if I came home. They needed me, and besides, I was not old enough to leave home.

Things did improve for a while. I found a little time to go fishing with local boys like Colin Turton and Allan Watson. We fished for eels in the Bass River and caught heaps. It was huge fun. We also caught minnows in the creek but it takes a lot to make a meal of them. This was valuable time with the neighborhood boys who took the opportunity to teach me the local folk lore. I was less enthusiastic over Colin's idea of fun, shaking the tee-trees along the railway line until the possums pissed themselves.

As hay time approached I arranged with a neighbor to borrow his horse drawn mower – he had graduated to a new tractor and mower. I began cutting the hay one hot day when my uncle Bill was due to arrive. By late morning the horses were tiring so I stopped mowing and began to remove the horses from the mower with the intention of watering them and allowing them graze for a couple of hours. As I was doing so, Stan and Uncle Bill approached. Stan must have temporarily forgotten the presence of Bill because he immediately took a swipe at me and began a tirade of abuse. According to him, I had knocked off too early. He was furious. He snatched the reins from me and put the horses back into the mower. They refused to move. Stan, oblivious of Bill, and now in a terrible rage, began to berate me and the horses for being such 'useless fucking bastards' and thrashing them mercilessly with the reins and a stick he picked up. Bill was horrified and called out, 'That's enough,' and, 'I'm going home.' Stan stopped as if struck. He had a dazed look of embarrassment and threw the reins on the ground before returning to the house with Bill. He had forgotten himself in the presence of a witness, a rare miscalculation.

The New Year of 1955 saw us all back to school, including Ross for his first year. Mum noticed something was not right with Ross. She felt he was unable to see or walk normally. A local doctor thought he had worms but she persisted. Something was not right. She returned to the Queen Victoria Hospital and consulted Dr Kate Campbell who immediately diagnosed a brain tumour from symptoms visible in Ross's eye. He was promptly admitted to Prince Henry's Hospital where Mr Curtis spoke with us in the foyer. By chance, I was with my mother that day and I can recall Mr Curtis telling us he held little hope for Ross's survival but he would do his best to save him. Miraculously, Ross survived the heroic surgery.

Mum stayed with her mother and stepfather at their home in Newport and travelled by train every day to and from Newport to Prince Henry's Hospital. She was also pregnant with a new baby due in October. I was indignant and questioned the wisdom of having another child in our present circumstances. She cried. We argued. How was she to explain to me the details of her predicament? We were both miserable. I felt worse and ashamed for seeming to resent the new child. I worried – was I simply being selfish?

With Mum away, conditions on the farm became unimaginably worse. Stan continued working and returned as usual after drinking more, too late to assist on the farm. Bruce and I battled on doing the milking and trying to maintain the routine of the farm. We survived in large measure due to the help of wonderful neighbours who plied us with food and clothing. They would leave casseroles and other dishes in the large mailbox at the roadside. The good will of these people and the community concern for us at this time has left an enduring memory I will value forever. Stan's helpless rage and frustration was now unchecked and he held me responsible for all of our woes. The abuse, ridicule and violence were now worse than ever. He wanted to fight me virtually on sight. My misery was overwhelming. Despite every attempt to run the farm Stan found fault with everything I did. Together with the now neglected state of the house, we were at a new low.

A saving feature for me was my new found interest in school, for this was my third year at Wonthaggi Technical School. I was in the 'Farmers Class'. Our teacher, Mr Trevor McEvoy, spoke quietly with authority and an amused smile. He was not judgmental and was always reasonable. He wore a tweed sports coat, well cut trousers and polished brown shoes.

He was an example of the man I wished to be, and perhaps, unconsciously, the father I wanted. There were only six boys in the class and I was enjoying the interest this new teacher had in me. He would summon me to his small office and discuss my work. I had been forever fighting other boys and getting into trouble with the other teachers but slowly my anger and confusion began to dissipate. Trevor became my adopted father figure. My school work improved dramatically. I suspect he was doing the same for other boys, however, my friendship with him was destined to endure for life. His example became a guiding beacon of how I would like to be perceived by others. I was able to respect him as a man.

On 14th of October 1955, Geoffrey Robert Cliff was born. Despite everything, there was a brief celebration and cessation of hostilities. The additional good news was that Ross was making a recovery after his grueling six month ordeal and was finally discharged from hospital. Mum, Ross, Pam and Geoffrey returned to the farm. Mum was elated with her expanded family but annoyed no one had visited Ross while she had been in the Queen Victoria Hospital having the baby.

Mum's return to the farm was a profound shock to her. The house, neglected during her time away, upset her and she remonstrated with Stan over the extreme neglect of not only the house but Bruce and me and our impending financial doom. Stan retaliated with his usual threats, abuse and violence. Mum was afraid because the fighting had attained a new level of savagery. I was maturing and becoming stronger, more able to defend myself and even more protective of Mum. I was able to appreciate she was recovering from the birth of Geoffrey and having huge difficulty with maintaining the home, especially given the primitive conditions we were living in. Our rubber boots were worn out and leaking. Our feet were constantly wet and covered in mud and our clothes were cast off's largely given to us by neighbours. We had no rainwear and wore men's old coats for warmth. There were no torches or kerosene lamps – we were adept at finding our way about the farm and visiting neighbors in the dark. My sense of frustration, disgust and anger with Stan was barely containable. He was not going to beat Mum anymore. The frequent fist fights nearly always started in the kitchen and become protracted affairs that terrified the little children and left everyone with enduring fears for life. They would scream and plead for it to stop. Pamela still remembers trying to hit Dad with her pink skipping rope during one episode.

About this time, Stan attacked me one day as I left the dairy. I responded by running up the hill behind the house where, although he was fit, he was unable to catch me. The terror of fighting him dissipated. I would just walk in and get it over, but he better watch out. The fear of fighting was replaced by a deep empty sadness. It is not natural to fight your father. It is a betrayal of trust. I wept.

Conversation was impossible in the home after the fighting. The tension was unbearable. At night I would visit friends or do anything to get away. I returned only to sleep but would lie awake wracked with despair and pray for intervention. Would someone, anyone, take control of Stan and free us from his tyranny? The prayers went unanswered. The good Christians we knew were too timid to help. They preferred to offer platitudes and wring their hands with gentle concern. In many ways we were invisible; our problems too incomprehensible. Surely, they thought, we must be exaggerating. The army accepted no responsibility for Stan. The Masonic Lodge in

Wonthaggi asked him to leave because of our mistreatment but, essentially, we were on our own. Where, I wondered, was God?

CHAPTER 5

STARTING WORK

Mum reluctantly conceded the time had come for me to find work. I felt responsible for the misery because by now even the sight of me set Stan off. I applied to the Archie's Creek Butter Factory and was offered a job in the butter room. I was assigned the position of box maker for four pounds seven shillings and sixpence a week. Mum arranged my board with a rural family over the phone. I would pay four pounds per week. Sight unseen, one Sunday shortly after the birth of my new brother Geoffrey I was driven to my new living arrangements in Blackwood Forrest about 7 miles from Archie's Creek on the steep Loch to Wonthaggi Road.

It was mid afternoon as Mum and I drove the Wolsley over the hills to Blackwood Forest. The gravity of our circumstances weighed heavily on us. Mum was upset that I was leaving school so soon but I was relieved and excited to be starting work and free at last from my father. We arrived around four o'clock and I was introduced to an elderly couple, Bert and Pearl. I was hoping there would be some discussion as to how I would get to work the following day, but after wishing me well, Mum drove away and left me to see the bungalow I was to occupy.

It was a pleasant little room behind the house. Inside was a bed, a chair, sideboard with drawers and a one bar radiator. Bert and Pearl retired to the house and I was left to explore my surroundings and unpack my few belongings. I found the wood heap behind the bungalow and started to split some wood to fill in time before being called to dinner. I thought it would be appreciated since this was a chore everyone I knew hated.

As if by telepathy, Pearl offered me the use of her bicycle to go to work. After the meal, I pumped up the tires of the old ladies bike in readiness for the next day. Next morning, my alarm went off at 6 a.m. I had a generous breakfast and set off for work – not having ever been over the road before. The ride of about 7 miles proved exhausting because the bike had only a foot brake and no gears. The going was tough, particularly where the sand built up into thick piles on the side of the road and corners. The steepest hills I had to walk up. I arrived on time to start just before eight o'clock. My working life was about to begin.

The foreman was 'Bluey Bayliss', a pleasant, quietly spoken man who directed me to the ceiling space above the butter room where the boxes were made and put down a chute for use below. My task was to reconstruct both new and used cardboard boxes with staples in the bottom and then paste labels on the side before feeding them down the chute. For a change, I made wooden boxes by folding them up and nailing them together. I mention the detail of this because my loathing for the job was in a way the source of my determination to find something, anything that might possibly be more interesting. The loft was freezing when cold and stifling hot in summer. The factory's appetite for boxes was insatiable – it was the only job on my horizon. I was told later, positions like this, where no alternative to survival exist are character building.

The Archie's Creek Butter Factory was in a deep valley with a long steep road up the hills on either side. The nightly necessity of riding home after an arduous day was taxing me heavily. In winter it was dark before I got home and I had no light on my bike. I contemplated a change and noticed a long sign on the fence of Rupert Bethune's pub across the road from the factory. It depicted a hen followed by three or four chickens and a rooster, under which was the caption, *'You have to make calls to get results'*. With plenty of time to reflect on this advice while riding home, I began to consider how I might improve my circumstances. Life with Bert and Pearl was to say the least, isolated. Although I was fed well and clean, I was lonely. There were no visitors and I did not use the phone at all. Apart from nightly excursions over the paddock to my friend Glen Payne's house, there was nothing to do.

At work I had started playing cards with the other men at lunch time and my circle of contacts was growing. Among them was another lad my age, Arthur Rigby. He was a great character with an irrepressible sense of humour. He said his mother had room for a boarder. Without hesitation, I accepted.

The Rigbys lived in a small cottage in North Wonthaggi where I shared a narrow back room with Arthur and his young brother Tommy. Now, to get to work, all Arthur and I had to do was walk across a vacant block to the main road and catch the factory work truck. Arthur's mother, Ellen was a large jovial lady with a heart of gold. His father Ralph, a coal miner was a little too fond of drink. However, Ralph was a happy and caring man who enjoyed the occasional mutton-bird for dinner. He was always kind to his family.

The talk of the time was the impending Olympic Games. Arthur's mother decided to buy a TV on time payment. When Arthur and I arrived home from work one day, we found the front room was standing room only. It was the same every night for weeks because the neighbours crammed in to watch the Olympic Games. They even took votes to decide which channel to watch but Ellen was unconcerned. It was a happy time for me because I was well fed and cared for by this warm lady.

I was soon transferred to the Archies creek branch factory at Glen Forbes. Mum was pleased to have me back as it had been difficult for them to keep the farm going in my absence. I was assigned a bed in the narrow back room I would share with Bruce. I was independent and would come and go as I pleased. My board money was also welcome. During my absence, Bruce had stepped up to the regular milking with Ross as his assistant.

The factory at Glen Forbes had been making cheddar cheese since it was built during the Second World War. It was a convenient collection point for milk – destined for the Melbourne market. Milk was collected from farms up the Bass Valley as far as Loch, Lang Lang and Nyora. Only cream could be picked up from Phillip Island because of the 6 ton weight restriction on the old suspension bridge between the Island and San Remo. While the transition had started for the collection of bulk milk from refrigerated vats on some farms, most was still supplied in milk cans picked up by tray trucks. On arrival at the factory, the milk cans were emptied into a vat where it was weighed and sampled. It was assigned either to large collection vats for delivery to Melbourne or held for cheese and or casein production. The milk supplied had a total butter fat content of well over 4 percent, so some of it was run through a separator to standardise it to 3.8 percent. The cream taken was a bonus to the factory. At the time this was an illegal but standard practice. The cheese maker, Les Rintoule, was an energetic pleasant man to work with. He had been trained to make the new line of rindless cheese at the Dairy Research Facility at Werribee. On completion of the painting exercise, I was made his assistant.

One gallon of milk makes about one pound of cheese. Les and I made 2500 lb of cheese a day seven days a week throughout the season. It was hot, arduous work but I enjoyed the comradeship of men working together under trying conditions. There were no facilities for tea breaks or a lunch room, no phones and almost no supervision. We knew what to do and did it. The additional task we all attended to was the firing of the large boiler which was our sole source of hot water and heat. Hot water was obtained by running cold water and injecting it with steam. The boiler was coal fired and the water feed was via a steam injector which required constant supervision to maintain water levels. Occasionally, when this was neglected or left to the less able, sheets of iron were blown off the roof creating a dangerous potential for explosion when water levels fell below the glass.

The foreman, Sam Pearson, was as pressured as the rest of us and in addition, was responsible for the maintenance as well. He lived in the adjacent factory house and was on call at all times. I was surprised to learn many years later it was Sam Pearson who informed the Masonic Lodge of Stan's mistreatment of the family. Thank you, Sam.

It should not be imagined we were following a chosen career path. To be financially independent at 14 years old necessitated taking the best paid position available. Once committed, the lack of education meant more enterprising career choices were unavailable. There is no doubt we were exploited by the factory. We knew it – but it was all there was. We received no allowance for overtime or penalty rates. I was not happy with what I was doing. Necessity was the driving force. The comradeship between the men and the ethos of hard work and taking responsibility ensured our work was completed to a high standard. To be known as a shirker or a bludger in a closed environment was a reputation to be avoided at all cost. We had such a creature in our midst and he was detested.

I was now 15 and getting about was difficult. I was used to walking or riding my bike to work but to go anywhere else, I had either to hitch a ride or perhaps catch the train. I frequently walked to see my friend Roger Dakin over the hill behind us and he had a similar problem. One day on an excursion to Wonthaggi with my mother, we were returning home and she stopped the car as we turned into the Gorge Road at Dalyston, 9 miles from home. She said it was time for me to learn to drive. We exchanged seats and I drove home. She didn't say a word. Apparently I was considered able to drive. From that time on I did most of the driving whenever it was required. I would take the younger children to church at Bass, join the Senior Young Farmers organisation and drive to the meetings in Dalyston.

During the next down time at the factory, we were put to work expanding the building, pouring concrete floors and laying bricks. These skills were taught to me by the Italian men who were working with us and who it seemed, had a natural aptitude for the task. I enjoyed this relationship and even learned to speak a little Italian. We had some funny arguments and exchanged much ribald abuse. It could be very loud and always involved much exaggerated arm waving.

After work, I occasionally found time to fish in the Bass River with other local boys. Our principal catch was eels. We learned to skin them by hanging them on a nail. We would soak them in fresh water to reduce the muddy taste before eating. Done well, they could be delicious.

CHAPTER 6
LIBERATION

The advertisement in the local paper caught my eye, '*Motorbike in good order, £25*'. My father prohibited it but by now what he thought was of no concern. A phone call later and I found myself walking out to the highway and hitch hiking to Bass. Ironically, Ernie Moore, the owner, was living in the oldest home in the district, built of bricks made by prisoners when the British settled near Corinella at the turn of the previous century. The bike appeared old as well but I thought it was beautiful. It was a green Arial, girder forks at the front, huge fish tail exhaust and a 500cc single cylinder side valve engine. I fumbled for the £25. It was mine – love at first sight.

After a brief lesson on where the gears were and, more importantly, how to start it, I rode home. One day soon after, I rode into Wonthaggi feeling pretty smart about my new found freedom. On arrival, I backed the bike into the steep gutter in front of Coles Store. After a short strut about the street, I returned and set the spark which was manually controlled. I gave it the best kick over I could because it was notoriously difficult to start. 'BANG' - there was a huge explosion and the bloody thing fell on top of me. A number of men ran to my aid and lifted the bike up. After a second try, I at last got going. The visit was not the success I had imagined.

We rode without helmets or even gloves. They were luxuries to be bought when we had the money. A number of other friends, including Roger, acquired motorbikes as well. In our spare time we roared around the district having many falls but miraculously escaped serious injury.

My relationship with my father during this time was strange. Although he continued to rant and abuse me, I was working and financially independent and was untroubled by what he thought. My concern was for Mum and the children. I did what I could to assist on the farm, even helping financially in addition to the board I paid. I came and went with complete indifference to Stan. I was independent.

One day Stan attacked me as I was kneeling on the ground while attempting to repair a small rotary hoe. A neighbour, Dick, witnessed the whole event. As I was crouched down over the machine and talking to Dick, Stan walked up, abusing me for the hoe being out of order and at the same time swinging a huge uppercut. I looked up to see the fist descending on me and instinctively swung a punch of my own as I stood up. It caught Stan right on the chin and knocked him out. I was as shocked as he was. He took some time to recover and while doing so Dick announced he was going home, predicting even greater trouble. On recovery, Stan became more circumspect and confined himself to verbal abuse and threats. Incidentally, I had not broken the rotary hoe.

In time, Bruce became the object of Stan's wrath, but Bruce had matured and was also able to defend himself. Previously, he had not experienced the verbal and physical abuse I received. Nevertheless, Stan continued to hold us responsible for the misfortunes of the farm.

We had lost a number of cows through death and culling so more were needed to raise the farm income. Stan managed to procure a loan from his uncle, Horace Greenroyd, to buy more cows. Horace was married to Edna, Anne Cliff's sister. They were childless and well off. Horace had been a successful builder before emigrating from the UK in about 1948. The additional cows brought the herd up to 35 head, which for a time did increase the income, but not enough to relieve the ever growing debt. Sometime later Horace asked Stan to account for what he had done with the money he had loaned. Finding the explanation implausible and ridiculous, Horace insisted on repayment immediately. After that, Stan was disinherited. The financial details of the farm, or what Stan had done, were never revealed to my mother.

Ross and Pam were now going to school and had many friends. A degree of normality crept into our lives. Bruce was doing most of the milking, assisted by Ross. I decided, on advice from an experienced farming neighbour, Frank Watson, I should plough the fern covered paddock in the gorge and plant it to millet as a supplementary summer crop. The land in its present condition was unusable because the old woody bracken ferns were a mass five feet high and blocking all light to the soil below. The paddock was also littered with the remnants of stumps from its tree clad past. This was an opportunity to recover about four acres of land and provide additional much needed summer feed for the cows since our hills dried out quickly at Christmas time because they were exposed to the prevailing winds of the south west.

During the early autumn, I harnessed the horses into the two furrow reversible disc plough that had sat idle under a tree and began turning the soil. At first it was difficult. The horses would lunge, first one and then the other, in an attempt to pull the load, which was great to begin with because the discs were rusty. After some time, and many false starts we became a team and were able to move off as one. The experience of ploughing that paddock became one of my most enduring pleasant memories.

I walked behind the horses in the deep furrow across the steep slope to reduce the load. The only sound was the gentle footfall of the horses and the muffled tearing sound of the soil as it fell away from the polished discs. At each end I swung the lever attached to the discs to return in the same furrow, always throwing the sod downhill. The sour smell of the opened soil and the sweating horses combined to complete a magnificent scene accompanied by a feeling of quiet achievement.

Having almost completing the ploughing, my hopes for a millet crop were dashed when Stan refused to buy the seed. It was unbelievable. I consoled myself with the thought I had at least reduced the crop of ferns on steep virgin country into tilled ground that could now support pasture.

Our neighbours, the Dakin family, treated me almost as

another son and I was there every chance I had. I was included in the different projects they were engaged in, like the growing and harvesting of maize or quarrying stone from their pit for the tracks. Sam Dakin was a powerful man who, despite his direct and intimidating presence was remarkably tolerant of the crazy stunts their son Roger and I got up to.

At 16 I discovered the Saturday night dances at Wonthaggi, about 14 miles away. To get there, a pattern developed where Roger and I rode a motorbike to another friend's place because he had a license and a brand new 1957 blue Holden FE sedan. John Slade, nicknamed Tex, was a year or two older than we were. Laconic, tall and possessing a great sense of humor, he enjoyed our company because he had an older sister and no brothers. Before the dance we went to Tabener's Wonthaggi pub, which was doing a roaring trade in the back rooms, despite the rules of six o'clock trading. Wally, the owner, had the best poker face in the business, totally inscrutable. He waved us in after informing us we were the guests of …: He gave a name, usually the train driver who stayed in the hotel overnight. By knowing this name and denying we ever paid for the beer, we were safe if the police flying squad dropped in. After an hour or two, when suitably relaxed, we felt ready to tackle the main event of the night, the dance in the Town Hall, or alternatively, the dance in the Fire Brigade Hall.

In the beginning, the dance in the Fire Brigade Hall was my preference because it was aptly placed, given the steamy atmosphere generated by the occasional performance of a madly attractive woman who sang 'Oh What a Night it Was'. She gave a new meaning to the song. The simultaneous release of collective sexual tension was addictive and we craved more. But the music stopped at midnight and the rush was on, hopefully, to take the girl of our dreams home.

My mother and I started going to dances and other social events regularly happening throughout the region. There were celebrations for every important occasion, the turning on of power when electricity arrived in different localities, birthdays, balls, and sometimes, simply to raise money for amenities like tennis courts. This was the way in which all young people learned to dance and it was great fun.

The older ladies would get us up to dance and soon we were able to do any of the common old time dances as well as rock'n roll. The larger ladies would grasp me firmly to their ample bosoms and propel me around as I grasped the bones of their corsets. It was most enjoyable and in many ways these well attended social occasions provided a welcome relief from the routines and isolation of rural life and a means of meeting other people.

Speaking of girls, at the dances I had developed an attraction to Sylvia MacKay, one of four daughters of Beth and Alec on their dairy farm in Woolamai. One Sunday I thought I would take a walk down there and see if I could further the acquaintance since her parents were such friendly, well known people. Just what I thought I would achieve I'm still not sure, but one has to try. I was pleasantly pleased when her father Alec greeted me warmly and asked me to have lunch with the family. Being new to this business it was a little more than I had envisaged because it is difficult to maintain a conversation with one girl in a large family when sat at a dinner table. Needless to say, they enjoyed my discomfort.

Alec, almost in passing, asked would I mind helping him after lunch. He had a job for men only. Anxious to ingratiate myself with him and impress his daughter, I willingly agreed.

After the meal, Alec and I left the house and went to his workshop. He instructed me on how to sharpen a pocket knife, first by rubbing on the course side of the oil stone, then the fine side until, when satisfied, he removed the final edge with a leather strop. To demonstrate he proceeded to show me how he could shave the hair off his arm. Then he announced where I came in.

I spent the rest of the afternoon running down piglets and holding them while he castrated them. On completion, I was covered in mud and blood and disinclined to pursue his daughter further. Had this been a warning to me or was he simply an opportunist taking advantage of male help? I have seen the different family members many times over the years since and we all enjoy a laugh about my visit, but I'm still no wiser as to Alec's intent that day.

One event we attended regularly for quite a time was Round Dancing that a group of people from Melbourne were teaching in the hall at Grantville. We met many wonderful people in this way, among them the Barker Family. Pop and Mum Barker, as they were known to all and sundry, were stalwarts of Grantville, he being a senior supervisor with the Country Roads Board in our region, and Mum, a mother to her large family and a friend to all. Both Mum and Pop Barker became the saviours of my mother for they began to closely monitor the threats and dangers Stan was fermenting at home on the farm. About this time Stan was asked to leave the Wonthaggi Masonic Lodge, because we were told, of his history of violence to the family. The only other official recognition of his problem was the recommendation by the Department of Veteran Affairs that he see a psychiatrist. Stan openly boasted he knew the answer to questions that might propel him in that direction. The true extent of our family's problems was soon revealed to the Barkers and they kept a close watch on Mum thereafter.

One Sunday I was asked to take Ross and Pam to Sunday school at Bass. It was something I had done a number of times before but unfortunately, while driving home after the service, we had an accident. Approaching in the other direction was a utility which tried to cross the culvert at the same time. Being too narrow for both cars we sideswiped. The Holden utility, careered off the road onto its side and the Wolsely sustained damage to the right hand side. The other driver was panicking as I helped him out of the window and although no one was hurt, he insisted on informing the police.

The local policeman, Ivan Porter, was familiar with my use of the car and motorbike although he had never caught me. He was also aware of the state of affairs at home. In due course we arrived home and Stan flew into a predicable rage. When Ivan attempted to discuss the whole issue he was amazed to hear Stan accuse me of stealing the car, because if true, it would allow Stan to claim insurance. It was Stan's turn for a surprise when Ivan turned on him saying it was a despicable lie and although unlicensed, I had not contributed any more to the accident than the other driver. Ivan knew I had been driving for some time and went on to give Stan a thorough dressing down. Mum was shocked and refuted the lie. She never forgave Stan for what she regarded as a new low in her assessment of him. The Wolseley was repaired but was soon replaced by a Morris Oxford utility. It had a bench seat in front but served as the family vehicle thereafter, kids in the back, of course.

The Young Farmers Organisation had a simple philosophy

designed to promote the three concepts of 'Agriculture, Culture and Social'. A balanced program designed by the education department for young rural men and women. There were many clubs throughout the state, all supervised by carefully selected regional managers. I joined the Dalyston club which was part of the Western Port District Council supervised by Mr. Bob Morgan. The meetings were run according to correct meeting procedures by the elected office bearers, supported in turn by Mr. Morgan and those parents, like my mother and others, who provided adult guidance.

We had a great time running a wide range of activities including, parties, dances, annual balls, debating teams, public speaking, agricultural trials and radio broadcasts. Despite our aim to be balanced in our program, we proved far more adept with the social aspects of it. Almost everything the club organised was well attended and always concluded with a sumptuous supper provided by the parents. There were a number of other clubs in the region and our social events, like dances and the annual balls, were attended by hundreds, each club supporting the others. The opportunity to meet a wide range of people was exploited by all.

When Bill Haley hit the airways with 'Rock Around the Clock', it started a revolution of both sound and lifestyle. Closely followed by Buddy Holly and Elvis, this intoxicating music had an incendiary effect on the teenagers of the time. The Young Farmer dances became alive with rock'n roll which went on into the small hours. A number of parents allowed our Young Farmers Club to use their homes for parties but none were more hospitable than Mr and Mrs Stuart Hollins of Dalyston who renovated their home with open hospitality in mind. The parties we held there were amazing for they had

great sound and the space to dance. Mrs Hollins did express
wonder as to how so many bottles managed to be in the garden
the next day. Overall they were tolerant and felt, I believe, it
was better to have us, including their two sons and a daughter,
under some sort of supervision than none. It was a happy time
and I was grateful.

All these events were happening for the most part at night
because I worked at the factory seven days a week through the
flush and for much of the season. I had been 15 when I had
started at the Glen Forbes factory. By now I was 16, beyond
parental control. Cheese making was hard and heavy work
with no distinction made between what was done by a man or
a boy, it was all the same to management. I was doing a man's
work so I spent my spare time and money in pursuit of a good
time to distract myself. While on the surface I was apparently
happy, inwardly I craved the guidance and intervention of a
stronger hand because I knew I was wasting time that might
otherwise have led to a productive, stimulating career. Like
my fellow workers at the factory, we were resentful of the
indifference and the poor conditions but opportunities were
limited due to our lack of education and in my case, the need
to be financially independent.

Another mutual friend of Roger and I was Ken McKenzie.
Ken was about 10 years older than us and owned a taxi he ran
in the bayside suburb of Hampton. He also owned a large
beautifully kept Jaguar in which he frequently turned up at
many local dances because his family lived in Grantville.
Between dances we would retire to the car for refreshments
and, as it happened, Ken always had a boot full. His generosity
seemed to know no bounds. Thus began a ritual that went on
for years and only ceased when girlfriends were able to provide

more compelling entertainment. Long after we had cars of our own we would take girls home and then meet at different agreed locations to party on through the night. Ken even had a PA sound system in the boot of his car. The usual six to ten of us had a great time with music while drinking.

One Sunday morning Mum came in to see me as I was recovering from such a night. She knew when I had drunk too much because I was unable to start the motorbike when I returned from Roger's place. They lived so high on the hill I could roll from there down the gorge to our gate and leave the bike lying on the side of the road. This morning she sat on my bed in tears, 'You will become a drunk like your Grandfather,' she said, and then asked who I had been with. I replied, 'I was with Ken.' She sniffed back a tear and offered the most amazing observation, 'Ken,' she alleged, 'is employed by Carlton and United to recruit new drinkers.'

In about 1957, during the slow time of autumn, Ken, Rochfort Abrahamson (known as Tex) and I drove to Queensland in the Jaguar, sleeping at night in makeshift camps on the side of the road. The holiday was an eye opener for unsophisticated country boys such as us. We called into the new development of Surfers Paradise before arriving in Brisbane. I recall the steam train we caught at Roma Street to visit the beach at Sandgate. Overall it was a wonderful, informative time and Ken bore most of the cost.

By 1958, I was entertaining all manner of different career choices but none created more angst than my attempt to join the Navy. In response to an advertisement, I applied for the position of trainee engine mechanic and was invited for assessment at the centre in Queens Road, St Kilda. I passed the physical examination and was then assessed for aptitude before finally having a psychological exam in which I was asked, 'How do you think you will manage the discipline?' I hesitated on this at some length, but, was finally passed and invited to sign on for nine years. I was not yet eighteen and I had to obtain parental consent. Mum refused to sign and an almighty argument ensued. She refused to sign because she felt I could do better and maintained I would never manage the nine years. My protestations were ignored and slowly the opportunity passed. Then I saw an advertisement offering the opportunity to train as a herd tester. I applied and was accepted. During my holidays, I attended the three week training program for herd testing at the Burnley Horticultural College and qualified. Ironically, the butter factory offered me a course at Werribee to train as a qualified cheese maker, but it was too late.

CHAPTER 7
THE HERD TESTER

Once qualified, I successfully applied for the position of herd tester with the Phillip Island & Archie's Creek Herd Test Association to begin on the 1st of December 1958. This was in anticipation of obtaining my driving license in January when I would be 18. To carry the equipment for testing, I bought a 1930, V8 Oakland car in almost original condition, but it succumbed within months to the extravagant demands I made upon it. Flush with a salary of £23 a week, I bought a Hillman Husky on time payment and became a reliable herd tester. The Hillman was essentially a small two door station wagon with a simple lift up rear seat when required. The small side valve motor ensured I had to be content with reliability rather than speed. Being a herd tester entailed working for the Archie's Creek and Phillip Island Association of twenty four farmers who received an incentive from the Department of Agriculture to test their cows for butterfat. The results of the testing provided an objective production record from which farmers could select and breed from the best cows. I carried ten test buckets with lids, a centrifuge turned by hand and about 200 test bottles with rubber stoppers set in tin trays of 24. For the sampling I had an assortment of glassware including a burette, a number of pippettes, graduated test flasks and a large carboy of sulphuric acid. The test buckets were placed in the line of the milking machine so that each cow's milk could be trapped, allowing me to weigh it and take a proportionate sample before tipping the balance into the large vat for collection by the butter factory truck. This was done for both the evening and morning milking.

I stayed on each farm once a month because the farms of the association were widely spread. The process was repeated every month. Farmers not in the association would also approach me and request a periodic test so for additional income, on completion of my regular round, I would test them also. For much of the year I worked every day either testing or doing farm work on an hourly rate. In Victoria at that time, the State herd average per cow was less than 300lb of butterfat. A number of herds in the Archie's Creek and Phillip Island Association exceeded 300lb while the top producer in our association, averaged over 400lb per cow each year.

The calving records required that all calves be tattooed in each ear so that each animal carried a reliable record of its breeding. The tattooing of calves could be great fun because it required the farmer to know which calf belonged to which of the cows that had calved since the previous visit. In general, it was the farmer's children or his wife who knew best because they were more often involved in the calf rearing process. The numbers put in one ear recorded the number assigned to the calf and the farm code, with a prefix for the year. The other ear carried the dam's number and the sire's code. It could be great entertainment running down frisky calves in all weathers while adjudicating the odd family argument about which calf belonged to which cow, remembering that every cow had a name as well as a number. On the larger farms at this time, it could mean up to 200 calves being born over three months.

The testing results were a valuable guide for the future breeding program of the farm for most, but for a few it was a chance to get their name in the paper because the results listing the top ten producers were published each month in the local newspaper. To be high on the list carried considerable kudos in a rural community, especially if it could be achieved consistently.

I would arrive on the farm around 3.30 p.m. in time for afternoon tea. I would then set up the equipment while the farmer gathered his cows. On completion of the milking, I would assist in cleaning up the shed, then myself, before having the evening meal. Most farmers were pleased to see me, although sometimes it was not always convenient for them. Testing did disrupt the routine and slow the milking a little. It was a business and as such, while pleasant to me, my presence had a nuisance value that was generally handled with tolerance and lukewarm indifference. I was not family and yet I was to be accommodated. The wives could be put out by my sudden appearance. There would be murmurings about changing beds, other guests, the food situation and other domestic inconveniences. Generally I was greeted with a warm welcome, but because I was a guest there was no helping oneself to the phone, fruit, snacks or drink from the refrigerator, unless invited to do so.

Over time, through familiarity, I merged with the wallpaper. I became privy to amazing family dramas that enabled me to see disputes did occur in other families, but most occurred without the violence I was used to. Issues of inheritance, sibling rivalry, religion, unsuitable suitors, politics, neighbourhood disputes and sport, beside the vexatious issues of life on a dairy farm, were all played out without physical violence and only moderate bad language.

Although I had a good car and was well paid, I dealt with my personal isolation by going out almost every night. I rarely managed more than five hours sleep because although some farmers started as early as 4.30 a.m., most started around 6 a.m. My coming and going was of little concern providing I was there for each milking and that I completed the testing and book work. Without a place within my own family and only this tenuous connection with the farm clients, I was a free agent. My belongings easily fitted in an old blue suit case held together with a leather strap.

Some of my friends might have envied my freedom. Inwardly, I craved the opportunities and stability I saw in the best of the families I visited. I was unhappy sleeping in a different bed every night and always being the visitor. Spare beds were invariably worn out and sharing a bedroom with other people's children is not homely. I was bored with the repetitious nature of the job but powerless to change it, or so

I thought. A few of the families were exceedingly kind, a fact I was grateful for.

During my free time during the day I visited my mother regularly or called on friends. One day as I was leaving my parents farm, I was hailed by two men I presumed were lost because they waved me down as if for directions. They introduced themselves as Senior Detective Bell from Dandenong and Senior Detective Seymour from Warragul. They wanted to know what I was doing one day the previous month when apparently I was seen in the bush opposite the Glen Forbes Butter Factory. I explained that, assisted by Roger, I had cut six feet of pipe from the disused piggery milk line to make a tow bar for the Hillman Husky. I tried to tell them I had obtained permission to do so from Sam Pearson, the manager of the factory, but they seemed uninterested. I gave them all the details of where and how we had got the pipe and felt that would be the end of it. Undeterred, they then went to see Roger, from whom they obtained a similar story.

To my amazement, we were charged with stealing the pipe. I couldn't believe it since I had permission to take the pipe and the pipe line belonged to the factory. I did nothing. I did not tell my father or my mother, thinking it would resolve itself when fully investigated. We were soon summoned to court. It never crossed my mind I should see a solicitor because I had no money. On the appointed day, I dropped into the local newspaper to speak to the owner, Mr. Tom Gannon. I did this because he knew of me and my involvement with the Young Farmers. I begged him not publish the story. It was a mistake I explained. He assured me he would not.

The bench was occupied by three Justices of the Peace. The charge of stealing was read to the court and I was asked to explain. Apparently, we were charged because the police thought we had been involved in stealing the contents of a house at Kilcunda the same day we had been seen taking the pipe. Detective Seymour then spoke in our defense, saying he had obtained character references for us both and that the pipe was worthless. He also confirmed I had permission and that we should not have been charged. Accordingly, the magistrates said there would be no charge so we were let off. Relieved, we went home.

The next week the headline on the front page of the local paper shrieked 'Honest Boys Let Off' in the biggest print possible. My father went into overdrive. He could be heard all over the district. All that concerned me was the ribbing I was sure to receive from everyone who knew me. Roger's father laughed the whole thing off. That was the beginning and end of our crime career.

On the visits to my mother our conversations were mostly of her problems and her concerns for the younger children. She was happy with her place in the community but financially things remained embarrassingly bad with accumulated bills and Stan's continued abusiveness. She was worn out and would leave if she had any way of supporting the children. She was concerned the grass had overgrown the area around the house, making it dangerous for the little children, Ross, Pam and Geoffrey. I bought a lawn mower and gave mum a little more money.

A family I herd tested on Phillip Island offered me other work on their farm. I enjoyed their sophisticated approach to both farming and life in general. Jeff and Ros Wilkinson had received private school education and travelled the world. Our friendship grew into my minding the farm while Jeff was away showing his stud pigs at the Royal Melbourne's Show in September. I worked the testing to accommodate that time and, indeed, was by now doing extra piecework for others in the hours between one farm and another.

The most common advice offered by the farmers and almost everyone I knew was that I should settle down and keep herd testing. In other words, suspend your curiosity and accept your lot without question. I should be grateful for the job I was doing and don't aspire for more. They were entitled to dream but I should not. It was a form of condescension that made me angry. I remain wary of people who expect others to do things they would not.

I had a girlfriend, Kay. We spent many nights of the week dancing while on other nights I was out with my mates drinking to excess. I wanted to belong somewhere and dealt with the frustration by filling every moment with activity, either by working or socialising. I doubt anyone knew the turmoil of my thoughts. I was angry with my father, worried about my mother, brothers and sister and dissatisfied with my work. I was an observer of family life, not a participant. Who, I wondered, gives a damn for me?

My girlfriend was not only beautiful, she was an excellent dancer. Despite having no formal training, she frequently won the 'Belle of the Ball'. It was wonderful fun and we were also good at rock'n roll. Her father played the drums as part of a band for the smaller dances. He seemed to enjoy the excitement of it all as much as we did. Her family was very hospitable to me and because her father was so much fun, we always had a hilarious time. Once when we were all around the table for a Sunday dinner, he was giving cheek to his wife Betty. In reply to his taunts and teasing, Betty turned from the stove and poured a saucepan of custard over his head. He sat there with an amazed look on his face before slowly wiping the custard from his eyes as it flowed over him. We kids just rocked with laughter. He was a genuine clown who had a theatrical take on all aspects of life.

Kay and her mother made their dresses, as did many girls at the time. They were beautiful concoctions of colour that accentuated their figures with numerous petticoats that occasionally fell to the floor while dancing. I realised we had gone over the top when one night I turned up in my recently acquired, near new spotless 1959 FC Holden sedan to pick her up for the district final of the Miss Gippsland competition. I was met by her younger brother, who instructed me to take the back seat out and replace it with a stool. Her grace arrived and sat enveloped by her magnificent new gown in the back seat. It proved worthwhile for we won, or at least she did.

By the winter of 1961 I was bored to tears and restless. I resigned from the Phillip Island and Archie's Creek Herd Test Association. The lack of a formal qualification, together with the boredom of repetitive manual work, had generated the fear I was destined to a life without choice, one laboring job appearing to be little different from any other. How I felt about anything had become irrelevant and an unaffordable luxury. Life, it seemed, was a matter of survival. I had learned I could do almost anything I put my mind to and I became unconcerned by what I did, provided I was paid.

The atmosphere in the community was subdued because of the almost daily reminders of the Cold War. The Berlin Wall was in the news, the threat of communism to the free world the subtext. The erratic ranting of Nikita Khrushchev fuelled the feeling of an imminent threat to Western democracies.

Chairman Mao Zedong, leader of the People's Republic of China, instituted his Great Leap Forward program which replaced the previous practices of farming with commune collectives, the result of which was a massive famine that, up until then, resulted in an estimated 30 million deaths. Despite the escapist fun of the rock'n roll era, there was a real feeling another catastrophic war was inevitable. The Russians and the Chinese, we were informed, were hell bent on spreading communism.

I heard of a training program with the MLC Insurance Company. I applied and after an intensive three weeks of instruction, was turned loose to sell life insurance. Amazingly, I proved to be quite successful, but I loathed it. I was too ready to empathise with the client. I quit after a few weeks. I tried selling cars at Korumburra and that lasted a few weeks. I was not a salesman.

CHAPTER 8

RESTLESS

A new initiative for the Bass Valley Region was the construction of a large dam behind Almurta. A plea went out for the people in the immediate vicinity to provide board for the men required to build the dam. To assist the finances at home Mum responded by taking another boarder, the foreman Tom Hourigan. Tom was pleased to be able to live close to his job rather than face the daily travel from his home at Traralgon, a 90 minute drive away.

Tom was a large happy man who wore his responsibilities lightly. Each day he returned home full of laughter and fun, appreciative of Mum's care. His presence brought immediate relief from Stan's unremitting verbal and physical control of the household. For the first time my visits home were a pleasure and I no longer left feeling guilty. The little children too became more relaxed and like Mum, we all became fond of this man who would clearly not tolerate a threat to any of us. Stan was isolated and inconsequential in his own home.

In early 1961 Town Road Constructions won the contract to lay the ten inch spun cast concrete lined steel pipes from the dam to Phillip Island. I applied for a job as a labourer. I was assigned to a stockpile of pipes next to the main road as it passed through the Koala Reserve on Phillip Island. My new job was to cut the pipes to different lengths as required for the pipe layers. I would set a pipe up so it was free to roll sideways, strap on a saw designed to cut through both the cast metal exterior and the concrete lining, and complete the cut. After several weeks of cutting pipes, my eyes felt intensely painful and began to stream with tears. The following day I could not see at all. I was taken to Doctor Hopkins in Cowes. My eyes were full of iron filings from the cutting process because, of course, we had no safety glasses. He stood me against the surgery door and removed the filings with a magnetic needle. My sight recovered in a few days but I had had enough. There was no future for me in what I was doing.

Despite our long working days, at night, and occasionally on a weekend, Roger and I managed to spend time together. He had bought a large 1952 Oldsmobile, an ex American Embassy car in beautiful condition. He was rightly proud of it. His fortunes had taken an upturn since he became a share farmer on a farm only a little further up the Dalyston road from the Dakin family farm. One Wednesday night we decided to go to the regular dance in Dandenong. When I finished work I called and helped him finish his milking. We let the cows go, and after a wash in a basin, we headed for Dandenong, taking a liberal supply of Roger's home brew with us. It was a pleasant evening when about 10.30 p.m., Roger whispered that he had won a heart. I would have to wait at Stevie George's café while he took this girl home. This was a variant of our regular arrangement. I waited patiently, taking the opportunity to have a meal of steak and eggs since we hadn't eaten earlier. About 1 a.m. Roger returned with a huge grin on his face. 'Well,' he explained, 'Things were going nicely until this God awful smell engulfed us. You could have reminded me to take the dog out of the boot after we put the cows over the road.' Apparently the poor thing farted and ruined everything. There must be a disturbed female in Melbourne who could recount this unusual happening.

We decided to go to the Korumburra rodeo, an annual event that promised to be a great day for us to catch up with friends. Roger and I travelled together, enjoying the luxury of his new car. There was a huge crowd and the mood of the day was party, something we excelled at. The day passed in a blur and then I woke up. Roger was sitting in a bed next to me with a grin mixed with concern. I asked where we were. 'We are in the Korumburra Hospital and you have a cracked skull,' was the reply. We had been driving on the road to Warragul late that day and had driven into the bank on the steep side of the road just out of Korumburra. Roger was driving and I was in the front passenger seat. The force of the impact had driven me into and under the dashboard in such a way the ambulance men had great difficulty getting me out. Roger explained with glee and my embarrassment that I had vomited all over them and the doctor summoned to help. Roger had sustained a few cuts and bruises but was otherwise unscathed.

My 21st birthday was celebrated in the Glen Forbes Hall in January 1962 and attended by many friends. Mum made a heroic effort to pay for the evening by selling a pig she had bought and raised in partnership with our neighbor, Mr Sam Dakin. She presented me with a watch I value highly. Somewhat embarrassed by the attention and resentful of my father's attitude, I reflect I may have been perceived to be surly and unappreciative of Mum's efforts, but nothing could be further from the truth. Stan contributed nothing and came late in the evening. Predictably, he fawned over the relatives who had made an effort to be there, promoting the belief he was the caring father. I was experiencing mixed feelings of guilt, anxiety and anger about the ongoing mistreatment of the family and the dim prospect for improvement. I was angry. It was a farce. My recurring unspoken prayer was: why doesn't someone, anyone, intervene?

Mum told me she was afraid for her safety and for the children, which worried me greatly. Bruce was still working for the Archie's Creek cheese factory and was rarely home. Mum was increasingly reliant on the presence of the boarders to maintain civility in the home. Tom Hourigan was still living there through the week but like the school teacher, he returned to his home each weekend. Mum was unable to leave without money or substantial support.

I met another girl at the Saturday night dances. Aileen was so attractive I could hardly believe my luck for I was far from feeling confident about my place in the world. She on the other hand was sure of herself and her maturity impressed me greatly. However, her interest in me somehow made me even more conscious of my lack of status and I cooled a little because I was drawn to the idea of escaping. Not from her but the vortex of despair I was feeling for my prospects and the worry for my mother and siblings. My presence had always made matters worse. Perhaps there was some flaw in me that made me the source of blame.

A fellow worker and casual friend, Don McRae, told me of his experiences working around Australia. He had worked all over, from Wyndham in the meat works of the Northern Territory, to Queensland on the sugar cane as well as picking fruit in Victoria. There was plenty of work and the pay was good, he said, what did I have to lose? I reflected long and hard. What indeed did I have to lose? I had exhausted the local opportunities and was sick of hearing the opinions of well meaning farmers who thought I should settle down and keep a steady job. I resigned from pipe laying, said goodbye to my mother and boarded the train with Don, destination Shepparton. We were going to pick fruit. It was about two weeks before Christmas, December 1962.

In Shepparton we approached a number of fruit farmers who informed us that because the season was late, we would not be required until some weeks after Christmas. Disgruntled and conscious of our fast disappearing reserve of cash, we caught the bus to Benalla and then the train to Sydney. Under Don's guidance we walked up Pitt Street and booked into the People's Palace. This was an entirely new experience. Here I was in another city with a companion I knew only briefly and almost completely broke. To top it off, I was propositioned in the lift by a prostitute.

Don had a little more money than I did, but that was not going to go far. We searched the papers for a job and found an advertisement for laborers required by Tooth's Brewery. In desperation we walked down the Broadway to Tooth's office and joined a line of men who appeared as desperate as we were. Eventually, I was ushered to a man sitting at a table inside. He began to take my details and asked me for my references. I said that they were outside in my case and he excused me so I could get them. Back on the street, I found paper in my bag and wrote a glowing report of my former employment. On my return, the man looked rather long and hard at me before announcing I was to start immediately, working in the smaller brewery where I would be assigned a position. I was relieved - it was a close call.

Don also gained work but was assigned to the larger Kent brewery. Flush with the knowledge we would be paid soon, Don suggested we should relocate from the Palace to where he had lived on a previous occasion. With no better suggestion, I went with him on a short walk to see his old landlady. We stopped outside a two storey terrace house in Cleveland Street, Redfern, opposite the parkland. The owner was a Mrs. Smith who said yes, Don and I could share a room upstairs with access to the kitchen facilities. We moved in straight away. My education began in earnest.

I reported to the office at the rear of the small brewery. It was housed in the corner tower of the high brick wall that almost surrounded the brewery. I was given a pint of beer before we started. It was a beautiful drop and made in this brewery. I believe it was called Tooth's Country Special, as good as I've ever had. My first job was working in the hop store in the tower many floors above the brewing process. My fellow workers were a rough lot who took pains to fill me in on the accepted work practice. 'You will be given a pint before we start work, another at morning tea, lunch, afternoon tea and knock off. From time to time throughout the day you will take your turn at the honey pot down at the landing.' At this point, I did not know what the honey pot was, but I soon found out when told it was my time to go down.

On the platform where the wooden barrels were filled for delivery, long spears set above the barrels could be pulled down into the barrels for filling. When full, the worker controlling the process would withdraw the spear and immediately drive a cork bung into the hole with a large mallet and considerable skill – but not every time. The occasional full barrel was rolled aside to the assembly of men waiting in the gloom, all anxious to pass judgment on the new product. This was the honey pot.

The pint pots were filled by gently rolling the barrel sufficient to pour it out and then we would linger to enjoy it before returning to our job, thereby releasing someone else for the trip downstairs. Well, you can imagine the effect all this beer had - we were drunk almost all the time. I lost favor with the men in the hop store when I refused to take my turn at the barrel. It ended in an ugly incident where I had to defend myself with a large knife while standing on a stack of hop bales. The workers had turned on me for being weak, which is not exactly the way they described me. I simply could not drink all day. A failure, I was shifted to another floor to clean the huge vats after the brew had been run off. Clad in a sturdy apron and rubber boots, I scrubbed out the huge stainless steel vats with a brush and caustic soda. Notionally, we worked in pairs, but I worked alone for the most part because my partner was quite at home spending all day at the honey pot. Men fell off ladders, cut themselves, were scalded, fell over and had every type of accident possible. The place was run by dipsomaniacs.

I was told one chap fell in a vat and got out three times for a pee before he drowned.

The living arrangements became strained after a few nightly visits to Don's old friends a number of streets away deep in Redfern. I was horrified to hear them calmly discussing a 'job' over the kitchen table. I wanted no part of that since I was already reeling with the mindless antics of the men at the brewery. A chap I worked with was glassed in the face over some minor matter. To top it off, one Saturday morning the couple in the next room with whom we shared the kitchen, had an almighty argument that went on for about three quarters of an hour and ended when she stabbed him several times with a carving knife. He staggered out into our kitchen bleeding heavily and pleading for help. The ambulance took him away and the police removed her. I had quite a lot to think about while mopping up the blood. What had I got myself into?

Soon after, Don announced he was going back to Brisbane. I declined to go with him because I had started to attend a school at night on the slope behind the Sydney Town Hall. I still felt the need to better myself somehow. I saw him off on the train with a sigh of relief because it had become obvious we had little in common. I wandered the streets of Sydney at night feeling lonelier than I had ever been. All I could see was the ugly, the superficial and outrageous behavior of the people around me. It was not that I was a prude. I had all the grog I wanted, I simply saw nothing attractive about the drug or sex scene. I began to mix with a group of young people who attended the church next to the park and even visited Luna Park with them, but I was conscious that while they had somewhere to go or someone to see, I did not. From the newspaper, I found full board and moved to Gladesville to a home on the main road. Although I had to travel on the bus each day to work, I felt more comfortable with my improved circumstances. I soon sent a note to Jeff Wilkinson who once said if he bought the farm next door he would like me to run it. One day, after I had been in Sydney about six months I received a letter from Jeff with that very proposition. I replied immediately and returned by train.

CHAPTER 9
THE FARM MANAGER

Since my first day on the Glen Forbes farm I had bonded in some spiritual way with the soil, the sight and the smell of this country. I was coming home – relieved and excited at the prospect of securing my future. It was about 9pm when I arrived at the Glen Forbes station. I walked up the road to the farm. My return was without notice so my family was surprised. Mum was pleased to see me. The old man simply grunted as he sat in front of the fire. Of course the children were excited to see me, but my homecoming was an anticlimax. Nothing had changed.

The Wilkinsons, on the other hand, were relieved that I returned. The plan they outlined was for me to run the farm, meaning milk the 100 cows, manage the piggery and in general do what was required. Jeff would oversee the details of the business and assist me where necessary. I would take only what cash I needed for my immediate needs and leave the balance with him for reinvestment in the farm on my behalf. Jeff and Ros' would move into the bigger home on the new property and later, the old cottage would be available to me. There was no formal agreement. Nevertheless, I was relieved and determined to make a success of this opportunity for it held the prospect of becoming a share farmer for people I knew and respected.

I moved into the small bungalow behind the larger home on

the newly acquired property. Otherwise, I lived with the family and this was a home experience better than I had known. The two little daughters were playful intelligent children and the atmosphere of the home warm and peaceful. The conversation and social intercourse with friends and neighbours was always congenial, I was happy and optimistic for my future as a farmer.

To my amazement, Aileen, the girl I had met before going to Sydney, agreed to see me again. I had left her without a satisfactory explanation because I could not articulate my concern or sense of shame. Now I felt I had something to offer. All I had to do was work and learn. I would progress from farm manager to share farmer and, who knows, have my own farm one day. Further, her belief in me instilled a confidence I would justify. I was in love. She had a halo of blonde curls, a slim figure, a flair for art and was intelligent.

The 100 cow dairy herd was milked with only four milking units in an old, small dairy. The milk was separated and the skim milk pumped down to the piggery where it was reticulated to the individual pens of the piggery. The piggery had been built to a design developed by the agricultural piggery advisor, Les Downie. The cream was sent to the Archie's Creek butter factory. Milking 100 cows in such a small shed was a slow business and took more than two hours. I found this trying, especially since I had worked in many more modern sheds while herd testing. The entire herd was joined by artificial insemination and that involved identifying the cows in oestrous and keeping them back after milking for the inseminator and subsequently releasing them. We were actively engaged in all aspects of herd improvement from feeding the cows while milking, herd testing and the supplementary feeding of crops like turnips over the summer.

Not only did we plant summer crops of turnips as part of the pasture renovation plan, we also grew barley we harvested with an old reaper Jeff obtained from the north of the state. The little Ferguson tractor was just able to pull the huge ground driven equipment. This fodder experiment was successful and provided a valuable source of feed for the piggery. The piggery was on the opposite side of the road to the dairy and consisted of a long rectangular shed containing ten sties each holding a sow and her piglets until weaning. The piglets were kept warm by lights suspended above them over an insulated floor. The sows were brought in prior to farrowing, cleaned up and the birth assisted when necessary. Designed and built well, the pig sties were easy to clean by daily hosing out. The effluent was collected in a large pit which I emptied and spread on the paddocks every week. The breed was pure bred Large White. There were about 40 sows and a few boars. With a gestation period of 114 days while technically possible to obtain three litters a year, in practice, fewer are achieved. Each litter generally consisted of eight to 14 piglets. When the piglets were weaned, the sows were joined again and turned out to graze in the adjoining paddocks. I enjoyed the pigs because they are intelligent, tractable animals that respond well to good husbandry. The smell takes longer to like.

I was enjoying life. The Wilkinsons kept a good home and treated me well. The farm occupied me completely. It was well run and we had good stock. The routine of the farm was constant but always interesting. It involved not only the husbandry of the stock but the maintenance and adoption of new techniques to upgrade efficiency. About two nights a week I would ride the motorbike, another Triumph twin cylinder 500cc, across to Wonthaggi to see Aileen. Occasionally I had a day off and was sometimes lent the Wilkinson car so Aileen and I could visit the beach or our relatives. It was a happy time and we planned our future together.

One evening, in the late summer of 1963, the Barker family picked Mum up in Glen Forbes and took her to an evening in Wonthaggi. They were members of the Scotch Club where they enjoyed Scottish dancing. This was a routine that grew out of their generosity and concern for Mum's welfare over previous years. That concern was genuine for they had penetrated the veneer of respectability Stan deflected others with. On this evening, their caution was rewarded. Pop Barker had driven his big green Humber Super Snipe up into the farmyard to turn the car around and drop Mum off. As he did so, the lights swung over the shed revealing a trip wire across the doorway in the back of the shed. On close examination, Pop found Stan hiding behind the door of the enclosed workshop. He was armed with a cudgel. Stan admitted his intention was to kill Mum when she fell.

News of Stan's treachery spread fast with the sudden realisation that the long held suspicion of our family's problems were deeper and more dangerous than many had chosen to believe. At the time those living on the farm were Stan, Mum, Bruce, 20, Ross, 13, Pamela, 10, Geoffrey, 7, and the local school teacher, Mr Don Jewell.

Soon after, Mum called saying she had left the farm with Pamela and taken refuge with an old family friend, Val Drayton. Val had come over and taken them back to their family farm at Labertouche, north of Drouin. Despite the many times we had spoken of her need to leave, the problem of having no money or anywhere to go had made it impossible. I was shocked but pleased, Mum had finally found a way. However, it raised new concerns for the safety and welfare of Ross and Geoffrey, who had been left with Stan. We considered Geoffrey was safe for the moment because Stan was fond of him, but Ross, who had been so ill, was vulnerable. Bruce was old enough to make up his own mind as to where he would go, indeed, so was I.

Ross and Pam later revealed what happened. Mum approached Pam early on the chosen day and said she was leaving and asked would Pam like to go with her. Pam said yes. The teacher was told Pam had had a recurrence of tonsillitis and would not be attending school that day. Ross had already departed on the school bus. He had just started his first year at the Wonthaggi Technical School and was unaware of the plan afoot. The workers left the home and then Val arrived as prearranged to take them to safety. Mum had organised a close neighbour, Dorothy Stephens, to meet Ross after school and see to his needs in the short term. Her intention was to gain custody of all the children but until she had established independent living, she could only take Pam.

Despite Mum's efforts to minimise the problems, Ross was traumatised. While Stan believed he was going to school each day following Mum's escape, in fact Ross hid in the bush down the old road for almost two weeks. By sheer coincidence, on his first day back at school, Mum arrived and had a talk with the principal, Mr Ted Shillinglaw, known affectionately to all as 'Two Bob'. Ross left with Mum and returned to Labertouche where he then began attending the Warragul Technical School.

Within weeks of being at Labertouche, Mum successfully applied for the position of house-keeper for a Mr Dawson whose wife was terminally ill at their home near Drouin. David Dawson and his wife Hazel had four children. They were aged from 2 to 9 years and he was having a difficult time trying to maintain his position as the technician in charge of telephones and communication for the Post Master General's network in Warragul, while managing his children and terminally ill wife.

Mum started work at the Dawson home mid May 1963. At first she found it difficult to work for David. He soon realised mum was a capable and compassionate person able to run the household and gradually forfeited a little of his control to her. Hazel, his wife, had been an active ambassador for the Jehovah's Witness church up until her illness. This had involved much visiting for the purpose and adherence to the dictates of the religion. In consequence, it had become a humourless home run on austere religious guidelines. Mum was far from comfortable with it all. The youngest daughter, Helen, aged 2, had been passed around among family friends while her mother was sick. The older children were emotionally stressed, but all began to settle under Mum's care. Sadly, despite the nursing and David's every effort to obtain medical help, Hazel died, leaving a family numb with grief.

David Dawson then invited Mum to bring Ross into his home for he had stayed with the Draytons since leaving Glen Forbes. Until then, Mum only had Pam with her at the Dawson home. Now she was asked to manage the home as one family. Ross moved in and began attending the Drouin High School while Mark, Pamela, Elise and Ian went to the state school. Helen was at home in Mum's care. The fight for legal custody of the Cliff children was yet to begin, for Geoffrey was still in the care of his father.

Back at Glen Forbes, Stan arranged the sale of the farm to a neighbour for an undisclosed price – hoping to settle the debts that would have consumed any remaining equity. He moved to a rented house in North Wonthaggi while continuing his employment at the Miller Cyclone factory. Bruce elected to go with him. Jointly they were looking after seven year old Geoffrey who was attending the Wonthaggi Primary School. It was a grim, marginal existence for them and I maintained basic contact out of concern for Geoffrey and Bruce.

My relationship with Aileen blossomed and we became engaged to be married with the approval of her family. We began regularly visiting Mum and the new family at Drouin. It was such a relief to see Mum happy and well treated by Mr. Dawson. He had assumed responsibility for her and the children and they were all thriving under his care. He was a clever man who could be formidable in defense of what he believed to be right.

Aileen's father Bob was a quietly spoken intelligent, introverted man. When not at work as a senior electrician with the State Coal Mine in Wonthaggi, he was working at home in his tiny workshop attached to the kitchen of their home. In his own time, he made a variety of welding plants he sold to tradesmen with specific requirements, like spot welding. I found I was spending time with him because I was intrigued with his knowledge of mathematics, physics and electrical theory. Each welder he made was designed and built with uncommon attention to detail and sold readily for extra income. He was given to telling me little stories – most had a message designed to invite further thought. He asked me one day had I heard about the man who was asked if he could play the violin. I said, 'No, what did he say?'. 'I don't know,' said the man, 'I have never tried.' The point was not lost on me. I enjoyed Bob's company and his instruction on many little projects. I especially enjoyed fishing with him in his little dinghy on Anderson Inlet east of Inverloch. I became fond of him and incorporated him into the image I was forming of my idealised composite father.

It was a pleasant surprise when I heard that with Mr Dawsons financial support, Mum had petitioned Stan for the legal custody of the three younger children. The matter was heard before Mr. Justice Little in the Supreme Court on 28th October 1963. The trial proved harrowing and became particularly nasty when Stan made counter accusations and lied about many issues as he defended himself against the charge of cruelty. Sadly Bruce, motivated by misplaced loyalty to his father, inexplicably took side with him. His Honor, Justice Little, summarised the hearing by making stinging comments about the credibility of the evidence led against Mum and then interviewed the children in his office before granting custody of them to her. He stipulated visiting rights and ordered Stan to pay maintenance of £2 a week for each child.

The court case passed without me knowing about it because Mum said she did not want me to endure unnecessary stress. She knew I felt responsible for the fights and abuse leveled at me over the years. I could understand her point of view but was disappointed. I had been denied the opportunity to make a statement removing all doubt of my father's unsuitability to raise Geoffrey. A copy of the transcript of the trial upholds the veracity of this account.

The decision to award the custody of the children to Mum was a huge relief and ensured the children had an opportunity to grow up in a stable, positive environment where personal achievement was expected and encouraged.

In November 1963, the terrible shock of President Kennedy's assassination rocked the world. I was milking the cows when I heard the broadcast. News of the assassination was a terrible postscript to the unrelenting anxiety of the Cold War that had hung over us all since the Second World War. John Kennedy had withstood the brinkmanship of Nikita Khrushchev in 1962 and the President's leadership at the time had been appreciated by all in the West. Now there was a profound sense of loss and an outpouring of public grief.

The farm seemed to be performing well despite sporadic episodes of erysipelas disease in the pigs. Caused by a bacterial infection, it is an elusive streptococcal infection of the skin and internal organs. Without warning it would render even the best of our animals sick, and sometimes kill them. The loss of animals in this way was confounding because the piggery was kept especially clean and the feed carefully milled by us and supplemented with vitamins and essential elements according to a recommended formula. The barley grain that formed the basis of their diet was either grown on the farm or Jeff bought from the north of the State. The bought graded barley was sent by rail to the Anderson Station from where I collected it with the farm truck. Our veterinarian, John Crawford, was a frequent visitor and friend who became as frustrated as we were that it was taking so long to control the problem.

Among the visitors to the Wilkinson farm was Mr and Mrs Rudolf Himmer. Rudy, as he was known, was a large man with a small goatee beard who drove a tiny Austin car. Retired and living in Cowes with his wife, he had been the musical director of the ABC. I forged a great friendship with this charming couple who brought fascinating insights of their bigger world into my life. They and been classically educated in Europe and had traveled widely. In addition, he was a gourmet cook. Aileen and I became dinner guests privileged to enjoy their sophisticated hospitality a number of times because of their gratitude to me for jobs I performed for them around their house and garden. It was a pleasure for me to go around to their home for an hour or two and clean out spouting or remove large trees and take away refuse, but they were grateful. He would select music from his huge collection and play it for us on the best of sound equipment while we ate sumptuous gourmet food served on Mrs. Himmer's collection of antique china. The experience was unforgettable and one I cherish because of its warmth and sincerity. I loved them and was grateful for the glimpse they provided of another way to live.

The Wilkinsons entertained a regular assortment of enlightened family and friends that enabled me to appreciate the wide variety of life experiences they were able to share. The combination of worldly people and progressive farmers enjoying good food, wine and music was a new experience for me. Herd testing had provided a global view of many ways to live and farm and I could see successful farmers were the ones who embraced change and valued continued education.

The arrangement of visiting Aileen on the motorbike was wearing thin despite the loan of Jeff's car occasionally. I felt it was time I bought a car of my own. I approached Jeff and casually enquired if he could advance me a few hundred pounds. To my amazement he said no. When I enquired further he said he was unable to discuss it. This uncharacteristic response unsettled me. Although I had been happy in my work, I had felt for some time I should be more involved with the financial side of decision making. Suddenly, I realised I knew nothing of the farm's financial structure and this inability to discuss it frightened me.

There had never been a hint of financial difficulty so I assumed all was well and that eventually I would be taken into confidence. Aileen and I were blissfully planning to marry and settle in the vacant cottage. The chill over my modest request was suddenly ringing alarm bells. After worrying for a week or more I turned to my neighbor and old friend Tom Hobbs. When I called it was afternoon and Tom was pleased to see me. We walked up to the cow shed where he lit a cigarette, always smoked in a holder, and invited my confidence. When I finished he took a long draw, gazed long and hard over his beautifully kept property and turned to me with a look of sadness on his face. 'Son,' he said, 'I think you had better get out before it gets worse.'

CHAPTER 10
NEW START

Shattered, I returned to the farm reasoning the problem must be serious for Jeff to be unable to discuss it. Whatever the cause, it was too confronting and painful for him to discuss with me. At stake was not only my job but the emotional investment we had made in each other. The Wilkinsons had become my extended family. I had found peace in their home. After a painful discussion with Aileen, reluctantly, I resigned.

Before leaving the farm, I went to see our local doctor, Dr Hopkins. He was a tall highly regarded man who was familiar with my family's problems because he had treated my mother many times. After eliciting my story, he regarded me carefully and said, 'All that's wrong with you young man is that you should have had an education.' I protested, 'But I'm too old.' He went on to explain he had been a teacher before doing medicine. He insisted he was sure I could do whatever I wanted, even at this juncture.

Determined to start fresh, Aileen and I made the decision to move to Melbourne. Aileen transferred to a branch of the bank in the city and I moved into a flat with my old friend Ed Featherston in Hawthorn. Ed had completed his training as a journalist in Wonthaggi and was now working in Box Hill. I applied for a position as a welder with FC Welding in South Melbourne. It was located in a huge tin shed roughly where the freeway interchange is today in South Melbourne. When I applied, the owner asked me if I could weld. I said yes, because it was something I had been taught by Bob while I was on the farm. He said, 'weld up those two lengths of channel into a box section.' On completion, he examined the welding and announced, 'You are a welder,' and employed me.

I was impressed with the skill of the men working there for they could straighten curved beams with heat and a bucket of water and weld beautifully in complex situations. A number of the men were Hungarian. Another was a German who had made submarines during the war – his work was superb. I was assigned to be his assistant after a while so customers with small projects would be directed to me. Although I worked under his supervision, I was in awe of his abilities. I learned a lot from him.

I started night school doing matriculation subjects at University High School in Parkville. This meant finishing at four o'clock each day in a filthy state after working all day on a dirt floor, then scurrying home to get clean before returning to Parkville in time for school around five thirty, three days a week. I had signed up for school in complete ignorance of what was best for me. At that time there was no one I could approach for that sort of advice and I was impatient to get ahead quickly.

The workload was crushing. Three subjects meant three nights finishing at nine o'clock, the need to study, and a heavy workload during the day. I moved from the flat with Ed to private board in Central Park Road, Caulfield, but not before Aileen ended our engagement.

I was devastated, shocked and hurt. My hopes for our future together evaporated – would nothing go right for me? Being attractive and possessing the freshness of a country girl, she was enjoying the attention of others now she was working in the city. I could see no alternative but to continue trying to improve my education. The separation, given the circumstances, was inevitable. Aileen too had been deprived of her dream and my prospects were undeniably poor. It took me a long time to understand and accept the situation, but gradually, the pain became endurable. I had learned what it is to love and be loved and how vulnerable it can render us.

Many years later I learned that her mother, having decided my prospects in life were poor, instructed Aileen to break the engagement.

Unfortunately, FC Welding relocated to Port Melbourne and this move further strained the logistics of my attending night school at University High School. My move to Caulfield was also proving to be a strain because the landlady was finding my working class grubbiness inconsistent with the demeanor of her other boarders who were bank workers she could entertain with high tea after work. Nevertheless, I persisted for about six months before I resigned from F.C. Welding and took a position as a steel salesman with Elders Goldsborough Mort in the city. I thought I was at last moving up in the world. The position was better paid, clean and easy because at the time steel was in short supply. All I was required to do was raise an invoice for those who ordered steel and then delete the stock from the inventory. After about six weeks of that I made an appointment with Mr Edwards the personal manager. I complained, saying I was bored stiff and needed a better challenge. To my amazement, he began laughing uncontrollably. He wiped his eyes and said, 'I have been here for thirty years and there are people on the staff I've never seen let alone tell me they are underemployed. Leave it with me.'

A few weeks later I was summoned to his office again. Mr

Edwards was visibly pleased, saying that as a result of our last talk, he had approached management with a scheme to take selected individuals from the staff and fast track them through the firm. The aim was to equip them to become managers of the regional offices throughout Australia. 'What's more,' he said, 'you are the first to be chosen.' I was promptly moved to the Finance Department.

In the preceding weeks I had also applied for a position with the Heidelberg Repatriation Hospital to work in the pathology department for I was nurturing the ambition of doing medicine since I was enjoying school so much. I was offered the position and resigned from Elders GM. I have never been so embarrassed. I was shunned by everyone at Elders. No one would speak to me. I crept away depressed – had I thrown away the opportunity of a lifetime?

CHAPTER 11
HEIDELBERG

It was spring 1964 and I had to find somewhere to live, preferably close to the Heidelberg Repatriation Hospital. For a few days I stayed at the Old England Hotel in Heidelberg in a small room facing the balcony on the first floor. Then I found board with a couple at Rosanna.

At the hospital I was assigned to the Haematology Department run by Stan Shelley. I felt comfortable immediately. I was shown how to perform many tests using machines and how to stain slides. Within days I was taking blood from the seemingly endless patients sent to us. In the hospital there were approximately 1200 male patients and 350 female patients. It was just 20 years after the Second World War. Outpatients in the thousands ensured we were always busy.

My fellow workers were a bright lot. The patients were wonderful and grateful for everything done for them. A lot were chronically ill, many terminally so. The war had exacted a heavy toll on a great many men and women who were remarkable for their stoicism. I felt privileged to be working with them. The task of going around the wards collecting the blood from the patients was, at times, harrowing. Those who were seriously ill would encourage me, despite the fact it was often difficult and painful to take their blood. At times it was even more difficult to stop the bleeding. I made many friends and was allowed to attend a number of autopsies, hoping to learn what I could about the disease that claimed them. I once saw an amputee who had lost both legs above the knee give a punch and Judy style performance using his stumps with faces painted on them. It was hilarious and hard to believe possible.

In the laboratory I was taught to make and stain blood slides, perform red and white cell counts and also became able, at a basic level, to differentiate different cells and ratios when viewed through a microscope. The whole experience was so interesting it whetted my appetite for more but I was getting ahead of myself. I needed to pass my matriculation subjects as a prerequisite for further medical training.

The wife of the couple I was now boarding with in Rosanna was proving to be a problem. She would burst into tears for no apparent reason and begin raving about all sorts of imagined happenings. Occasionally, she was unable to prepare a meal at night but all was revealed when her husband explained she was drunk. The poor soul was a dipsomaniac, with all its attendant problems.

David McKenzie, a fellow worker, invited Karl and I to share a rented house with him in East Coburg. David had been a pharmacy student for a few years but had opted instead for a career as a biological scientist. Karl had started medicine at Monash University but lost favour with the department for his involvement in student politics. Instead he was completing a range of subjects at the Royal Melbourne Institute of Technology (RMIT). We had a great time together, partying with an ever increasing circle of friends who were mostly working in the medical field, including of course, the nurses.

I was despondent about my schooling. There were many deficiencies in my scholastic background. I had not quite completed my ninth year at technical school and it was little wonder I was finding it difficult. I failed and repeated English, struggled with biology and had difficulty with physics and chemistry. My study methods were simplistic and inadequate. There were no student counselors. I was just treading a path of my own making. In retrospect, I should have done basic mathematics and worked up to matriculation which would have solved many problems because to this day, I have never had a formal lesson in mathematics. I was advancing slowly with occasional help from Karl, and blind determination.

I received a substantial cheque from Jeff Wilkinson about this time. It was the money he kept on my behalf while I was on the farm. There had been no records and now no explanation of what had happened. I accepted the money knowing it must be correct. My feelings were of profound loss for the way in which our partnership had ended. It was no consolation to me that the Wilkinsons had also been obliged to rebuild their life. I hoped I had not contributed to their pain.

I had maintained close contact with my mother and family at Drouin. She was happy and even thriving despite providing care for the combined progeny of two families. In the May of 1965 Mum and David Dawson married at a ceremony in the garden of their home. It was a happy occasion that seemed to secure the future of everyone in the family. Their mutual love was apparent to family and friends alike. The seven children were making progress at school, Mum was safe and David was free to provide a living. Bruce and I, being so much older than our younger siblings, were independent but always welcome to the family home at Drouin. Concern for the family abated.

Early in March 1966, I was working in the bacteriology department of the Heidelberg Repatriation Hospital and still attending at University High School when Glenys, a young woman working in our laboratory, approached me, she said her father was a patient in the Royal Melbourne Hospital and asked if she could travel with me to visit him when I left for school. I agreed because the school was just behind the hospital and involved no delay. We travelled this way a number of times. The following week we received notice her father had died suddenly at the age of fifty two of complications arising from the operation on his carotid artery. Glenys was distraught with grief. She was alone in Melbourne with little money and no car while her family were frozen with the shock of her father's untimely death. I picked her up from where she was boarding and took her to the grieving family in Grovedale.

Glenys and I became friends. I admired the way she coped with the death of her father and was drawn to her quiet intellect. Shy and quietly spoken, she had hardly been noticed while working in the laboratory but our chance meeting revealed great qualities that drew me to Glenys. For a time we continued our work at the hospital. I was moved to the laboratory dedicated to tuberculosis detection which, while interesting at first, quickly become routine and boring. My frustrations arose from a number of sources. Although I had learned many laboratory techniques and was stimulated greatly by the intense clinical background of my colleagues and the hospital, the question of the 'why' could only be addressed with further education. I had yet to complete my matriculation and was tired and disheartened by the effort it was taking. My frustration wasn't helped by the long drive into the city after work. I would sit in class without food or drink until after 9 p.m. before driving home to prepare dinner and further study.

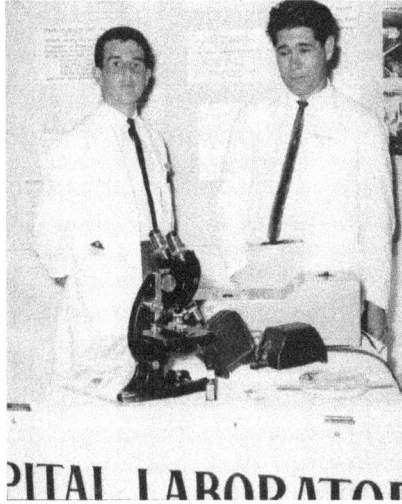

Glenys was also frustrated with her lack of opportunity. She accepted a position as a computer assistant with the Shell Company in the city while I moved to the Gas and Fuel depot in South Melbourne to work in their laboratories, I figured I would be closer to school and earn more money. Glenys and I became engaged in October and for a while we thought we were making progress. She did not like her job with Shell because it was so boring for her. Then one day I fell while taking gas samples and severely damaged my ankle. Unable to work, I went home to Drouin to consider the options.

The headmaster of Drouin High School was Mr Clarie Wilson, a former teacher at the Wonthaggi Technical School. I made an appointment to see him in the hope of receiving some advice because my attempt to gain an education was beginning to founder. He was helpful and suggested that as I was still only 25 perhaps I would like to go back to school full time providing I could earn enough to support myself. The prospect appealed to me so I began to look for a job that would support my return to school full time.

I heard that Bill Gallus, who owned the local dairy, was looking for someone to learn the delivery round in Drouin. I phoned and he explained that he was too old to continue the round and agreed for me accompany him for a week to learn the routine. If I proved satisfactory I would continue on and manage the depot for which I would receive the appropriate wage. This time I had a real chance of success. I could attend school and complete my matriculation in a regular way while still working, because so far, I had only passed two subjects.

The job started around 4 a.m. with harnessing the horse into the two wheeled float and loading the bottled milk. Bill turned up as planned for the first week and I quickly learned the round. After three or four weeks by which time I worked alone I asked for my salary and he refused to pay saying he had changed his mind and it was only a trial. He closed the business.

I couldn't believe it. Thwarted again, I went home to the family in deep shock that yet again I had failed, and worse, was humiliated by the duplicity of this man. I learned 20 years later from his son and daughter that he was just as duplicitous with them. Overcome with anxiety, I crashed in tears. This was despair of the worst kind. I was taken to the local doctor, a friend of my stepfather, who transferred me to the Hobson Park Psychiatric Hospital at Traralgon.

On admission, I was heavily tranquilised and my mother's permission obtained for treatment. The intention was to induce a hypnotic state to allow me to converse without inhibition under the influence of intravenous drugs. I have little recall except of receiving the injection and awoke feeling hungover but content to take the medicine prescribed. I was put on tricyclic anti depressants and gradually returned to near normal over the next ten days.

Mum was debriefed by the doctor and was horrified to learn I had been molested as a child along with other details of my childhood and the rejection by my father. She was furious and her hatred of my father intensified. She would never divulge the details of what had been revealed. Whether or not this decision was hers or on the advice of the psychiatrist, I do not know. I attempted to ask her again a number of times in subsequent years but she remained adamant and became upset. Gradually, I recovered. Although I could recall little of the experience, somehow, a burden had been removed.

A few weeks later I returned to the outpatient clinic and saw another doctor, an Indian man who discussed my case. He asked me what my intentions were and when I replied I wished to do medicine. He scoffed and said that would not be possible. He said I should keep on with the medication and pursue a less ambitious career. I left determined he was wrong and that I would never succumb to such a problem again. I stopped the medication because it made me drowsy and confused.

Unable to go to school and in need of a new job, I heard

of a family near Drouin who urgently wanted a share farmer. The father had died suddenly and the son was too young to manage. My credentials were excellent for this sort of work so I became a farmer again milking 100 Dairy Shorthorn cows. Glenys, who had been supportive while I was in hospital, was happy for me to take the position because the farms second house was in a just livable condition and the job would give us time to consolidate our prospects. The bereaved family, numb with grief, was unable to communicate anything but the most basic of instruction, left the running of the farm to me.

Glenys and I were married on the 13th of May in Geelong, after which we enjoyed a caravan tour through the Riverland of South Australia before visiting the parents of Christopher Murray, a friend we made while at the Heidelberg Hospital. Chris had a studentship arrangement whereby while he was at the University of Adelaide he was obliged to work where directed by the Commonwealth in his vacation time. Chris insisted that should we get to Adelaide, his parents would want to meet us. Alice and George Murray proved to be a remarkable couple. He was totally blind and she, a tiny wisp of a woman, fussed around him with the nervous energy of a little bird. Glenys and I had a laugh because they provided us with separate beds on our honeymoon. We did not know it then but we were destined to return and occupy the unused half of their home.

Our marriage had been timed to coincide with the school holidays which enabled the son on the farm to manage because the cows were dry at that time of year. We returned to the farm in time to calve down the cows through the winter, a process hampered by poor conditions and the outdated farming practices I was expected to pursue. The fences were in disrepair, there was no money for materials and conditions were miserable. With no wish to confront the bereaved mother, we considered the reward for effort was too little and resigned in the September. The worms of ambition were still biting.

We moved to a flat in Glenhuntly, Melbourne. Glenys obtained employment taking blood at the Red Cross and I began driving taxis with the intention of returning to school. At first I started with Yellow Cabs because they had a training program that led to an advanced driving license, a new innovation, the result of recent scams in the issuing of licenses. I passed the advanced driving examination without problems. We were required to know the different location of principal venues throughout the suburbs and the most direct route to and from different places.

Over the summer, I become a day student of George Taylor and Staff School in Flinders Lane in the city. I changed to driving taxis for a family who had a number of cars with the Silver Top group. Based in South Caulfield it was convenient to our flat in Glenhuntly. The taxi owner paid me slightly more than the standard 40 percent of the gross take which varied from $30 to $60, depending on the business of the night.

The school year of 1968 began and I quickly made friends with a group of fellow students trying to repeat their matriculation exams. Geoff Combridge, Simon Sheed and Joel Fink. Although older by about six years, I was the weakest student because they were all repeating Year 12 after attending other schools. The teaching standard of the school was high so we made different degrees of improvement. Occasionally, we would have a drink together and enjoy a laugh but I was stretched from the demands of driving the taxi every night at 5 p.m... The others had independent means.

Driving taxis was an eye opener. I thought I knew a little of the world but was often amazed by the antics of my passengers. Most customers were ordinary folk but often those who used the taxis were low life without a vestige of concern for anyone. Drunks, violent, irrational and frankly crazy people who did not know their destination or have the fare. They would argue, threaten and abuse the driver regularly. I did learn tricks to minimise exposure to obvious problems. Like driving past a person waving the cab down so I could observe their walking toward the car. Any evidence of staggering and I was away again because I was tired of cleaning out the car after passengers vomited, or had sex in the back seat. Responding to radio calls where we were expected to pick up drunks lying in a hotel bar was also a source of wasted time.

Glenys became tired of the bloodletting and moved to the Weather Bureau in Exhibition Street, ostensibly as a computer operator. However, she spent a great deal of time laboriously hand copying charts and other tedious work. Meanwhile, disgruntled, she sat the Public Service exam and waited to hear the outcome.

Glenys did particularly well in her test and was offered a choice of positions in the civil service. One option was to work as a computer operator with the Weapons Research Establishment (WRE) in Salisbury, near the Edinburgh airfield in South Australia. This had immediate appeal because we were aware of how much easier it would be to live and work in Adelaide, especially if I gained a place at university. Glenys accepted the position. The only problem arising was that she would have to start months before I could finish my exams in Victoria. We contacted the Murrays in Adelaide and were thrilled when they offered us the rental of the unit that formed one half of their lovely old home in North Adelaide. Glenys would go before me and start work. I would finish my exams and join her as soon as possible.

CHAPTER 12
ADELAIDE

In December 1968 after exams completed, I packed the trailer with all I owned, including the canary in its cage, and drove to Adelaide. Glenys was already comfortable living in Adelaide but I had to find a job. The exam results from Melbourne were yet to be posted so I searched the employment columns of the papers. I soon began work with the Newbold refractory brick company, about five miles west of the city, making and stacking bricks for $40 a week.

Meanwhile, I applied for entry into the undergraduate department of Adelaide University pending my exam results. When at last my exam results were posted, I had passed but my scores were inadequate to obtain a place in the medical faculty. There were no allowances for a mature age student. After a consultation with Professor Crammond, the Professor of Medicine, I was advised to complete a South Australian Matriculation because competition for places in the faculty was intense.

I was disappointed and resented a system that made no concessions to mature-aged students. I had paid fees for everything I had done and received no consideration from anyone. The system was unfair. Nevertheless, I arranged to complete a South Australian matriculation of five subjects, physics, chemistry, biology, English literature and modern history.

Glenys and I were happy living in Adelaide. We made friends with Peter Mayberry, a friend of Christopher Murray. Peter was a physicist with the British Tube Mills. As a child he had contracted a form of TB that damaged his spine. Although shorter than normal with a hunched back and barrel chest his spirit was indomitable and his intelligence was outstanding – as was his lively wit. We formed a friendship for life. His wife, Helen, had had few opportunities in life but her support for Peter was unwavering. Later, while raising their family, she qualified as a primary school teacher – a commendable effort.

Sharing the house with the Murrays proved to be convenient and inspirational. Although completely blind from 16 years old, George had become a basket maker with the Institute for the Blind and then in a private capacity later in life. The baskets he made were of every conceivable design and made to a rare standard of excellence. Each evening Alice read him newspapers, magazines, practical handbooks and the classics. In addition, he participated via tape recordings with other blind people who added and subtracted segments from the sound tapes in circulation between them.

The Murrays belonged to numerous societies like 'Bird Watchers' and 'Sailors Around the Horn'. They attended public lectures on every subject imaginable. The first time I fully appreciated George's blindness was one pitch black summer evening when I was strolling in the big backyard. A small shed on one side with an awning over the door was covered with a dense creeper. I heard some banging in the shed, felt my way to the door and asked George what he was doing. He replied, 'I am making legs for a table.' I was staggered. Here he was in pitch dark, measuring, planning the wood and fitting legs to a table. He was happy – this was his world. I was in awe of this man who seemingly could do almost anything. His one fear was that his hearing would fail to the point of total deafness. Thankfully, it never did.

At the brick yard the main product of the time was a fire brick made for the aluminium smelter at Point Henry in Victoria. We made extruded wire cut bricks by the thousand and then packed them into pallets for the trucks to transport to Victoria. It was hot, heavy, dirty work for which I received $40 a week. I was annoyed with myself. Despite my efforts, I had not come far.

I soon applied for the position of storeman clerk with the Chrysler factory at Tonsley Park, a suburb south of Adelaide. My new job was clean and better paid. I was one of three receiving clerks for car components delivered to the factory. The office was in an annex of the receiving platform at the rear of the huge factory. Pallets of goods were tested for conformity to specification and checked off against the invoice. It was simple repetitive work and boring in the extreme. I was attending school two nights a week in different locations, Mitchell Park High and Adelaide Boys High School in Fullerton. This was a source of amusement to my fellow workers who routinely fronted the bar of the Tonsley Park Pub within five minutes of knock off.

Our living standards had improved markedly in Adelaide. It was not all work. Glenys and I were happy. Although she worked shifts at the Weapons Research Facility we were making friends, saving money and enjoying the comparatively relaxed Adelaide lifestyle.

George Murray had a fishing boat he kept at the small boat club behind Torrens Island. His boat was about 22 feet long, clinker built with a half cabin and powered by an ancient one cylinder marine engine. Peter and I were soon co-opted into taking George fishing on a regular basis. We were astounded the degree to which this blind man could be independent. From the moment we stepped on board he was able to look after himself, from refueling and starting the engine to sorting his own tangles. We soon learned this was the way he preferred to be. No fuss, no concessions – just free to be one of the boys. It was a wonder we didn't drown George because it was so easy to forget he was blind. At home he was the gentleman with impeccable manners, but with us, the inner boy was unleashed. We loved our time with him and often stopped off at a pub after fishing to share him with other men.

CHAPTER 13
PARKE DAVIS

In 1969, while perusing the papers each week for a better job, I spied a position advertised for a medical representative with the Parke Davis Drug Company. The interview was held at a motel in Fullarton by an executive from Sydney and the South Australian sales manager, Graham Spencer- Smith, a pharmacist. I was nervous because I was reaching high and attempting to capitalise on my improved education. Somehow, I managed to impress the executive who asked me to join the firm. Evidently they valued my time in pathology.

I was sent to Sydney for an intensive period of training. No expense was spared and the tuition was rigorous. Parke Davis was determined its representatives would behave in an ethical way and provide useful valuable information about its products to the medical profession. On return to Adelaide, I found myself receiving additional tuition on the art of being a sales representative from Graham at his home. He threw a box of matches on the table where we sat and said, 'Sell me that.' I stared, incredulous. Why I wondered, would he ask me to describe something so obvious? What was I to say? I was at a loss to understand how to answer the question. That's how naïve I was.

My job was to detail the many Parke Davis products to the doctors and specialists in my territory which was everything north of the river Torrens and part of the city itself. Every six weeks I had to travel out to Border Town, then Narracoorte to Mt Gambier before returning via Robe, Tailem Bend and Murray Bridge. I also visited the towns of the mid north and later Broken Hill and Wilcannia. It was frustrating work in that I had to be available when the doctors were free. This often meant many hours sitting in waiting rooms with perhaps only a three or four minute conversation when we finally met. Sceptics might wonder how useful our contribution was. However, Parke Davis was an entirely ethical company which went to a lot of trouble to see what we gave the doctors was useful, relevant and clinically proven.

The doctors held our products in high regard and for the most part were amenable to keeping abreast of our research and product improvement. I was well received almost everywhere I went. However, I was warned of a woman gynaecologist on North Terrace in Adelaide who would offer a lolly once the conversation started. If foolishly accepted, you would have a gob stopper in your mouth that put an end to the detailing. She had a wicked sense of humour.

The representative I replaced was a pharmacist who, with

some other friends, had just started the Ganymede Wine and Food Club. At first we were a small group but it grew rapidly to become a diverse mix of over 60 pharmacists, dentists, doctors, lawyers and business men. With occasional ladies nights, it was a huge success and an opportunity to widen our circle of friends. The format was for two members to arrange the monthly meetings at a venue of their choice, consult with the chef as to the menu and select wine to complement the meal. We experienced the hospitality of many fine restaurants all over Adelaide.

Glenys and I continued our studies. She was studying mathematics while I was slowly mastering my new matriculation subjects, some for the second time. I particularly enjoyed modern history, which explored the origins of the different major revolutions and also the origins of the First and Second World Wars. I became intrigued with how intellectually challenging it was for Thomas Jefferson, ably supported by people like Benjamin Franklin, John Adams, John Hancock and George Washington, to write the American Constitution. In effect they crystallised the aspirations of all those seeking to free themselves from monarchy and rampant authoritarianism. The result was a magnificent document remarkable in its time. It was the beginning of my enduring fascination with history.

Strangely, despite my mathematical deficiencies, I also enjoyed the study of physics because of the clear thinking and regard for the logical progression of ideas. I loved the dictum, 'When the model or theory becomes too complicated, find another way.'

The studies were going well and I knew that despite my travel time away and working full time, this time I had a chance. Glenys and I had a lively social life and my work was both interesting and well paid. I actually felt on track to gain entrance to university. The looming problem was how were we to create an income if I was accepted? It was early 1971 and students were still required to pay fees.

Glenys and I had bought and paid off a block of land at Piccadilly, near Crafers, next to the new freeway skirting Stirling and the lower slopes of Mt Lofty. We cleared the block of fallen trees and scrub with the intention of building a house, for which we had drawn up plans. The buying process had been a worrying business because, on the advice of our bank manager, we had instructed a solicitor he recommended to handle the conveyencing to ensure the title was clear of encumbrance. We handed over the full price and left it to the solicitor. About six weeks later, we received the title. To our amazement it had a private road across the block giving the right of use to the other five or six titles in the court. At first the solicitor denied liability. I was obliged to point out I had strong reason to doubt if the Law Society would agree with him. He then conceded and at great cost to him, removed the private road from not only our title, but reference to it on all the other titles. At last, we owned a valuable block of land.

The search for an alternative income was intense. We considered many small business enterprises then came across a notice advertising the sale of a mixed business located opposite the hotel in Crafers. The business was being sold because the English family who bought it was grief stricken after the husband had fallen ill and died suddenly. The wife and her elderly mother were unable to cope. There were a number of children, including a disabled, incontinent son. We bought the business, with change of ownership to occur after Easter.

For the Easter break Glenys and I went on a tour of some

of the towns I visited for Parke Davis in the mid north of South Australia such as Riverton, Hamley Bridge, Balaclava, Saddleworth and Eudunda. We then went on via Mildura and back to Inverloch in Victoria where we met up with all my Dawson family. My younger siblings had adopted the surname Dawson. We had a great time with the family who had rented the enormous holiday house owned by the CWA quite close to the main street and the beach in Inverloch.

On our return, we moved into the shop and were horrified by what we found. We had bought the business on the basis of its profitability and potential. The living space when inspected had been a terrible mess and we had naively presumed it would be cleaned up. When we arrived to take over it was late in the day. The family sat silently around the long kitchen table covered with food and cooking utensils, their cases piled in a corner, a more miserable scene was hard to imagine. They were a totally demoralised gathering. No attempt had been made to clean. They stood up and took their leave with only a few suitcases, headed directly to the airport for their return to England. It was a tragic scene, the dispirited remnants of a family whose attempt to make a new life in a new country had failed dismally.

Glenys and I were staggered by the filth and the wrecked furniture. Acutely conscious of our need to open the shop at eight o'clock the next morning, we threw out everything the family had left and I literally mopped the walls of the kitchen in an attempt to reduce the smoke and grease encrusted on them. Open hours were 8 a.m. – 8 p.m. every day and we could sense the potential to improve the business dramatically, despite the comments of some who felt we were being bypassed by the freeway. In fact, the shop serviced a large community of discerning people who had moved into the region to escape suburbia 16 miles away.

Glenys bravely ran the shop with the help of a girl we put on full time. Others we employed casually as needs varied. Part of our commitment involved picking up seven lunch boxes from the local primary school each day. Glenys prepared the preordered lunches and returned them in time for the lunch break. This was quite a commitment while trying to meet the growing general demand and lunch trade of the other small businesses in the area. While I was still employed by Parke Davis, on at least three nights a week I had to descend to the warehouse in the suburbs and buy all the groceries necessary to replenish the shelves. Glenys would send me off with the order book she compiled. I would return in the old 1957 FE Holden sedan that was our backup vehicle, packed to the roof with groceries. Then of course, we had to put the goods on the shelves with prices attached. Our aim was to recycle our money as often as possible without accumulating slow or unwanted items.

My matriculation studies were suffering as a result of all the demands on my time but success was in sight. I had especially enjoyed attending the English literature class the year before. Like all classes at the beginning of the year, it was full of well intentioned people but by mid winter the class shrunk to seven – of whom I was the only male. On those bitter cold winter nights our teacher would read poetry and passages of the classics to us in a way that warmed the soul. I had been a reader all my life but his insights were moving and highly motivating.

The shop was a rapidly growing newsagency, grocery, delicatessen, bank and dry cleaning agency. It also became necessary to carry a range of green groceries because we were using so much salad in the lunch trade. This required me to go to market before five o'clock, three mornings a week. Despite the early rising, I enjoyed those visits because I found the buying a challenge, especially in learning to deal with the sharp operators who abounded at the market. I learned to haggle well and buy only top quality goods.

Soon I learned by accident that there were different levels of buying price at the wholesalers. When I tumbled to this well guarded secret, a huge argument ensued in which I insisted on access to the better price structure. Suddenly, all the deliveries, like small goods, delicatessen lines, cigarettes, soft drink, milk and even groceries could be added to the one account, thus qualifying for prices and services reserved for larger businesses. Most of the groceries would now be delivered, which saved a huge amount of time. Speaking of accounts, the only person we extended credit to was Lady Mawson, who lived near the summit of Mt Lofty behind us. We would receive her order on the phone and when ready, I would deliver it to the property which had a cottage inside the main gate. Regrettably, I never met her in person, unless she came to the shop where I did not recognise her.

Despite having the shop and work commitments obliging me to travel away a quarter of the time, my matriculation subjects were falling into place. As exam time came around I was conscious I would have to resign from Parke Davis if I managed to get a place at university. The real excitement however was the impending birth of our first baby, due in January.

I had to choose what course I wanted to study at university. My first choice was medicine, but I was concerned. If I put

Medicine as my first preference and I failed to get in, I would have to do Science. I felt I had not endured all the years of night school to do that. On the other hand, quite a number of my friends in the wine club were dentists. They convinced me this was a better option because for the most part, the dentistry course was run parallel to medicine. I agonized over the options before finally choosing Dentistry 1, Medicine 2. This would avoid missing out and not getting either. The results came out and I was accepted for dentistry. I rationalised this was wonderful but nurtured a misgiving. Had I in the final moment gone to water and chosen dentistry because I was afraid to believe in myself?

I resigned from Parke Davis. The state manager, Graham Spencer-Smith, was astounded. How could I give up my generous salary, the car and the expense account to become a university student? I had just turned 31, was expecting a child any day, and had a shop to run seven days a week to provide an alternative income. He thought I was mad and said so. It was beyond his comprehension that anyone would give up such a prestigious position to become a student.

CHAPTER 14
FIRST SON

During the night of January 6th 1972, Glenys woke me. The baby was coming. We rushed to Adelaide's Queen Victoria Hospital where our son David Graham was born in the early hours of the next day. It was an unforgettable moment. I was present for the birth and deeply moved by the experience. Glenys did a great job – It was her moment. She recovered from the birth and Mum and Dad came over to help. It was the summer vacation so I was able to help with the shop and we hired additional staff. We were excited and very happy.

In February, I began my life as a university student. I was working as hard as I could from the beginning, but not feeling in control. I was picked up each morning by David Shaw, a medical student who lived in Crafers. David was a gifted student with remarkable maturity and a great sense of fun, destined to be a successful physician. The long drive in his old blue mini each day allowed for a useful exchange of ideas.

My lack of mathematics was embarrassing. I found I could follow the concepts but was frequently at a loss to solve problems because I was unable to do basic processes. I scrambled to teach myself algebra and calculus while becoming proficient with a slide rule.

It was an eye-opener to me to see so many young people having such a good time and achieving with so little effort. Sometimes it even made me angry that eighteen and nineteen year olds did so little. I knew of students doing only two subjects. They seemed to drink a lot of coffee and be uncommitted to anything. There were a few protests about Australia's involvement in Vietnam, but even they seemed half-hearted. However, like others in the community who had thought Australia's involvement in Vietnam was justified, I was beginning to believe we were misled. Our involvement in the war might be a mistake.

In 1969 Chairman Mao had declared the Chinese Cultural Revolution over. The spectre of yellow hordes aggressively pushing south to threaten our freedoms was replaced with a more realistic assessment and respect for the resilient people of Vietnam. Indeed, it slowly emerged that through ignorance based on misinformation and fear, the Australian people had made a serious error of judgment. We had no right or need to be in Vietnam.

One of our shop customers was Paul Richardson who I came to know well. He was a shift worker with the Metropolitan Fire Brigade who in his spare time had a lawn mowing round of 27 selected clients. I was surprised when his wife started driving their four wheel drive with him lying in the back. Sometimes he was able to walk, but only then with a lot of pain. I asked, 'Can I help?'. Clearly, I thought, he can't cut lawns and must therefore be falling behind with his customers. Paul was relieved and said if I would do the work he would come with me and teach me the tricks of the trade. Soon after, I offered to buy his equipment. He was relieved, a reasonable price was agreed to and I acquired this new regular source of cash income. Being young and fit, I could readily cut seven or eight lawns at a time with the wide self propelled reel mower and the conventional mower.

The optional first year subject chosen by most medical and dental students was Psychology. We were asked to form pairs to run our own experiments so I partnered with John Gilbert for an experiment where we were given a rat to train in order to replicate the behavior and statistics of gambling.

The cooperation in the experiment with John enabled me to observe how clever he was. At the time I was struggling with my other commitments and was aware my study process was inadequate and frustrated by poor mathematic skills. Physics in particular was proving difficult. Then the exam results were posted. I failed physics and just passed chemistry. I was devastated, but not surprised.

John Gilbert's results however, were outstanding. My new friend and companion in lectures was a gifted student and although pleased with his results, he was disappointed for me. With so much at stake, I was shaken and afraid I might lose my place. In humble desperation, I asked John how he ordered his study and prepared for examinations. The question might have seemed ridiculous to some at this level, but not to John who readily agreed to help me.

He explained by showing me samples of his work. Each subject, he said, could be broken down into topics and each covered by a number of lectures. Every night he would read laterally on the subjects lectured that day and expand the notes taken. As each topic was completed, he would summarise and file it under the subject heading. As each subject developed, he would periodically summarise the whole work aiming to complete the process for each subject by the beginning of SWATVAC. Said quickly, it seems straightforward, but in practice, the plan requires many hours and self discipline to meet the deadlines. The process of lateral expansion before condensing the work as described ensured the syllabus was covered and reduced to essential elements which meant it was understood. John's success was no accident. I was allowed to repeat physics and chose to repeat chemistry for my own sake.

To make some additional money over the summer holiday of 1972/3 I bought an Austin six ton truck so that after examinations were finished, I would go back to Drouin and cart hay with my brothers who were either at school or University. We found plenty of work in the December and early new year before returning home taking Geoffrey with me for a holiday. We had made money and saw an opportunity to do better next year. In the remaining weeks of the holiday period, with Geoffrey's help, I replaced a large section of the shop floor and built a new modern sandwich bar equipped with lights and a glass front. We bought new deep freezers and refrigerators for soft drink all of which with some painting, improved the presentation of the shop. The business was growing steadily and the truck sold for a profit so we were optimistic for the future.

David, by now a strong adventurous little boy, was keeping us entertained and busy now that he had started walking. I adopted the study system John Gilbert had shown me and with only two subjects this year my work improved dramatically with a corresponding improvement in confidence. The problem was how to balance the demands of the shop and study with spending time with the family.

Meanwhile, the Dawson family moved from Drouin to San Remo Victoria where they had bought a lovely old home overlooking Western Port Bay. It had a view extending from Newhaven to Bass Landing which encompassed Churchill

Island and the southern end of French Island. The block extended down a steep path to its own private beach – a perfect place to retire.

CHAPTER 15

DERNANCOURT

During the autumn, we advertised the shop for sale and began looking for a house in the suburbs. We had been in the shop just over two years. It had become a strong, viable business and we calculated that with the proceeds of the sale we would almost have enough money to pay for a reasonable home. The shop sold and after payment of accounts we had $10,000. At auction we bought a three bedroom house in suburban Dernancourt on the north side of the Torrens River for $11,000.

The shortfall in the price of our home was accommodated by the Bank of Adelaide which happily transferred the balance from the loan of the previous owner to Glenys and me. It turned out to be between $1000 - $2000 at 2 percent. We figured that Glenys would return to work at WRE, and I would be a full time student who cut lawns and earned money during the holidays.

The year was racing away again and I was reflecting on how I was going to make more money out of hay carting the next summer. My brothers were keen because Mark was at university in Canberra and Geoff was working for Neville Hewson, a dairy farmer at Buln Buln near Warragul. Neville was in the process of relocating his interests from dairying in Gippsland to grazing on a property he had bought at Goomalibee on the highway between Shepparton and Benalla. Being a particularly wet year, he was reluctant to transfer cattle on to the recently inundated farm near Benalla so decided to cut the entire new farm for hay and agreed to pay us 13 cents a bale to cart it. This suited us because we knew the season there would be a month ahead of Gippsland so we would start at Benalla. Mark was a student at the ANU in Canberra, Ian was completing his final year at school in Wonthaggi and Geoffrey was a student at Glenormiston Agriculture College. I had this little army of strong experienced hay carters on standby, all desperate to make money.

University exams finished in early November. I packed and left for Benalla to meet with my brothers. On that one farm we carted 23.000 bales before moving on to others in the region. I bought another truck similar to the one we had so our efficiency became known. By mid December the Benalla season cut out so we moved back to Drouin as arranged with Jimmy Robinson the previous year.

Good news from Adelaide: I passed physics and chemistry

and was set to begin the clinical component of the course the next year.

We had left the shop management with staff so Glenys drove across with David and camped in the Drouin Caravan Park for the summer. She was a big help and supplied us with food – Glenys knew the appetites of men engaged in carting hay. There were a few incidents we still laugh about, like the man-hungry farmer's daughter who stood staring at Mark's manhood before inviting him into the house. We encouraged him to go but he declined the offer, evidently preferring to cart hay. Or, the farmer's wife, a recently married English rose who arrived with what she thought was a huge farm lunch hamper. To her amazement, the contents of the beautifully decorated basket disappeared with indecent haste after which the boys jumped into a water tank on the corner of a hayshed. I was embarrassed as she packed only minutes later – clearly shocked by the boy's appetite and behavior.

By the end of the season we had carted 63,000 bales. We distributed the proceeds of over $8000 amongst ourselves after costs were deducted. It was desperately needed money. Mark was a financially strapped student of Forestry at the National University in Canberra. Geoffrey was a student at Glenormiston Agriculture College and Ian was about to complete his final year of school at the Wonthaggi High School. Dad had maintained he could only afford to educate the children to final year high school and if they wanted to go further they would have to support themselves. It was understandable given he had seven children to educate, but it was a problem for some, especially Mark, who had enormous difficulty providing for himself in Canberra.

Despite the difficulties, five of the nine children in the

family completed tertiary studies and all became successful in their chosen employment. In later years Mum spoke of David not being surprised when any of us did well. He simply expected us to. His wise and thoughtful approach to life, together with the support of mum, had enabled everyone to maximise their potential – a worthy aim for any parent.

I returned to our house in Dernancourt in the better truck and sold the other for a profit. The university year started and I felt good knowing this was the first time I had ever been able to study without working full time. Fortunately, I made firm friends with other dedicated students like Lyndsay Richards, Nils Broders and Eddy Ng who helped me maintain perspective. Nils was married to Ilsa, and they had four boys. Eddy was married to Lyn. I was still cutting lawns and worked most weekends.

I noticed a sign at university saying there was an officer who would assist students with problems they might have. I made an appointment and saw a young man who welcomed me with a reassuring manner. I explained my problem and asked if the university had any means of helping students who had children in need of day care. His ineptitude amazed me. There was no provision or assistance and I left feeling angry with what I thought was a discriminating service. Surely, there were other student parents having similar difficulties? We would solve the problem ourselves.

Glenys went back to work for Weapons Research Establishment on shift work which suited us, because either of us could pick up David from day care. The lady running the day care centre was a gem. She was Dutch, had trained as a kindergarten teacher and was way ahead of her time. The facilities were secure and first class, the activities were supervised and constructive, there were no television sets and the children all had a sleep after lunch. David was a happy, secure little boy.

The work load at university was enormous and stimulating which strained my study schedule. The Professor of Physiology would spring mini exams and viva voce tests on us regularly. Failure to take them seriously, even for as little as 1-2 percent of the final result, could be fatal.

There were about 94 students in second year. Many had to fail because there were far fewer places in third year. The senior demonstrator and manager of laboratory work was Les Reynolds. To be a dentist requires an understanding of dental materials and their uses which are many and varied. Les patiently turned our clumsy efforts into creditable work. This had the additional benefit of making us use our hands. It cannot be assumed everyone has the ability to do fine exacting work with their hands.

Despite the pressure of university studies, as the year progressed my concern was how to make money over the coming summer holidays.

CHAPTER 16
THE KIOSK

My brother Ian had became disillusioned with school and left to work in a bank in Cowes on Phillip Island. Living at home with the parents, he was impressed with the entrepreneurs he came across in the region. Ever on the alert for an opportunity, he became aware the beach kiosk in Cowes was without someone to manage it for the next summer. The kiosk and the mini-golf beside it were owned by Mrs Stein. Following a conversation with Ian, I phoned her and discussed the details. It was agreed, I would rent the complex which was equipped with an American made hamburger machine, refrigerators and a doughnut making machine, and yes, we would manage the mini-golf as well. Some months before starting, I sent Ian about $1500 to buy some basic stock such as sweets and groceries. I felt this was a good opportunity because I had seen the tourist influx to Cowes over summer in my previous life as a farmer on Phillip Island.

The instant the exams were over, I moved to Cowes and erected a large tent of Dad's in the caravan park near the kiosk. The boys and I planned to live there for the summer. Glenys would come across with David and stay with Mum and Dad in San Remo when she was able to have her break from the Weapons Research Establishment. I then went around and opened the door of the kiosk. The entrance was blocked with a stack of bags that rose over six feet high in two piles behind which were two or three enormous cardboard boxes marked 'Minties.' The large hessian bags were marked 'Downey Flake doughnut mix'. I was completely thrown and asked Ian how could this be? Apparently, according to the representative for Downey Flake, if the entire population of Melbourne came to Cowes for six weeks of summer and they each bought three dozen doughnuts we would need that amount. As for the Minties, they were his favourites. Ian had been conned. I became a wholesaler of doughnut mix for the remainder of the summer. We did manage to use three or four bags of doughnut mix. I phoned doughnut makers far and wide with a deal they couldn't refuse.

Exam results were posted -- I passed. The relief was wonderful, the formula had worked. I could enjoy the summer and make a little money.

We were having great fun. The crowds came and some from different ethnic groups actually camped in their cars on the road facing the beach. The ice cream, drinks, cigarettes and mini golf were in great demand and on the hottest days we sometimes replaced the entire stock of ice cream and drinks.

A side benefit of the business for my brothers was the attraction they provided for the girls who gathered nightly. Instruction on the mini golf, teasing and loud music featured well and helped the time fly. We were quite aware this was only ever going to be at most a six week experiment but the volume of goods we sold amazed us. As the weeks flew and people started leaving we had to run down the stock. We devised a 'Mongrel Award' whereby the person serving would endeavor to switch the client's request from what they asked for to something we still had. Mark won the award for the sale he made to a young boy who came up with 10 cents for lollies. Mark sold him two loose Minties, all we had, and a box of matches. We waited with some trepidation for the angry father, but he never came.

Geoff maintains I was the worst because one evening, a man who was clearly gay minced across the road and with a flourish of the hand and an earnest look into my eyes, asked for a 'Gay Time'. According to the boys, I told him to 'piss off'. How was I to know it was an ice cream? The boys sitting on the floor behind the counter were in fits of laughter and have never let me forget.

It was the summer of 1975. After a little time with the parents in San Remo, we returned to Adelaide and were relieved to hear I was entitled to a student allowance. It was an initiative of the new Federal Labor Government, led by Gough Whitlam who had swept to power in 1972 to fill the vacuum created by the Liberal Party who had fallen asleep at the wheel. I sold the lawn round and began my third year of dentistry. Glenys went back to shift work and David was still going to day care. Through the week I caught the bus each morning for our first lecture of the day at 8am and became totally engrossed in study. Now we were doing introductory work on patients. With my little coterie of friends, all equally engaged in the work, we went to additional clinical lectures for graduates held in the Royal Adelaide Hospital. Lindsay and I attended a few additional autopsies in the hospital to improve our knowledge of anatomy.

The days were long. In addition to the lecture program, we had to complete the laboratory work needed for those patients who required new dentures. Each clinical step was rigorously examined and our laboratory work had to be of the highest standard. This meant many dentures had to be remade and fitted, all within our crammed schedule. The only time for the repeat of laboratory work was our lunch hour. Somehow we managed to keep up.

The student common room in the basement of the hospital was a large room equipped with a billiard table and chairs where students were able to relax. It was also where the infamous student parties were held. The Students Union had a graduate president and an undergraduate president. Dr Tom Wilkinson was our president and I was elected undergraduate president for three years, with Lindsay Richards as secretary. I became the Student's Representative and was accorded the honor of attending the Dental Faculty meetings run by the professor and graduate members of staff.

Being an undergraduate student at 34 years of age overlooked the life experience I had gained in the 20 years since I started work. What I wondered, can be reasonably expected of 20 year old students who for the most part, had not worked or been made to be accountable at all. I was not the average student. Some students had remarkable maturity while a few were indulged and given to excesses students are known for. It was not my place to pass judgment but I had to overcome feelings of impatience and disgust when I saw laziness and overindulgence. Perhaps I was jealous. I found I could easily identify with senior staff so I worked hard to obtain their respect and avoid perceptions of favoritism. At faculty meetings I was encouraged to put the student point of view as I understood it. The professors and other faculty members readily sympathised and were tolerant of all the issues affecting students that were put to them. Overall, I gained a respectful regard for the integrity, energy and concern given to the teaching of dentistry.

I soon began employment with The Adelaide Advertiser newspaper. Starting at 6 p.m., my job was on the classified advertisements floor. Classified advertisements at the time were set using print from metal slugs produced on linotype machines. The script was on one edge of each metal wafer and a number of slugs formed the text to be printed. When the text was printed, it was proof read and then sent for inclusion in a page of the paper. If a correction was required, it was returned to me, the runner, wrapped in a scrap of paper on which the printed advertisement was made and I would take it to the appropriate linotype operator for correction. One evening, I was summoned to the manager's office. I was met by him and an agitated union representative insisting I be sacked. The manager read out the complaints with a weary perplexed tone. 'The Union alleges you started work before knock on time and you touched the metal slugs although you are not a tradesman. The union insists they are prepared to go on strike if you are not dismissed. What's your explanation?'. I replied, 'Each evening on arrival, I walk past the return chute from the proof room and automatically remove the contents, dropping my coat and bag at my home station on the way to the linotype machines the material was directed to. I doubted that I had started work early since I had to rush from the university half a kilometre away and struggled to be on time at 6 p.m. Our official finishing time was 2 a.m. and we generally finished at 1 a.m. I couldn't possibly exceed my minimum hours of work. As for touching the metal slugs,' I asked, 'How was I to read the text under the metal without removing them first?' Apparently my explanation was satisfactory and I was told to go on doing my job, but it was another example of a self-important union man exercising power and wasting everyone's time.

Having worked in many different factories, I observed it was often the most garrulous man with a chip on his shoulder who became the union representative. Rarely could they be relied on to present a real issue to management with any sense of credibility.

The study program, although demanding gave me confidence. Now I studied every aspect of the work and not just topics I enjoyed or found easy. I have heard many people say they can't handle examinations, but in all probability, they were making the same mistakes I was. Poor organisation and too little time spent on fully focused work. As for the pressure, who wants to be operated on by someone unable to work under pressure? My exam results for the year reflected the value of John Gilbert's advice. I passed with a Distinction, two Credits and two Passes.

We travelled back to Victoria for the Christmas and summer and enjoyed our first holiday in years. Glenys was pregnant again, expecting the birth in late July or early August 1976.

Glenys's job at the Weapons Research Establishment helped keeping the computers churning out data concerned with Australia's development of guided missiles and rocketry. Security issues prohibited talk about her work and I suspect her understanding of what I was doing was equally obscure. We were unable to share matters of common interest. That is, apart from David, whose development we enjoyed immensely. Despite the demands of my study program, I would be there for him; only after he was in bed did I return to the books. We awaited the birth of our new baby with great anticipation.

Fourth Year at the dental school became more demanding. In third year we had been assigned patients in need of work suited to our limited competence. To the initial patients more were added thus becoming the foundation of a mini practice for which we were held responsible. Now we were encouraged to do more complex work. Each step of both clinical and practical work had to be approved before moving on, and of course, things went wrong to frustrate both student and patients alike. One requirement was that we make and insert at least one gold crown before progressing to final year. As mentioned, we had to make the crown ourselves and that process frequently became a saga. My friend Geoff, who had a cubicle back to back with mine in clinic, had to remake a crown a number of times until finally it was approved for fitting. His patient was made comfortable in the chair and the temporary crown was removed. Geoff thought he should try the new crown on before cementing it in place. He put the crown in, but with a gulp, the man swallowed it. Gasping and coughing, the man sat up. But the crown had disappeared.

Geoff, anxiously solicitous, explained the crown would turn up and could be recovered but at that point the patient lost control. 'Never mind about the bloody crown,' he cried as he jumped out of the chair 'I've had to catch the train from the southern suburbs seven times for this bloody crown and now you want me to sieve my shit, I've had enough,' and stormed out. I don't know how it was sorted out but Geoff qualified with the rest of us and is a good dentist.

CHAPTER 17
GRADUATION

With our second child due in August, Glenys had arranged to retire from work in June. Without warning, in the late evening of 25th July 1976, Glenys said, 'The baby is coming.' I drove her to Burnside Memorial Hospital where our obstetrician met us and delivered our baby without undue difficulty. Glenys had done everything possible to facilitate the birth and lay back exhausted but elated. We had another son, Stephen. As daylight broke I asked the doctor how he scored our baby for vitality and he said nine out of ten on the Apgar score but, as a precaution he would have the pediatrician examine him. Glenys and I were as happy as only new parents can be. A safe delivery and all well. After notifying family and friends, I went off to university without seeming to touch the ground.

That morning I was listed for my first case in theatre

extracting all of a patient's remaining teeth while under general anesthesia. A specialist oral surgeon looked on as I managed to extract some teeth while others broke off, a typical student effort. I then removed the remaining roots surgically and closed the wound in the prescribed way. The watching teaching staff were satisfied and began to drift away when suddenly I was paged for a phone call in the final seconds of the operation. I was excused and stepped out of the theatre to take the call. 'It's the pediatrician here Peter, I have transferred your baby to the Queen Victoria Hospital and I have to tell you he is not expected to survive. You should come to the hospital.' I stood transfixed with shock. The blunt statement that our baby was expected to die flattened me.

I rushed to the Queen Victoria Hospital and began a vigil of watching and waiting. Helpless, I observed him now in a humid crib, our son and so beautiful. I willed Stephen to keep breathing. I left and went to see Glenys, still in the Burnside Memorial Hospital. She of course was in shock as well as being physically exhausted. I hardly knew what to do next. David was being cared for by our wonderful neighbours, but beyond that, we had no one else to call upon. Glenys was under instruction to express milk and I was required to carry it to the other hospital. I was especially concerned for Glenys who was sharing a ward with mothers nursing their babies while her own was in another hospital and not expected to survive.

Gradually, we regained our senses and learned that 1-2 percent of babies born slightly premature develop hyaline membrane disease where they lack the protein surfactant that the normal full term baby's lungs secrete. The surfactant protein acts as a wetting agent that allows the alveoli of the lung to expand and contract – without it breathing is extremely difficult and sometimes impossible. Our Stephen was in big trouble.

Some family members came over from Victoria in the days following the birth. The details became a blur as I visited Stephen and Glenys in their different hospitals while keeping contact with David and the dental school. There was little change for eight or nine days until improvement was noted. About day twelve when we were allowed to take Stephen home. This emotional experience has allowed me to empathise with parents anywhere who have lost a child.

Glenys naturally had stopped work and we decided to manage financially by borrowing against the increase in the value of our home, pending my expected return to the workplace as a qualified dentist. The decision to borrow money was a calculated risk designed to allow Glenys time to mother both boys full time. We were heartened by the results of my forth year exam results. I passed all five subjects with a credit for General Medicine and a distinction for General Surgery.

It was February 1977 when I walked David to his first day of school. He proudly wore his ABBA t- shirt and Mickey Mouse school bag while I watched him bravely join his new class mates. I was bursting with pride and unable to foresee his embarrassment when a photo of him in this outfit surfaced for his 21st birthday.

Peter and Helen Mayberry also had two children. We were able to exchange visits and take the children to different events. We were pleased with ourselves and optimistic for the future.

It was hopefully my final year and I had many patients, quite a number for whom I had made gold crowns and completed other complex work. While all students were required to complete at least one crown, most managed more and, some of us many more. The better organised the student the more they could achieve. My friend Nils Broders, who had trained first as a teacher and then a trainee pilot, was easily able to exceed the minimum. Edie Ng likewise had a degree in zoology. Both men were married, Nils with three children and Eddie with one. Maturity has its advantages.

Exam time came all too quickly. Some examinations had several components, each of which had to be passed. Assessments had been made of our practical abilities in differing disciplines, such as denture making and surgery. The oral medicine exam required us to attend an oral examination. Since we were examined alphabetically I had little time to wait while standing nervously in line at the door. On entry, I was confronted by three senior oral surgeons and the visiting English examiner, Professor Poswillow, all sitting behind a large table, in silence.

The room darkened and slides appeared on a screen. 'Tell us what you see,' said the professor. I did as requested and an exchange occurred in which further answers were given, slides changed and the process repeated. After what seemed a lifetime the Professor said, 'This is very good.' He asked more questions before saying, 'Now one more.' When I answered he clapped his hands, as did the others, and I almost died of fright thinking they were being facetious. I fell out the room to admit the next student.

When the exam results were posted I was bowled over. I was given an unheard of Credit in Restorative Dentistry, a Credit in Preventive Dentistry and a Distinction for Oral Medicine and two passes. The top student was a young woman who had already completed a dentistry degree in Malaysia but

I was somewhere among the top two or three students.

My gratitude goes to John Gilbert, the young medical student who took time to advise a confused and desperate older student. No one in my seven years of night school had ever discussed the preparation for learning and consolidation of material in such a systematic way. I have observed many times since that the secret evades many students and some teachers to this day. Of course, there are other ways to study successfully but I suspect better students adopt some variant of the method outlined to me. But while the study technique was a key component of the success formula, it was Glenys's unwavering support on the home front that made it all possible. For the ten years since our marriage her unstinting help had supported me in every way. In addition, she had born the two boys and became an exemplary mother. My gratitude is boundless.

I was flattered to be offered a position as assistant in a prestigious Adelaide city practice owned by a highly regarded dentist who was a visiting examiner. This opportunity carried the additional prospect of postgraduate study but, Glenys had supported me long enough. I needed to earn a proper salary and gain dental experience. I turned down the Adelaide offer and accepted a position in Wangaratta Victoria where I hoped we might prosper. I would work in a practice owned by Dr Mark Heesh and start during the Christmas holidays of January 1978. I was 37.

CHAPTER 18
WANGARATTA

Initial attempts to rent a house in Wangaratta were unsuccessful. In desperation, we accepted unseen a vacant house on a farm at Bobinawarra, a 20 minute drive east of Wangaratta. With the trailer loaded high I left our Adelaide home for the last time.

The rented house was 200 metres beyond the more substantial farm owner's home. The drive in from the main road to both houses followed the Hurdle Creek, a tributary of the Oven's river. We took up residence in this basic house perched on the west bank of the creek. Margaret, the farmer's wife was pleased to have another woman close by because she had two young children and her husband was frequently away. They warned us to beware of snakes because we were so close to the creek. It proved sound advice for hardly a week passed without a snake being found in or around the house. The favorite place for them to hide was next to the hot water service, especially once the cold autumn nights the region is famous for set in. I disposed of the snakes with a shovel or the rifle because with children around the risk was too high.

My working career as a dentist began with Dr Mark Heesh in Reid Street, Wangaratta. I could hardly believe so many people could be having dental problems. The practice staff made me feel at home straight away. My assistant nurse, Kathy, was a young girl with the natural aptitude and common sense country girls are known for. Within weeks of my starting, Mark announced he was taking a long overdue six-week holiday with his wife and six daughters. I was at a loss to see how it would be a holiday with six girls but the poor man had not had a break for years. I was beginning to learn what a strain he had been working under.

The patients came from the distant mountains in the East to Yarrawonga in the Northwest. I was slow to begin but with the help of experienced staff, I managed to provide an up-to-date dental service that they said was appreciated. On my way home I stopped off at the Milawa pub to clear my head and expand my knowledge of local history. The sudden absence of study made me restless so I began woodwork classes at the Wangaratta Technical School. This time I made a coffee table with an inlaid tile top.

When Mark returned, I took the opportunity to learn all I could about denture making because the practice had a good dental mechanic on site and Mark had vast prosthetic experience. He had a great sense of humour too and conducted a running bragging session with Arthur Sweney, the solicitor next door. He would pick up the phone and invite Arthur to inspect his tomatoes in the back yard; in response, Arthur would brag about his pumpkins. Then I discovered that they would buy the vegetables – the largest available and tie them on the plants. There was no end to it. An unrepentant practical joker, Mark even left a sign on a fellow dentist's door, 'Butchers Picnic, closed for half a day'. That was not so well received because the dentist was inclined to take himself seriously.

One day I asked Mark why he arrived at work so early only to sit and read The Age in the laboratory. He invited me to consider what it was like to share breakfast with seven women every day. He then went into a pantomime act miming the dialogue from home to simulate the arguments and demands of his six daughters: 'I'm never going to speak to you again,' and 'You wore the jeans yesterday,' all interspersed with pleas for quiet by his wife. The technician and I thought it was very funny.

At the Wangaratta Hospital I had my first experience since graduation of extractions and dental work done under general anaesthesia. I was determined never to do that sort of work in the surgery because of the potential risks. The first time I removed a patient's teeth at the hospital I asked for the denture I had made so I could insert it following the extractions. I was handed a tiny denture that the staff insisted had shrunk. I began phoning the surgery and anxiously trying to find what had happened until it dawned on me that this was a big joke engineered by Mark. Finally the real one was found and the patient woke up with a denture that fitted. Being new at the hospital, I had wanted to impress the staff with my professionalism so was a ripe for such a trick.

After six months, I approached Mark asking if I could buy into the practice as an associate and share a proportionate percentage of the management costs. He had been paying a huge amount of tax each year and while some new equipment had been bought, I considered the whole surgery needed updating. With careful management, that could be achieved by minimising his tax liability while receiving cash for my share of the goodwill. In that way I would contribute half the cost of the upgrade. He refused to discuss the proposal, insisting I remain his assistant. He was enjoying the returns from my work. Rather than argue, with reluctance, I resigned. Mark was not happy. But, at 37 I could ill afford a leisurely approach to supporting my family; Glenys and the boys deserved better living arrangements.

Following a conversation with my stepfather, it was decided we would go on an extended caravan holiday and consider the next move. I bought a caravan and we headed north. Our little cavalcade meandered along stopping in time to give the boys some exercise and to set up camp. It was so pleasant to be with Mum and Dad who were equally pleased to have time with the children. We enjoyed our first stop-over in the park close to the radio telescope near Parkes in NSW. Each day we moved on and eventually came to Walgett where we stopped for lunch at the hotel. Somehow, someone realised I was a dentist. We were amazed when the mayor introduced himself and invited us to look at the vacant dental clinic in the town. He was so insistent I agreed to look when we had finished lunch.

The surgery was a fully equipped room in the front of a house facing the main street. The house and practice were available for occupancy immediately and he was prepared to be reasonable with regard to rent. Unfortunately, my family was not the slightest bit interested in living in Walgett. We moved on. Mum insisted for years that we could have become the mayor and mayoress of Walgett.

Eventually we reached Brisbane and managed to navigate to Tennyson, the suburb where my brother Geoffrey was renting a house with his girlfriend Robyn. Tennyson is right on the south bank of the Brisbane River and coincidently, next door to the Queensland Veterinary Research Farm where he was destined to be the site manager. At the time however, he was working as a plumber's assistant installing Solar Hart panels by the thousand. It was quite a reunion, especially because Mum and Dad had made the effort to drive that far towing a caravan. It may not sound much, but Dad's driving skills were marginal. Mum maintained her fitness on the trip with the involuntary exercise she derived from the phantom braking she performed for him.

After meeting Robyn's parents and an excursion around

Brisbane, Mum and Dad turned south, while Glenys the boys and I headed north. We completed a circuitous route via Barcaldine and Charters Towers to Cairns before returning to Melbourne down the coast. Along the way we studied caravan guides which described the towns we might be interested in living and listing the population. By comparing the population of a town with the number of listed dentists we were trying to identify an opportunity to start a practice. The number of dentists in a town was listed in the Australian Dental Register. We preferred to stay in Victoria and decided the imbalance we were looking for was in either Bairnsdale or Warragul, both in Gippsland. We decided Warragul would be best because we knew the region and it was only an hour from Melbourne and San Remo.

CHAPTER 19
WARRAGUL

I visited Warragul and began my search for a site in which to start a dental practice. I knew the area of old and some of the business people. I approached real estate agents with my problem. The agents drove me around with much enthusiasm and arm waving but one had an inspiration the others missed. On his advice, I approached Cliff Wilkinson who had a large menswear and fabric shop in the main Street. Cliff was most obliging and showed me the large space above the shop with an access via a stairway from the street. It was just what I was looking for. I found a builder who immediately set to work making two surgeries and an office in the space overlooking the street.

A dental supply firm eagerly fitted the chairs and supplied the instruments required. Six weeks later my nurse Helen Foster and I opened the door. To say I was worried would be an understatement. I had leased everything and my family's fortune was at stake. The trickle of patients became a deluge and the fear gradually subsided as I acquired more staff to cope. Financially it was a strain because a modern properly equipped dental practice cost a lot of money and my cash flow was immediately put under strain by patients accustomed to pay on account - a rural custom that took years to eliminate. The need for additional staff was an easier problem to solve because we were able to attract the best of country girls who became loyal, diligent assets of the practice.

We rented a house in Warragul North and moved from Bobinawarra. David enrolled at the Warragul North State School, which was over the road. Glenys and Stephen were at last able to relax, free of snakes and able to enjoy the convenience of the town.

There were two other dental practices in Warragul in 1978. The oldest had been established for years by Dr P Wooley, who was ageing and increasingly unwell. He was a cultured man who was for many years the town's only dentist. I was confronted now with an endless number of people presenting, if not with toothache, at least with advanced dental breakdown. I could sympathise with the terrific service Dr Wooley had provided, despite the complaints I heard about his extraction technique. To have an appointment book crammed for months ahead, and then fit emergencies in each and every day, meant he had worked under great pressure performing a largely thankless task.

I had just graduated from a dental school committed to preventive dentistry. Here I was, Dr Wooley's successor, trying to convince a community there was a better way than dentures by 25. The other colleague in town, Dr R. Osborne, was in a similar position and had made a little headway. Essentially, with regard to dental education, the people of the region were ignorant. My appointment book filled rapidly, as did the demand for emergency treatment. I hated having to treat so many small children who would invariably present with a number of teeth in an advanced state of decay. I knew that even if I were able to successfully repair or extract one tooth, subsequent treatment would be an unpleasant experience for us all, the child, the parents, my staff and me. Then the parents would complain about the cost. Despite this, most were appreciative of my efforts to confront the old expectation of dentures by the age of 25. From the outset I had some conversions and they increased exponentially over the next 30 years. I was aided by my colleagues of the Australian Dental Association (ADA) who also promoted the message that dental problems are, for the most part, preventable.

Ironically, one aspect of dentistry I enjoyed and had a lot of fun with was the making of dentures. Although hard to do well, It was a change of pace and less stressful. The patients were generally older people who had either lost or worn out old dentures. All had a story to tell. One old lady heaved herself into the dental chair and tipped a bag full of dentures on the bracket table. When asked how I could help, she began selecting, with shaking hands, different components from the five full sets of dentures she had tipped out. With eyelids fluttering and her face contorted with concentration, she tried the different components before announcing that a particular upper denture would or would not work in combination with the lower dentures she selected. The combinations seemed endless. When I asked what she would like me to do for her, she demanded, 'Make me a new set.' I declined – It was obvious my new ones would also go in the bag. After persuasion, I convinced her we had to pick the best set of what she had and progressively solve the problems they were causing. The whole performance was rewarding, fun and successful.

We had been warned as undergraduates not to be over critical of a colleague's work because one can't be sure of the difficulties they might have had. My nurses were an integral part of the whole effort to re-educate the public and we had a lot of fun. We were often rewarded with gifts, and the loyalty of the patients was encouraging.

My accountant, Kevin Thompson, quickly had the business restructured. The shelf company I acquired was called Tyrannasour Pty Ltd. The name became my trademark around the town and with dental suppliers. Kevin nominated me for membership to the Rotary Club of Warragul and so began a long and rewarding friendship with the businessmen of the town.

Glenys and I bought a pleasant family home in Drouin. It was on a corner with access to the yard from the side street. There was a small swimming pool and I had a shed put in the back yard to house my tools and the horse drawn jinker I was busily restoring from the damaged remnants of the original.

The boys were growing fast. David was at school and Stephen was going to kindergarten. The Drouin Pony Club held its meetings in the paddock opposite our house and this created a natural interest in riding ponies. We bought a pony called Midas and David quickly became a competent rider and a keen member of the pony club. Glenys took a great interest in the club's operation and training program and our circle of friends gradually widened. Glenys found her talent for teaching the children to ride which in addition to her understanding of the rules and regulations of the pony club organisation, made her readily appreciated.

Throughout this time we maintained close ties with both Glenys's family and mine. I was taken by surprise when Stan, my father, made an unexpected visit to see me. I had not seen him since 1965 and he had been careful to keep his distance from that time. He was remarried to Dora and invited me to visit them. They lived in Doveton, near Dandenong.

I have to admit to being intrigued. Had Stan any sense of remorse? I considered it would be good for the boys to meet their grandfather. I also knew we had to be careful. He was capable of fermenting discord and telling lies that might confuse the boys.

After careful consideration, I visited them in their rented home in Doveton. Dora was a nice lady who had a troublesome leg. She had a number of pleasant mature age children herself and seemed to have Stan under control. They were gracious hosts and eventually they took in and cared for my grandfather, Emanuel Cliff.

I visited Stan and Dora again and was pleased to see my grandfather looking so well, he was almost 96, but still able to walk to the shops and play bowls. I asked him how he was and he explained by demonstrating that sometimes he had to straighten the fingers of his right hand to pick up his bowls, otherwise he was well. I was delighted to see he still had that engaging way of looking at me, eyes twinkling and fully alert to his circumstances. I was so proud of him and especially pleased with his accepting and peaceful frame of mind. I decided it would be good for the boys to meet both him and my father, but I would not let them out of sight during the visit.

Not long after, I called in with my family and we enjoyed afternoon tea. We returned home pleased the boys had at last met two significant family members. The timing had been fortuitous because in July 1980, I was informed my grandfather had been admitted to hospital. I visited him and found him sleeping peacefully. He woke and recognised me. We talked quietly until he paused and looked at me with his steady gaze, the twinkle now replaced by a tear 'Son,' he said, 'I should have done more.' Here at last was the recognition that he knew and understood the problems his son had caused in our lives. In that moment he passed the baton of family leadership to me and I accepted his love and apology. I aspire to be as good as this man, Emmanuel Cliff, who died 24 July 1980, aged 96.

The practice continued to grow. I became keen to have an assistant dentist to cope with the demand. However, it required a large consistent demand for dental work before I could justify employing another dentist full time, meantime, I was doing my best to cope with my over busy one-man load. Then tragedy struck, Dr Frank Turner, the dentist who had looked after me as a youngster in Wonthaggi, died suddenly, aged 56.

I had known him well as a boy. I visited Frank's widow Dawn and offered any assistance she might need. She explained he had built up a practice in Leongatha at the expense of the one in Wonthaggi which was now reduced to two days a week. She was devastated. Frank's death had been sudden and unexpected. It had left her financially vulnerable.

How I wondered, was she to sell a small town dental practice, manned part time by a dentist past retirement age? I suggested she have the Wonthaggi business valued by a dental supplier and, if she wished, I would buy it at that valuation providing I could pay by monthly installments over two years. Dawn agreed to this proposal and I took possession of the practice as agreed.

My intention was to employ another dentist and leave him in Warragul with me working between the two as demand dictated. An additional problem was that the public dental facility at the Wonthaggi Hospital was also left without a dentist so I was persuaded to provide an emergency service every Wednesday morning. The hospital's demand for our services was enormous and impossible to meet.

I saw patients who came from as far away as Lang Lang to Tarwin Lower. Many were in pain or had injuries or denture problems. At times there were 15 to 20 patients waiting at 9 a.m. each Wednesday to greet the nurse and I who travelled from Warragul to Wonthaggi, a journey taking at least an hour. The private component of the Wonthaggi practice grew rapidly as well. In time, I was able to entice another dentist to Wonthaggi and he stayed for about six months but unfortunately, his wife disliked the locality and they returned to Adelaide. I resumed the service for a time but then sold the Wonthaggi practice because I could no longer cope with the work load.

In the meantime, the Warragul practice had grown so I employed other dentists. However, they found the work too difficult and would move on saying they preferred to work in the city. I had to dismiss two dentists for unsatisfactory work standards. Other rural professions were having a similar difficulty. It was hard to find competent committed professionals to work in the country. After a few attempts, I managed to secure the services of Lindsay Bishop, who became a valued colleague.

To avoid losing the considerable custom we had from towns east of Warragul, I bought commercial premises in Trafalgar and established a new branch practice. There had been a practice some years before but that had closed when the main road had been realigned for the new highway. My concern was to preserve my customer base because meanwhile, a young married couple, both dentists, bought the practice of Dr Wooley who had died in Warragul. Demand for service was leveling off. By securing the Trafalgar custom I could afford to employ another dentist and have them work between the two towns which were only 15 minutes apart.

Our social life tended to centre on the Rotary club and the pony club. In 1982 the Rotary Club of Warragul gave me the responsibility of liaising on the club's behalf with the local Shire to organise the centenary celebration of Warragul. Being so busy I neglected to involve other members and organised the procession on my own. A few months prior to the event I was prodded to reveal what progress had been made. I assured the club all was in hand and urged the Shire to provide space and entertainment for the enormous crowd I expected on the day, in particular when the procession arrived at the Showground. The day arrived and I allocated tasks to all the willing Rotarians who came along. It was extremely hot and the participants began to arrive. The fruit of hours spent throughout the year writing and talking to hundreds of individuals, clubs and interest groups came to fruition.

Even so, I had not realised it would be so enormous.

Steam trucks, road rollers, car clubs, marching girls, bands, the Army Light Horse, heavy horses, the Reserve army, the list was endless and more than 35,000 people lined the streets. In secret, I had prearranged with a theatrical group to enact an armed hold up and kidnap the Mayor as he finished his speech to the people and climbed into a waiting Cobb and Co coach. The mayor, who had a wooden leg, was being helped into the coach when my outlaws burst out of the crowd with guns blazing and robbed him of his possessions. I was three blocks away still directing the procession so missed seeing the hold-up, but was told, when the guns went off there was some panic until it was realised it was part of the fun. My boys and Glenys were on the coach with the driver and reported that the mayor was absolutely thrilled so many had turned out for what was the biggest event Warragul had ever seen. It took more than two hours for the procession to pass the dais on route to the Show Grounds where the crowd continued to enjoy festivities.

Despite my busy schedule during the previous year, especially with the organisation of the procession, I was surprised to find I was having difficulty reconciling the books for the practice. Instead of a little being left over after paying the bills, the cash flow had slowed significantly. One Friday night, as I packed to leave, a nurse who had been with me for less than a year was watching me with interest as I put the books in my bag. She asked what I was doing. I said I would take them home and try and see if there was a problem. She asked what I would do if something was wrong. I said I doubted if anything were wrong but if I found there was, I would contact the police.

On the Sunday, we were getting ready to leave for a visit when I received a phone call. It was the nurse, asking if she could come and see me. There was something she wanted to tell me. I had not looked at the books but realised something serious was about to happen. She was a woman in her late 20s and very attractive, according to many of my male patients. When she arrived I asked her in and waited. Nervously she explained she had taken money for some months and also altered the books in an attempt to hide the evidence. When I asked her how much was involved she said she was unsure, she thought it was at least $4,000.

I was shocked and annoyed with myself for not having been more careful. I had become preoccupied with organising the centenary procession. Until then, I had never had reason to be suspicious of staff. She asked what I was going to do about it. I declined to comment until I thought about it. I feared if I had her charged I would never see the money again and in addition would cost more to have the books audited. I discussed it with a policeman friend and agreed to leave the matter with him. The woman was visited and she chose to return $4,000 if she was not charged. By the time the money was returned, we realised considerably more had been taken, and for a year or more later, anomalies continued to surface in the bookwork. In all, the amount stolen was more than $10,000. I now wish I had charged her because she was caught subsequently, stealing from a ladies fashion shop in Warragul and a food store in Trafalgar.

Our lives were busy but the longing for a farm had grown. My additional concern was how to raise boys given my childhood had not equipped me to understand urban living. I did want the boys to pursue tertiary education should they prove capable. But, I also wanted them to experience the pleasure and satisfaction that could be learned by living on a farm. Glenys and I discussed the consequences of having a farm with the boys. They were told on a farm they would be expected to contribute without complaint. I had a large dental practice to run and their mother would need support with milking and the rearing of calves because only a dairy farm could provide the cash flow needed to pay for it.

CHAPTER 20
THE DAIRY FARM

Glenys and I began our search for a farm. We heard of one about to be put on the market on Lardners Track at Torwood, some 10km south of the railway line. We requested permission to inspect and the owners agreed. It was just what we were looking for and the price at the limit of our budget. We bought the 63 acre farm of once magnificent blue-gum country on the north facing foothills of the Strezlecki Ranges, 16km from Warragul.

The land was essentially a rectangle lying lengthways across the lower slopes of steeper hills to the south. The house and dairy were on the corner where the road divided. The house in Drouin sold immediately and the proceeds became the deposit on the farm, with nothing left to buy stock. A loan was obtained from the Drouin Butter Factory allowing us to buy a herd of dairy cows. The proceeds of the milk return would repay the loan. I restored the dairy to working order with the help of friends. That required the building of a brick wall to provide a walkway for the cows to leave the six per side herringbone milking parlor. The milking machines were cleaned, rubber-ware replaced and a secondhand refrigerated milk vat acquired and installed. The collection room was painted out and a pleasant working dairy was the result. With the help of the previous owner who was a cattle agent with an eye for cattle, we assembled a herd of 55 cows.

Glenys was a first class dairy farmer. She had the cows so quiet they were like pets. While standing to be milked they chewed their cud and I often watched and wondered what it was they were thinking about. I suspect it is not much, provided they are left alone to eat and digest food. It is their only preoccupation. Contented cows produce the most milk. There were problems however. Some had come with mastitis and they had to be identified and treated. To Glenys's credit, she eliminated all trace of mastitis in the herd and achieved the lowest consistent cell count of the suppliers to the Drouin Butter Factory.

There is no pretending it was without strain having to run the dental practices and the farm. Dentistry takes a toll, evidenced by their sharing with psychiatrists the dubious distinction of having the shortest working life of all professionals. While I enjoyed the patients and the clinical demands they presented, the farm for me, was a peaceful retreat.

Within two years we repaid the butter factory and at long

last received a milk cheque each month. The financial strain eased. The culled cattle were now ours to sell and they too returned a little money. By having the farm we were able to offset the earnings from dentistry against the costs of the farm. The tax savings were contributing to our improving prosperity.

Built in the 1950s the farmhouse was structurally sound although parts of it were dated and small. To modernise, we hired a caravan to serve as the kitchen while renovations were being completed. I hired a carpenter and demolished the kitchen and dining room after which all were rebuilt and modernised. A deck and verandah were added on two sides of the house and the garage upgraded to include a new laundry and second toilet-shower facility. The result was a comfortable and convenient home for family living.

We had a number of ponies to match the boys as they grew. Jasper, a Connemara about 14HH, was an amazing jumper who when bored with a paddock, simply jumped into the next. He had uncommon courage that allowed him, even as he aged, to perform at a high level of competition. Then we bought Cassie from our farrier. She was a 15.1HH super athletic chestnut stock horse with an almost unbeatable fast walk. David, already a competent rider, had moved on from his earlier ponies and was now enjoying the freedom of riding around the farm and the district. One day we attended a special sale of horses at the sale yard in Warragul. I had no intention of buying and took only passing interest until some Australian ponies bred by a well known local farmer were on offer. Unbroken, they were being sold for very little. A cute little 11.5 hand high mare was bought in. Too beautiful to refuse, I bought her for $150.

The breaking in process of the pony was a learning exercise

for not only the horse, but the family. The pony was an excellent pupil and it was not long before I had her walking around with me driving her with long reins. Soon after David, then Stephen, rode her everywhere. She was called Lindy and in pony club circles, became a legend for her stamina and tractability.

My typical day would start early with getting cows in to milk and attending to outstanding problems like blocked water lines or feeding out hay. After a shower and breakfast I went to the practice for the day. My dental day would often start before eight o'clock treating a child at the Warragul Hospital under a general anaesthetic. There were so many decayed, infected and broken teeth and the dental neglect so rampant, for some it was the only way I could manage them. I loathed the work because I knew it was preventable, but as yet, the public did not. Then I would start my day at the practice, each day booked out with general dentistry. My colleagues were in the same predicament. The initial practice above the menswear shop became too small so I relocated to a larger ground floor premises with four dental chairs, a laboratory and two offices, next to a busy medical practice.

A difficulty for patients in Gippsland was the absence of specialist services for the provision of orthodontics or oral surgery. The provision of orthodontics is not as imagined by many, just to obtain an aesthetic outcome, rather, it is to provide a functional dentition that with care, will last a life time. Teeth deemed ugly up until this time were usually extracted thus disfiguring and or necessitating full or partial dentures.

By coincidence, while visiting Adelaide for the wedding of my brother Mark, I called on Richard Edwards a friend from wine club days. He had completed his training as an orthodontist during the time I was an undergraduate. Richard was having a rough time. His marriage had failed and his practice in the Adelaide Hills was slow due to an oversupply of orthodontists in Adelaide. I told him of my problem and explained I had asked a number of orthodontists in Melbourne to come to Warragul. All had declined preferring to stay in the city. I offered the use of my practice for Richard to consult in. I assured him he could stay with us when he came over and the air fare could be covered by adding a few dollars to each consultation. Richard agreed to come, sight unseen. I was pleased because the district acquired the service of a specialist orthodontist and I knew his future was assured. Similarly, the treatment of serious oral pathology was better managed by a specialist and patients requiring these services hitherto had to travel to Melbourne.

To entice an oral surgeon to Warragul was a somewhat similar exercise. I prevailed upon my former tutor in oral surgery, Dr Jock Herd, who was under employed in Melbourne. He accepted a similar offer to the one I had made to Richard. At last, I had the services of competent specialists with whom I could interact to provide comprehensive modern dentistry.

With specialists providing service, better diagnostic tools were necessary. I bought the first orthopantomograph machine or OPG, to be installed in Gippsland. It allowed me to take lateral and panoramic view's (X-rays with very low exposure) of the face thus providing an enormous amount of detail with minimal exposure. Successful orthodontics, like all branches of medicine, is dependent on the correct diagnosis. The improved radiography provided an accurate noninvasive basis for the assessment of what we call the malocclusion and could also preclude pathology. The cost was claimable on medical benefits so for the first time in the region, full specialist care could be provided. In later years, the hospital was able to provide the radiographic service.

Richards's orthodontic practice blossomed overnight. It began with a few days a month while staying with us, but soon, he moved to Warragul to live. He bought my old premises above the menswear shop for a fraction of the usual set up cost.

Meanwhile, Jock Herd arranged regular access to the Warragul and Neerim South Hospital where he removed troublesome wisdom teeth and treated other pathology. Although I was a visiting dental surgeon at the local hospitals and doing a lot of general oral surgery, I was always disposed to referring patients to a specialist when it was in the patient's best interests to do so. I had more than enough to do without overreaching my competence as a general practitioner.

From the beginning, I maintained a close interest and attendance in all aspects of further education for dentists. The big dental event was the annual conference held in a different state each year. The Australian Dental Association would arrange for outstanding guest speakers from local and overseas to bring to us the best research and reviews of dental and medical science. It was also a chance to meet and exchange views with colleagues to overcome the inherent isolation of a busy country practice. The second tier of ADA further education involved the regional groups – ours being the south east division of the state. This enabled us to meet a number of times a year and to organise a weekend conference where specialists from Melbourne would donate their time and lecture us on topics chosen by the group. Generally the wives and partners attended and this provided a great opportunity for a barbecue or fine dining after the lectures. The combination of lectures specific to our needs and the opportunity to socialise with colleagues and their partners provided an important network of support to individuals who work to a large extent in isolation. I was proud of the profession, and enjoyed the company of all in it.

My assistant dentist expressed interest in buying into the practice as an associate. We had worked well together and he was keen to earn more now he had a wife and a young family. We agreed he would buy half of the Warragul practice and I would retain the Trafalgar practice. The proceeds of the sale further increased our equity in the farm.

A new secondary college started in Warragul. Saint Paul's Anglican Grammar School had been established by an energetic few having the foresight to see the need for a high quality independent school. Glenys and I had registered our boys with Caulfield Grammar School but here was an opportunity for a private school education without the need for them to live away. The creation of Saint Paul's also coincided with David's graduation from primary school. He was enrolled in the first year classes of the new school, which had only begun the year before. To begin it had started in the hall at the rear of the Anglican Church in Warragul but the building of a new school had started. It proved an excellent choice for a number of his friends also enrolled. This meant that while living at home, he was still able to maintain his social network while ensuring he received a thorough education.

The combination of good teachers and children from stable farming families meant the standard of education attained by the children in primary schools was high and achieved with little drama. Stephen and a girl of similar age who lived close to us were the last generation of kids to attend the Lardner School riding their ponies. The sight of this small boy riding home from school, alternatively racing and dawdling on his little white pony, is a memory I cherish.

The farm was doing well. We were milking 55 cows and rearing about 23 calves each year. There were a considerable number of young cattle to be accommodated besides the two horses. It became necessary to rent more land and distribute the livestock between properties. I bought an old Bedford three ton cattle truck because it would enable us to transport not only the horses to the different pony club events but the cattle too.

To an outsider it may have seemed we worked all the time. Although almost true, it was interesting and mostly enjoyable. David learned to drive the tractor after spending a week restricted to first gear and progressing week at a time to the others. He had his own 'business'. He bought some chooks and was selling eggs. He had a number of customers, among them the artificial inseminator John Pollard who also collected semen from bulls. The egg white containing albumin was used to dilute the semen, making John, David's best customer.

In a practical sense everything was running well but I was strained and to some extent dissatisfied with dentistry. I had made the mistake of my life not doing medicine. It was easy to rationalise that what I was doing was great but I felt my natural curiosity in medicine could not be fulfilled. While I was improving the dental status of a large number of patients and spreading the preventive dentistry message, it was failing to challenge me.

From the time I left the farm on Phillip Island I had dreamed of doing medicine. In many ways my checkered career had equipped me to empathise readily with people who were having difficulties in their lives. In addition, I had acquired the basics of medical practice together with a wide practical experience in general dentistry. This combination inevitably led me to see beyond the more obvious symptoms patients presented with. Lay people joke that a dentist cannot converse with patients because patients have their mouths open, but it is far from the truth. A successful dentist has to earn the trust of a patient from the outset because we work within the patient's personal space. For many, the mouth is their most personal space. For those suffering acute anxiety or who are unable to co-operate, the dentist is faced with a challenge – overcome the fear. To achieve that, it is necessary to communicate not just with words, but with body language, empathy, and, a caring attitude.

Patients recognise these qualities and let down their defenses with little reserve. I was privileged to share my patient's concerns about their health and private lives but my natural impulse was to participate in the resolution of the health problems. I had chosen the wrong career.

Of course, one continues to learn with experience and further study, but my interests were widening. My reading of history had grown as had an interest in philosophy and politics. The frustration of juggling time between the farm and the practice led me to think that as a family, we needed to break the cycle, perhaps take a holiday. I discussed the possibility with Glenys who had supported me in all we had achieved. She too, felt in need of a change of scenery.

I put the practice on the market and a buyer appeared in no time. A friend of Lyndsay Bishop, my associate, bought my half of the Warragul practice and Lyndsay bought the Trafalgar component which was separate to the associate arrangement. Relatively cashed up and still only 45, Glenys and I decided we would have a look at the world. The idea of having just a few weeks off seemed just as difficult as taking months off. The logistics were the same. As to the cost, we only live once. Our good neighbors the Haywoods had sons who agreed to manage the farm in our absence. It was arranged we would go while the cows were at the end of their milking season, from early March to July. Because the practice sold in late 1985, I did some locum work with a colleague in Traralgon for a few months while we arranged the details of our intended world adventure.

We considered where the boys were with their schooling and concluded the experience of travel would more than offset the temporary suspension of formal education. Following a talk with their teachers, we agreed to supervise some mathematics and have the boys keep a diary.

Over the years Glenys and I had hosted Rotary exchange students, a lad from Denmark and a girl from Finland. They were great ambassadors for their country and a pleasure for us to have in our home. They had fitted readily into our lifestyle making the whole experience a happy exchange of cultures. On hearing of our intended holiday, their families extended an invitation for us to visit them. We planned our travel with a view to visiting Eva in Finland and Fleming in Denmark.

Prior to leaving, we chatted about what our priorities would be and discussed the purpose of our trip. The boys and myself were open to almost everything, Glenys had a general interest in History and our common ground was all things rural.

CHAPTER 21
AROUND
THE WORLD

We left Australia on 12th March 1986 soon after the nuclear power station explosion at Chernobyl in the Ukraine. The nuclear accident in the reactor had created a fear of the fallout throughout Europe leading to wild speculation as to what the ramifications would be for the wider world. Not only for those affected directly, but also for people of other countries whose crops and communities were affected by the radioactive fallout which dispersed itself in the atmosphere. Reports we saw indicated the radioactive clouds moved west and north causing anxiety in the UK. Undeterred, we left rationalising the risk to us would be minimal because we would be moving quickly through countries that were for the most part only marginally affected by fallout.

Our only accommodation booked for the trip was the first night in London at the Astor Court Hotel in Hallam Street, close to the home Dickens once occupied. By prior arrangement we organised to hire a car from a man in Romsey on the advice of other friends in Rotary who had enjoyed his cooperation in the past. During the few days we were without a car, we visited the Tower of London, the principal museums, Fortnum and Masons, Churchill's war room, Westminster and generally enjoyed the ambience of London. Then we caught the train to Romsey, where we picked up a Volkswagen Golf. Our aim was to have a two week excursion around the south of England before our scheduled flight to Stockholm on 26th March. We used Bed & Breakfast homes while visiting horse farms, museums, the salvaged ship the Mary Rose at Southampton and every other place of historical interest we could fit in. We quickly fell into a happy routine, taking enormous delight in savoring this wonderful opportunity to see and observe an endless variety of people and their way of living.

For example, while driving west through the rolling farmland of Devon, we planned to stay at a farmhouse B&B selected from the book we had bought for the purpose. We had phoned ahead. On arrival, about 5.30 p.m., the lady said she would honor her commitment but asked tentatively would we mind going to another B&B if she could arrange it? She said some family matter had arisen that she would like to be free to deal with. Her manner was genuine. We agreed and the phone call was made. We would be accommodated for the same modest fee and the directions were given to us to find the new address some distance away in the village of Hooke.

The journey proved difficult and required crossing many small country roads which meant by the time we arrived, it was 6.30 p.m. and dark. Hooke was tiny, a few houses on the corner of deserted crossroads. The house might have once been an inn, for that was what its shape suggested. I stopped the car in front of the door and knocked, unsure of the reception at the late hour and such little notice. The door opened and immediately we were enveloped by the glow of a hall light. Framed by the light was the silhouette of a middle aged lady whose face, as our eyes adjusted, revealed the features of an intelligent and slightly eccentric lady. She ushered us in with a disarming smile. Apologising for being slightly disorganised, she asked if we would care to freshen up and share a drink with her before dinner. She had phoned her chef on receiving the phone call and he had come in immediately from across the road to prepare the dinner. A large beautifully decorated dining room was adjacent to the spacious lounge in which we sat sipping a magnificent French red wine while waiting our meal.

Our hostess entertained us with an account of how she ran her boutique restaurant under normal circumstances which clearly did not normally include an Australian family dropping by late in the day. It was her passion she said, to entertain senior naval and merchant mariners who by arrangement would come from ports nearby to enjoy her menu and scintillating conversation. She was not only the hostess but an informed participant. She said, it was her privilege to entertain us. And entertain us she did.

We took our places at a table set with fine silver arranged with precise exactitude. Our hostess offered apologies for the restricted choice of menu, a necessity she explained, of the little notice given to her chef. This rare and wonderful lady made entertaining an art form. She extracted our history and spoke with special attention to the boys who were as enthralled as Glenys and I were. Her knowledge of the world and her familiarity with the classics and English history left us deeply grateful for the experience. The next morning she introduced the boys to her pet donkeys that she led to fresh pasture nearby. I was able to capture them on film before moving on again. But each of us, I am sure, has an enduring memory of our time in Hooke. The charge was so modest I was embarrassed -- it was the standard tariff of the farmhouse B&B.

We returned the car to Romsey before flying to Stockholm on 26th March. In Stockholm we booked our place on the ship to take us overnight to Helsinki, Finland. Because it was the Easter weekend, the Viking ship was almost booked out with Swedish tourists taking the opportunity to party for the weekend. The freedom to drink alcohol on board was in stark contrast to the restrictive alcohol laws in force throughout Sweden. Glenys and I chose to sit up in the large lounge chairs provided for the purpose to avoid the expense of a cabin since there were four of us. A thin layer of ice covered the sea and the waterfront around us was dotted with other vessels. It was a beautiful scene that evoked memories of an older world silhouetted as it was against the mustard coloured Scandinavian architecture in the background.

Light fell as the ship threaded its way past many small islands. The crowd aboard moved to the enormous entertainment rooms and the party began. Entertainers performed and the drink flowed freely. By accident, I became involved with some Finnish soldiers returning from military exercises while Glenys looked after the boys. Meanwhile, the ship developed a slight constant shuddering motion as it thrust its way through the sea ice, but I was enjoying the party too much to be bothered. By four o'clock in the morning I was in the piano bar with many hopelessly drunk Swedes. Eventually, one by one, they toppled off their chairs and lay comatose on the floor. Meanwhile, Glenys became seasick on the lower deck and the boys ran between us to report the phenomenon of men lying where they fell all over the ship.

The ship arrived at Helsinki the next morning and decanted

its inebriated passengers who like me, were pale and unwell. The chill in Helsinki registered 20 degrees below freezing which was almost as cool as Glenys. I received no sympathy from her as we bought our bus tickets for the roughly 100km journey east to our destination Loviisa where by arrangement we would meet our Finnish hosts for the long weekend.

My impression of Helsinki was how I imagined a Russian city might look. We had little time to dwell on that as a large loud and officious lady called Helga explained in broken English that our baggage would travel on one bus while we would be aboard another. The seats were assigned in a bus with no toilet. I sat transfixed with agony and a growing horror that I might disgrace myself before arrival in Loviisa. The added difficulty was the language barrier for we could not negotiate toilet stops or even ask how long the journey would take. The bus labored slowly through thick snow, only stopping from time to time to pick up and drop off passengers. I thought I would die. Glenys looked positively hopeful.

On arrival, I fell at the feet of our waiting hosts muttering, 'Where's the toilet?' They were wonderful and understood completely. The ablutions performed, we packed into their car and headed home, where I was put to bed. Eva, the daughter, was thrilled to see us, as indeed were her parents. They were wonderful hosts and took us to see a Finnish dairy farm where the cows were kept inside a large barn for most of the year. We visited their small holiday home near the Baltic coast and even drove out on to the Baltic Sea where we saw men fishing through holes made through the ice.

The real highlight was, as always, the dinner we enjoyed with their friends. While we sat to feast on traditional foods, they talked and explained their customs. The traditional dish for Easter is 'Mammi' -- essentially a bread pudding with dark molasses and dried orange peel that is allowed to rest and sweeten before baking. After baking it is refrigerated to be eaten cold with vanilla ice cream, sugar and cream. We learned reindeer steaks were common, the meat usually fried in butter, but it was not on our menu. They explained a depression creeps over the people during winter that they call their 'winter head'. Alcoholism is a problem in Finland but despite everything they endure, doing what they can to keep alive the crafts, art and the literature of the culture they value highly.

On the 1st of April we retraced our path to Stockholm on a ship of the Silya line. The entertainment was more sober and Glenys was not seasick. In Stockholm we spent the day exploring the city before taking the train south to Denmark. The weather was clear and we spent pleasant hours looking at passing country until we reached the Baltic coast again at Helsingborg. We left the train and moved onto a ferry for the trip across the strait to Helsingor in Denmark. We arrived in Copenhagen on a Sunday evening, about nine o'clock. We were extremely cold and hungry. There was a kiosk open on the station with a sign indicating it sold hamburgers and soup. When ordering the hamburgers the man reached into a refrigerator and handed us cold ones, then proceeded to ladle the soup into cardboard drink containers. The soup was almost devoid of anything solid other than a few perfectly white round meat balls floating on top. Desperate as we were, we consumed the lot while considering where we might find accommodation.

The hotel board listed huge prices for the rooms on offer. In desperation, Glenys decided to phone a youth hostel. We had joined Youth Hostels Australia before leaving as a fallback measure only. Glenys made the call. A short taxi ride later, we were pleasantly surprised to be accommodated in a clean establishment. The boys loved it because they could play snooker and relax with other young people, all keen to talk to the young Australians.

We spent two or three days exploring Copenhagen and it was everything the brochures had promised. It was a beautiful little city with unique charm. We made contact with the parents of the Danish boy we had hosted and were assured they would love us to visit. We caught the train in Copenhagen for the ride west to Denmark's Jutland Peninsula. The family lived in the village of Ru, a little south of Aahus, where we left the train to be warmly greeted by the Holst family. Bengt and Hanna Holst made us right at home and readily offered their second car for us to explore the region. They lived in a fine home they had built over many years and eagerly put on a special dinner in our honour to meet their many friends.

A visit to the Holst family friend and dentist left me reflecting on his complaint about paying taxation that was well over half his income. He explained that the highly organised social system meant many people felt trapped in a benevolent political system that removed the incentive to do more than the minimum. A career change was almost unthinkable because one had to have authority to do so. For instance, the dentist could not become a farmer without a green card. Subsequently, I attended a Rotary meeting with Bengt and met a large group of businessmen who expressed similar reservations about what they regarded in their political system as the disincentive to excel. The standard of living was obviously high, but these heartfelt laments about the system of government left me with something to think about.

We left on the train to go south over the border into Germany, through Hamburg to Koln, or Cologne as we know it. I had arranged to attend a dental conference there and on arrival we booked into the youth hostel on the east side of the Rhine River. Glenys and the boys spent a few days on a discovery of Koln while I attended a conference remarkably similar to any I had been to in Australia, no surprise for much of the premium dental equipment was made in Germany. I was entirely comfortable at the conference and even the language barrier proved insignificant. After inspection of the magnificent Koln Cathedral that had miraculously survived the intense Allied bombing during World War Two, we boarded the train again. This time the destination was Rotterdam in Holland.

On arrival we made our way west on the suburban trains to Zwart Waal, where we were met by Trixie and Paul Vandenboom, the brother of a fellow Rotarian in Warragul. The Vandenbooms made us most welcome and extended generous hospitality to us. Paul took us out to see the huge Rotterdam dry docks where he held an important position.

Over the next two days the Vandenbooms took us to Holland's oldest city, Brielle, still entered via a gate into the walled town. Designed originally to repel invaders, the town was specifically fortified to resist Napoleon during the French invasion. The Dutch are rightly proud of this beautiful walled town with its canals and each April it celebrates its liberation from the French. From Brielle we drove to see the new fortified dykes being built to keep the North Sea out of the Dutch lowlands. While our time with Trixie and Paul allowed us to gain a well informed overview of their view of Dutch politics, it also afforded us a valuable insight into the complexity of the inter-trade dealings and how interdependent the component countries of the continent are for their general prosperity.

Glenys and I considered the next part of our tour of discovery. It was decided we would take a train to Paris because a car would simply be a hindrance in the traffic there. We would spend a few days and then catch a train back to Brussels where we would hire a car and complete our plan to drive through France, Italy, Switzerland and Germany before returning to Brussels to drop off the car. Our flight to London would complete this part of our tour.

We arrived in Paris on Tuesday 15ᵗʰ April and went directly to Hotel Crondsadt, 10 Rue La Martine. Our time in Paris flew as we explored all the destinations we read about at home. Too many to list, we would most certainly return to this fascinating city. We left Paris for Brussels a few days later where we arranged to pick up a car and head for the English Channel to plan our next move. To optimise our travel experience, we were learning to seek accommodation by late afternoon so we could rest and plan our next movements. We stayed near Ostend. The next day we visited the historic small town of Bruges which had a large civic square at its centre with a high tower overlooking it. The tower was built in 1254. The top was reached after climbing 360 steps. Later, in England, I was to learn from my elderly uncle that he was stationed in this tower during World War Two when he was an army clerk keeping track of supplies for the Allies.

The boys were more impressed with the dunking chair suspended over the canal. In medieval times women accused of witchcraft were strapped into the chair and lowered into the river, their survival depending on their innocence. Following a tour of the village in a horse drawn Landou, we moved on to Passendale and Ypres to inspect the World War One sites where many Australians had lost their lives.

No account can truly convey the feelings one experiences when visiting these sites. I determined to read and study the history more closely before returning to pay my respects at another time because I was conscious this was where my grandfather had been wounded and his brother killed. The number of graves, irrespective of the occupant's nationality, is so staggering all I could think of was the futility of war.

We travelled east, staying at Cambrai and then on to Verdun, where we visited another World War One site a little north east of the city. Fort Douamont was a component in a ring of fortification built to protect Verdun in 1883 and is on the highest ground on the northern perimeter of the city. A memorial park today, it had been fought over many times, changing hands in the process a number of times. It was eerily still, undulating country carpeted with bomb craters through which light scrub struggled to grow. Signs throughout the park provide a staggering statistical record of the men killed and of the armaments, shells and bombs, dropped on the area. I was moved by the immensity of this testament to human depravity

We drove 794km south, stopping periodically to enjoy the French cuisine and to visit to the Ponte de Guarde. A Roman aqueduct, it is a structural marvel that bore a sign saying that Napoleon, in the midst of his troubles in 1812, had decreed with amazing foresite that it should be preserved for posterity. Moving on, we returned to the motorways until we reached St. Tropez, a beautiful harbour town on the Mediterranean Sea -- the famous nautical playground of European celebrities. Enormous luxurious boats lined the quay, all kept in readiness should the owners have a little time to spare.

From St. Tropez we drove east into Italy headed Mestre, the town on the mainland adjacent to Venice. We found accommodation at the Hotel Koppa and travelled on the bus in stifling heat to the ferries. Venice can only be entered via a variety of ferries that serve as buses taking people to their destinations along the waterways of this ancient Byzantine city. We took the ferry to the island of Ling. We explored there before returning to St. Mark's Square, where we had lunch. Then we visited the glassworks for a demonstration of glass blowing and to see how Murano glassware is made. A ride in a gondola was a must. We had a 40 minute excursion of the waterways which took us via the back streets to the home of Marco Polo. The experience of drifting gently through this ancient city and then seeing the home of this historic icon was unforgettable. The opulent homes and small palaces were built in the early part of the 15th century, many in the Renaissance style, a reflection of the fabulous wealth generated by the Byzantium trade with the East.

I found it difficult to imagine how many of the buildings which showed damage from the ravages of the sea, could be restored and preserved for the future. What I saw was a fragile economy, heavily dependent on the tourist industry. This was a sobering footnote to what was a remarkable day walking and floating by landmarks like the ancient bridge over the main canal, a scene I had only seen in books.

After an early night we drove north into Austria where we noted, after crossing the border, the Teutonic love of order and cleanliness. It was a 604km drive that day and we reached Wein (Vienna) and our youth hostel, which was on the south west periphery of the city. The following day we took the train into Wein, one of the most beautiful cities I have seen. We spent three days exploring every feature listed on our mustsee list, including the Spanish Riding School located in one of the many wings of the Hofburg Palace. The palace is an enormous architectural wonder that has been the seat of Austrian Government since its first occupancy in 1279. Open for inspection to the public, it faithfully conveys a sense of majesty and awe upon its visitors. We were impressed with the efficiency of the public transport and the overall beauty of the city. We resolved to visit again with the intention of attending the Opera House to hear the music of Mozart, Brahms and the other masters.

We moved on to Salzburg, the boys readily preferring to stay at the Youth Hostel again. Salzburg is divided into the new and the old cities by the River Saltzach (salt-river). The hostel was in the new town and we had a pleasant evening exploring. The following morning, we crossed the river and went to the old city, famed for being the birthplace of Mozart and popularised by the film 'The Sound of Music'. It was a glorious morning and the old city sparkled just as I had imagined from the travel brochures. To stand and reflect on Mozart's music while contemplating the circumstances of his birth in his modest home is a moving experience. We rode the cable car to a plateau above the old town on which the remains of the old castle sit. We were greeted by an Oom'pah band that was entertaining the crowd who were enjoying the view and a casual lunch. We descended again to the old city below in the square where people were playing chess with pieces almost the size of a person. On leaving, we headed for Innsbruck where we enjoyed an evening at another youth hostel before moving on to Munich. The beer halls of Munich were passed without note because of the boys and we moved a little to the north for a visit to the former Nazi concentration camp, Dachau.

The first of many concentration camps created by the Nazis in the early 1930s, Dachau at first housed political prisoners and later different ethnic minorities declared the enemy of the Reich. It is said to have held a total of 206,000 prisoners, of who 33,600 died a documented death. The camp had facilities for gassing prisoners, plus a crematorium. When liberated by the Allies in 1945, it held 30,000 prisoners and contained piles of bodies. The deaths were the result of starvation, beatings, typhus and execution. The statistics have to be regarded as conservative estimates only for there is considerable evidence, including the fate of those who were consigned to the satellite camps, many more who died are unaccounted for.

We continued our tour of discovery through rolling farmland to Passau in the southeast, close to the Czeska Republic, then north past rich dairy farms interspersed by private and state forest areas. The small villages we passed through were notable for their neatness and the saw mills we saw in the region. We turned west and circled north of Nuremburg to Neustadt where, as had become our custom, we stayed in the youth hostel.

The following day we visited Weissenburg, where I attended a lunch meeting of the Rotary club while Glenys and the boys explored the town and the local museum. The guest speaker spoke of his recent visit to Namibia, West Africa. His talk served to illustrate vividly the good work Rotary was doing throughout the world. I was made most welcome and enjoyed the fellowship extended to me.

From Weissenburg we traveled via Ulm, Lindou and Ravensburg to Zurich. The weather was perfect for travelling and the light just right for viewing and photographing the outstanding scenery for which this region of Europe is renowned. Glenys and I were observing the behavior of the boys. The cities, they decided, were largely similar except where a museum, castle or outstanding feature took their attention. They preferred a rural setting. For the most part they participated with interest in all our discussions and contributed greatly by asking questions that frequently obliged us to consult our maps and historical references to provide the answers. It was obvious the boys were coping well with the mass of new and challenging experiences each day presented. The boys soaked up every opportunity we came across. After Zurich, Glenys took us on a tour over the Jaunpass at 1500m then back through Gstaad to the Chateau de Oex, a youth hostel in the mountains around which light brown Simmental cows wearing bells around their necks grazed greedily on vivid green pasture. After our evening meal we went for a walk and ended our day by talking to a French riding instructor who ran a nearby riding school.

The next morning the sun was shining on the paddocks and the sky was cloudless. We began our descent from the chateau. The encircling mountain tops glistening with snow. Below, on the slopes, the picture postcard green paddocks all reflected a different shade, dependant on their orientation to the sun. At the lower altitudes we passed terraced vineyards so steep all work done was by hand. Some even had flying fox devices to convey the pruning's and fruit to the road below. We passed through Aigle to Montreux, an elegant village on the eastern shore of Lake Geneva. Dreamily still, the lake had a mist over the water, the edge defined by a garden brimming with tulips of every colour.

I arranged with our contact in England to meet us at the airport on our return to London on 7th May, only a few days later. Meanwhile David and Stephen made friends with two boys holidaying from Brighton, England, who were riding their bikes around Europe.

From Delemont, we went via Basel onto the Black Forest route which runs north through the mountains before turning west across the Rhine into Belgium. Our intention was to catch up with friends near the border with Holland before returning the car in Brussels. The Black Forest belied its name for the deciduous trees were stunningly beautiful in full autumn colour. We dawdled through this fascinating country before crossing the Rhine a little south of Frankfurt to stay at Rudesheim, where we were had another magnificent view of the river from the youth hostel. My diary record indicates how inexpensive it could be staying in these hostels. We were charged 40Dm for the family that night, whereas we were asked for 100Dm each for rooms in the township.

Monday 5th April saw continued mild weather and we drove north along the Rhine to Koblenz, where the Moselle River forms a junction overlooked high on the east side by a castle built in the 11th or 12th Century. The boys were intrigued when told the locality was once ruled by a feudal prince who exacted rents and tolls from the river boats that passed. The money enabled the prince to maintain a small supporting army which in turn provided safe passage on that section of the river.

A short drive the next morning took us over the border into Belgium across the rolling country taken so rapidly by the German army in World War Two. Now it had regained its claim to manicured perfection. To my farmer's eye it was stunningly beautiful and dotted with neat homes, many of which had flower boxes in which exuberant brilliant red geraniums grew alongside dark blue lobelia. We found our Belgium friends. Sadly, Han's was very ill and Anna was having great difficulty coping. Our visit was welcome for they were childless and elderly. We conveyed news of their Australian connections, a welcome temporary distraction from the routine of their lives. It was a happy but emotional parting for us all as we returned to Brussels for our flight to London.

At Heathrow Airport we were met as arranged by Les Richards and resumed our former clockwise tour of England after returning him to his home in Romsey. It was strange to be among people who spoke English after having spent so long with other languages. I must say it had been no hardship for, although driving on the opposite side of the road, I had adapted quickly. What I had missed was the ability to converse about history in detail, to understand the foreign humour or to have a cup of tea. The latter was rectified at Les's, after which we continued our journey to Beer on the south coast of Lyme Bay.

Summarising our next five to six weeks, we meandered down to Lands End, then along the West Coast to Bath and Bristol before following the coast of Wales to Pembroke. We visited museums, horse farms, cathedrals, locks, mines and Roman remains. Each day had become an opportunity to see and explore something new. Our family, far from home, was happily employed examining travel guides and the information we were collecting.

At Fishguard, Wales, we took the ferry to Rosslare in Ireland. It was an unpleasant trip on a lumpy sea just subsiding from a storm. The stench of vomit hung heavily over the ship from its previous voyage. On arrival we planned to circle clockwise around Ireland back to Dublin before taking a ferry back to Holyhead on the northwest coast of Wales. Our immediate impression was of the beauty and quaintness as we meandered through Waterford, Cork and Kerry, each night staying in B&Bs. The people received us enthusiastically and we were mutually entertained by our different accents and customs. The Irish economy at the time was flat. This meant the people of necessity persevered with dated farming and transport methods, like carts drawn by donkeys and the practice of driving the tractor to the pub. The signage was often a source of amusement to us because the Irish use of language has an unfamiliar logic at times. But what a stunningly beautiful country it is. As we drove around the Ring of Kerry, the sun was setting on the heaving ocean. It provided a soft filtered light that contrasted the many shades of green on the hills surrounding this large inlet. Back in Killarney we were met with a festive air because preparations were underway for a music festival.

We sampled the festival then moved on with pleasant memories of Irish people who know how to enjoy themselves. On through Limerick, over the Shannon to Galway Bay, seeing familiar names, tempting us to linger and savor their atmosphere and charm, but always the imperative, move on, or we would never get home. The hills of the Connemara were sparsely occupied and seemed to provide subsistence only to the people we saw cutting peat from the many bogs right across the region. Small donkey carts laden with cut rushes could be seen from time to time, used we imagined, as bedding for animals. It was a timeless place, the inhabitants apparently poor and worn out by their fight with the elements.

I rounded a corner in the road and was confronted by a large machinegun directed straight at me. We were flanked by a number of heavily armed British soldiers. On high alert, they remained tense but politely businesslike until satisfied we were indeed an Australian family travelling on holiday. Then their attitude changed. They were happy and wanted to chat about Australia and give the boys an explanation of what they were doing. The troubles of Northern Ireland were at a low point in Irish history. Bombings, assassinations and violence were almost daily events and these soldiers were here to prevent the movement of weapons and undesirable people. They advised us to take care.

As we entered Londonderry I stopped to refuel the car. When I paid, the owner said there had just been an explosion somewhere behind us. He was clearly fearful and surprised we would visit the region. Approaching the township centre was a shock – it was a war zone unlike anything we had seen. The boys counted and found one in six homes were uninhabitable due to fire damage or being bombed. High wire fences surrounded the police station and an air of watchful fear hung over all. I had no wish to stay. We moved on, looking for a place to have lunch. We skirted east across the River Foyle, then around the high bluff overlooking the large inlet where the suburbs appeared untouched. We found a hotel and entered to find the front dining room occupied by people eating noisily. The woman in charge asked us to wait. We stood patiently for some time and were a little uncomfortable since her attitude was polite but curt. Eventually she asked us to follow her and we were shown into a larger more formal dining room. Her attitude changed to one of warm friendliness and cooperation. The meal was enjoyable but as we ate we reflected on what had happened. The wait we concluded, was to observe us because we were strangers. Once we were perceived as a family and no threat, we were invited into the part reserved for regular trusted clients.

Glenys and I were moved by the almost palpable fear these people were living with. I had read 'Topaz', a history of Ireland by Leon Uris. How were the children of Northern Ireland to grow into well adjusted citizens in an environment filled with such fear and hatred? It might have been sectarian in origin but fortunately despite all, many individuals were warm and gracious hosts.

We stopped on the north east corner of Ireland near Balley-castle to see the Devils Marbles, the rock formation of the cliffs contracted when cooling from its liquid lava origins to form regular concentric forms. Looking across the water toward Scotland, we could see the Mull of Kintyre, a headland made famous by John Lennon of the Beatles. Our Irish experience was turning into one of emotionally charged concern for an intensely likeable people. For generations this poor but beautiful country had exported millions of its people to America and Australia.

Our next stay was at Larne, then Belfast. We chose not to explore Belfast with our usual thoroughness and instead contented ourselves with driving through the streets, which were scarred from the troubles. Many houses had been bombed and boarded up, a spectacle almost as devastating as the damage we had seen in Londonderry. We departed from Northern Ireland with feelings of sadness for the people and their future with a selfish tinge of guilty relief because we had witnessed the war zone without harm to ourselves.

We returned to Holyhead on the ferry the next day then

drove south along the west coast of Wales. The Welsh residents were hospitable but reserved. They too were finding it difficult to survive. Their villages and homes were neat and functional and they took pride in living in this remote but beautiful country.

Back in England, we headed for Bradford where we had arranged to meet the surviving members of the Cliff and Thornton families. Colonel and Alice Thornton were cousins on my grandmother's side. They had two children, Tony and Brenda, who were about my own age. Throughout World War Two my mother had sent them food and clothing parcels regularly and I was excited at the prospect of meeting them.

Alice and Colonel, both in their eighties, lived in the suburb of Saltaire, a little North of Bradford. The meeting was emotional and deeply stirring. They had kept contact with our families through the years and had resisted my grandfather's entreaty to emigrate and join him. In time, Alice and Colonel had come to regret they had not. Both were highly literate students of English history and contemporary affairs. So began a highly rewarding four days of sharing stories of the family history with them.

Colonel took us to the former homes of the Cliffs who had immigrated to Australia in 1920. The houses were essentially the same Colonel said. Still occupied, they were of a standard considerably better than I had imagined them to be. My grandfather, Emmanuel Cliff, had married Anne Thornton and had owned a bakery, a shop now run by a pleasant Pakistani family who appreciated our contribution to its history. Why or what I wondered, had happened that caused them to leave this apparently stable life and come to Australia with two young children?

In 2010 I learnt Emmanuel Cliff's cousin had married a Mr Luke. They had emigrated and settled in Clayton, Victoria, where they ran a successful market garden. Enticed by their success and assurance of support, Emmanuel had followed with his wife and two children. It is the common story of many enterprising people. The anguish of leaving an established life for an unseen opportunity so far away intrigued me. Would I have had the courage? Did they regret the decision? From all I can remember and ascertain, my grandparents had a happy life in Australia, especially since they were able to return to England a number of times and maintain their link to family. Colonel and Alice were important components of that link, hence the reciprocal love and exchange of stories between us.

It was with a sense of sadness that we had to leave to continue our tour of discovery. Our aim was to go north into Scotland along the west coast and return via the east through Edinburgh. From there we would wend our way south to complete our UK holiday.

We skirted around Glasgow, regarding it as just another industrial city. I know this judgment was unfair, but a trip of this sort has to have priorities and ours was to see the highlands. Our youth hostel guide listed a hotel at Loch Lomond that became our destination for that day. It was a surprise to find a grand old home with views across the Loch from the upper floor. The common room on this level was large, with big windows and comfortably furnished with couches and a grand piano. There were few people about. Glenys took the opportunity to review some Maths and English with the boys while I perused the maps. It was still only about five o'clock.

I hardly noticed a man come into the room and take his place at the grand piano. Then he began to play. He was a concert pianist who treated us to an astonishing performance, the better for the ambiance of the setting and its unexpected happening. After at least an hour he began to play the score of 'The Sound of Music'. At this point, his children, until then unseen, came in one by one to sing their part of the 'goodbye' song. The few people present besides ourselves were as enraptured as we were. It was a moving unforgettable musical experience. When he had finished playing, I approached the man and was surprised to hear his American accent. He explained his name was Smith, an executive of the Church of Latter Day Saints in Salt Lake City. I thought he was in his early forties and he had a large young family. He added that his expertise, beside the piano, was in finance and he was on a mission to South Africa to help restructure the church. He extended to us the hospitality of the Church in Salt Lake City and urged us to visit. Although it was most dramatic and unexpected, it was only one of the many truly wonderful experiences we had in our travels. There were too many to recount, each a vignette of unforgettable generosity and human interaction.

Stories like 'Ring of Bright Water' by Gavin Maxwell had long whetted our appetite for at least a glimpse of the islands off the coast of Scotland. The stories were of a man who had lived for a time in the Outer Hebrides where he had found and befriended otters. His descriptions of the people he described as crofters and their customs had sown the seeds of curiosity in our minds. However, the best we could manage was two days on the Isle of Skye. Day one was cold and wet. We caught the ferry and toured the island. The place was alive with hikers, seen everywhere trudging along and clearly having a great time, apparently unconcerned by the weather. It was so common a sight throughout the UK we now understand it is a national passion. Permanent inhabitants were few. There was a small village at Portree, then little sign of habitation until we reached the northwest tip of the Isle where we found a crowded youth hostel full of spirited young hikers having a great time. The sea was churlish and the sky was scattered with rain storms driven by a cold strong wind. I was unable to see across the Little Minch strait that lies between the Isle of Skye and the Outer Hebrides.

The rugged islands had usable land divided into paddocks by stone walls. These were the tenements held by the Crofters who with their families had farmed here. We saw sod-roofed stone huts where they once lived, and given the bleakness of our day, I was unsure whether to admire or pity a people obliged to endure with so little in such a wind swept cold climate. The scenery was beautiful. Even the scudding clouds and rain squalls had a beauty of their own as they swept in from the sea. With the car heater on, we retreated to the mainland, marveling that people would choose to live in such inhospitable isolation.

We drove along the north side of Loch Ness. The boys were disappointed they did not catch a glimpse of Nessie, the monster said to inhabit the lake. The hills of the region are typical of those throughout the Grampians -- steep, grass covered on the lower slopes, not especially high and with barely a tree to be seen. Rumour has it that the hills were once covered with valuable oak trees that were ruthlessly harvested during the reign of Henry V111 to build ships for the Royal Navy. Perhaps if I were obliged to live there I too might invent stories like that and also the one of the Loch Ness Monster to help while away the long cold nights.

We passed through Inverness and then to Aberdeen on the east coast, all the time hoping to catch a view of some Aberdeen Angus cattle like we were breeding at home. There were none to be seen but while exploring Aberdeen I spied a Land Rover with an Angus stud sign on the door. I approached the owner and introduced myself explaining our interest in the breed. He was most apologetic and said there were almost no cattle left in the region because they had been plagued with disease and economic difficulties that rendered stud farming non-viable.

Near Perth we detoured to visit Glamis Castle, family home of Elizabeth, the Queen Mother. Born Elizabeth Bowes-Lyon, she had married George, affectionately known as Bertie, the second son of King George V and Queen Mary. The reign of King George V1 and his Queen Elizabeth had coincided with my childhood and I had been imbued with loyalty to them.

Edinburgh proved as fascinating as we had envisaged. The view of the castle from Princes Street had the boys clamouring for a visit. We walked up the steep access roads and were surprised to find the space on which the Edinburgh Tattoo is staged was quite small and on a considerable slope. A walk around the back streets bought us to the Inn and statue of Grey Friar's Bobby, the little dog now immortalised in film. Further on I felt a surge of envy for the opportunity the young students had that I saw entering the old Medical School, part of Edinburgh University. It bought back visions of grave robbers and late night clandestine dissections once practiced here. What a stimulating intellectual environment it would be, the very buildings conspiring to exact one's best efforts in a quest to become a worthy medical practitioner.

Our return to London was punctuated by detours like visiting Nottingham Castle and a walking tour of Cambridge where I was drawn to the many fine book shops in which we all became lost in our individual quests to find a gem to bring home. The conducted tour proved a wonderful investment because our guide imparted a lifetime of experience by both showing and explaining to us the historical significance of what we saw. Again, each building we passed had a story. I experienced pangs of envy. How I would love to have had the opportunity to live and study in Cambridge.

Our visit to the UK was complete -- at least for now. We would return for more.

CHAPTER 22

HOME

Our return was a reality check -- a time of mixed emotions. The joy of reuniting with family, friends and animals was an abrupt change from the ultra stimulation and passivity of our around the world journey. The trip had been an amazing experience, with profound ramifications for the rest of our lives. It had not always been easy and required work to take advantage of the opportunity. Travelling on that scale had been exhausting on many occasions but we coped well as a cohesive family. Apart from what I had learned of the world, the unexpected bonus was sharing time with the family, it was the standout feature of our holiday. We had seen, heard and stimulated to think and observe how other peoples of the world live and cope with life. The seeds were sown for thinking of our opportunities in a global context. It had been the best investment we could have made and the boys had been wonderful participants in the whole adventure.

The neighbours lads who had looked after our farm had managed well, especially since they had the misfortune of having to cope with a particularly wet winter. There was little time to waste and we returned quickly to our familiar routines, but now I was unemployed.

I approached a colleague Max, in Morwell offering to buy half of his practice since, in the past, it had been run by busy popular partners. After consideration, Max eagerly sold me half of his business. I started work immediately and my half grew almost overnight into a full time concern.

Max was a popular dentist who was living in extraordinary circumstances. While he rented a house in Morwell where he lived alone, his wife and three daughters lived in Sydney in a rented house on the North Shore. For most of Max's career, since his graduation in Sydney, the family home had been in Sydney but, for reasons unknown they had come to Gippsland. Thoroughly spoilt and overindulged, the family resented the move and returned to Sydney to live in rented style beyond Max's capacity to support them. One daughter, who possessed her own credit card, was attending a private school in Melbourne while living with Irish friends of the family. When Max received the account for her credit card one month he discovered she had spent $1,300 at the chemist and was not ill. The same girl was told she must stay in Sydney with her mother and attend school after the summer break. Instead, when school started, she took a first class flight to Melbourne to attend her old school -- paid by credit card of course.

At the end of each day Max would take a large pocket full of cash from the desk and send most of it to Sydney. He enjoyed a drink or two and, being a raconteur, his mates would eagerly await him each night at the pub. He had trained for the priesthood in his young life so with a lively wit and irrepressible love of conversation tinged with Irish humour, he was an interesting but impecunious man.

Max's antics were legend in Morwell and he was encouraged by an irascible solicitor, a scholarly couterpart with a love of the drink. This fellow would turn up regularly and sit in the waiting room where he insisted on staying until he had been seen for imaginary toothaches. He was Max's friend so I was able to avoid him on most occasions.

Morwell was the home of electricity generation in Victoria and the heart of the Latrobe Valley. Because of this, unemployment was historically low and the town prosperous. The people were quite prepared to pay for and maintain their dentition. The drive to work each day from the farm took forty minutes and I found this time useful to keep up with current events on the radio.

Glenys and I decided to we would start breeding Angus cattle. To begin we borrowed a young Angus bull from friends who were successful livestock breeders. Then we bought a line of springing (pregnant and close to calving) Angus heifers. These were well grown animals with great conformation that produced beautiful calves that became the basis of our Angus Stud. We added to this line with a selection of cows bought from other studs. To accommodate the increase in stock numbers, we leased more land. The weekends became even busier. One afternoon, we were informed by a worried neighbor that despite my warning, David had had taken the new unused farm four wheel motor bike from the locked shed and had an accident. He was badly hurt in hospital but mercifully not critically so. When crossing a drain at speed the bike had turned over dislocating his right leg from his hip and causing other minor injuries. Stephen, who had been watching had only just been able to lift the motorcycle off David and then run to neighbours for help was also distressed by the experience. The six weeks of traction in Hospital taxed David's patience but resulted thankfully in full recovery. As concern turned to relief we joked that the boys hearing may have improved by the incident.

I was asked to become a director of the Saint Paul's Anglican Grammar School in Warragul where David was a student. The school had secured a large site and built quite a number of rooms, the nucleus of a promising school had been established. The principal, Des Parker, had assembled a group of effective teachers but resources were stretched to the limit.

The demand by parents for places was increasing rapidly while space for the students to move into the higher years was badly needed. There was a building program in place but space and support equipment for the teachers was under great strain.

To obtain the essential funds the school was working within a complex formula set by the Government that allowed little room to fund needs such as teaching aides, sporting facilities and office equipment. The formula was designed to deliver an education to people with the lowest possible fees and any attempt to raise them would result in a penalty occurring somewhere else in the funding. Despite the limitations, the principal made a great start. It was now time to take stock and plan for the future. The directors agreed to hire Phillip Roth, a specialist public school consultant to chair our meetings over the summer with a view to deciding our ethos and planning in detail strategic issues such as how big the school should be, and implicitly, how and what subjects would be taught.

The goodwill of all participants was infectious. Our meetings were charged with uncommon energy and interest. Phillip's broad experience allowed us to decide relatively quickly on many issues. It was agreed for instance it was the aim of the school to enable every child to reach his or her maximum potential. Then we had to build from the ground up the facilities, appropriate staff and systems to achieve the aim. We had some money intended to reduce a loan with but Phillip cautioned us about applying normal domestic and business solutions to the running of a school. He pointed out that although in a private capacity we would normally attempt to pay out all loans quickly, it was not incumbent on one generation of parents to pay for all the facilities of the school. His advice was to allow the loan to run so we could use the money in hand for other purposes. Similarly, he advised against the natural trend where principals and school boards build empires thinking that 'big is better.' On that score I decided to research the reason our present senior teachers had abandoned other schools to join St Paul's.

There were many other issues and I was impressed with the energy some parents expended to support the school in its early development. I gained an insight into the complexity of running a school and the dedicated hard work better teachers put into trying to develop the potential of students. There can be no better investment by a community than ensuring the best possible education for its children.

The economy and how we were coping with it was a frequent topic of conversation during the declining years of the late 1980s. To expand or diversify a business, or to invest in property or shares, were all issues of interest. Two of my fellow Rotarian friends, Des Dillon, who owned a large dry cleaning business, and Richard Edwards, an orthodontist, decided to accompany me to a course on entrepreneurial business management run by the Caulfield Institute of Technology. This involved driving to Melbourne one night a week for a semester or two. The content did extend our understanding of business management and alerted us to the potential for building on opportunity.

Unfortunately, although Glenys and I had achieved a great deal, serious cracks had appeared in our relationship in recent years. Communication at the personal level was strained and almost impossible on all but practical matters. I found the situation upsetting because Glenys had contributed so much through difficult times and should now be able to reap the reward. Tensions arising from the problems began to fester and manifest in decisions necessary for the running of the farm.

One practical issue was the need to be able to transport horses for the boys and cattle between the home farm and the leased land in two different locations. A horse float would necessitate a four wheel drive car and not be suitable for the cattle. It would also mean we would have too much money invested in vehicles. We already had a family car and a utility. In the absence of discussion or an alternative solution I suggested a second hand truck which eventually I bought for $10,000. It was a Mazda with a 6 cylinder diesel engine able to carry four tons. The truck proved to be a great asset able to quickly and comfortably transport both cattle and horses safely.

Glenys had become the district counselor for Pony Club and the boys were occasionally riding in different events in their quest for more adventurous riding. We were still involved with the Drouin Pony Club, which had provided great family involvement for many years. I had been president for a few years but it was Glenys's role as the district counselor that was the most demanding. She knew the rules and details of the organisation better than me.

The dental practice at Morwell had changed since Max had left. I still owned my half of the practice and the other half had changed hands twice. The first dentist had such profound personal problems he had been obliged to sell again within six months of his arrival. My latest associate was Dr Peter Kingsbury, who came with his own senior nurse and turned the ailing fortunes of his new practice around. He was an experienced operator with a sound reputation.

By 1992 the Victorian Government had sold off the State Electricity Commission and the power houses of the Latrobe

Valley were privatised. The future for Morwell and its sister city of Moe became less certain, as indeed, was the state of my marriage to Glenys. My anxieties at home had become overt and no longer suppressible. I was unhappy and sensed I was sinking irrevocably into a broken marriage, the very thing I feared most given my past life experience. Soon after, Peter Kingsbury approached me and said he would like to buy my practice. He knew of course how sound it was and given my concerns, I immediately engaged my accountant to transact the sale for me. On leaving my practice in Morwell I soon accepted a locum position at Leongatha, ironically, the larger remnant of the Wonthaggi practice I had bought in 1979.

Glenys was the one doing most of the milking while I had been flat out with dentistry and at the same time attending to the peripheral issues of farming. All this while trying to maintain a social life had taken its toll. My concerns and entreaties to change the direction of our lives were met with a deadly silence. The inability to communicate distressed me greatly and I became angry and resentful that I could not obtain the agreement needed for us to get off the relentless treadmill of exhausting work. I believed Glenys was in a similar position but the inability to communicate created a resentful silence that had festered for years before finally erupting into an exchange beyond which further resolution seemed impossible. Despite an attempt at reconciliation it had to be accepted, we had to separate.

Attributing fault serves no purpose. For inextricable reasons we lost our way. It was tacitly agreed, for the sake of our boys and out of mutual respect, we would not denigrate the other and co-operate over the distribution of our assets. The farm was sold and a settlement agreed upon. Unfortunately the high land prices of the 80s had become unattainable. It was nearing the end of 1992. David was at Latrobe University, where he had begun a degree in economics and the marketing of rural products. Stephen was about to complete his final year of secondary school at St Paul's in Warragul. I had thought the tensions between Glenys and me were secret. I soon realised the boys knew the relationship was in trouble for some time. I had a great deal to be thankful for. Glenys had never wavered in her support for me and she was a wonderful mother to the boys.

Glenys found work with the Australian Securities Commission and I assisted her to move to a unit In Warragul. The plan was for me to maintain the farm while the stock and equipment were liquidated. We had agreed to use the one solicitor to divide our assets fairly.

I had continued to work as a locum dentist while maintaining the denuded farm which was in great condition. It sold readily toward the later part of 1992. Like everything else, it made an unexceptional market price. The high land prices of the previous 18 months had moderated.

The solicitor divided the proceeds and congratulated us on the amicable manner of our separation. The emotional toll was enormous. Somehow we had managed to co-operate on all levels. In January 1993 we celebrated David's 21st birthday with a huge party at the farm. It was great fun and a memorable last time together on the farm. David returned to university and Stephen began living with Glenys for his last year of secondary school. I put a question to them – would they mind and manage if I were work in the UK for a year? No, they said. They were under control. There seemed to be nothing more I could do.

I had no farm, home or practice and was single. I needed time to adjust to my changed life. I had to create a new life and be available to the boys when they matured. For the moment I needed to stand back and reconsider my options. I had a British passport and there were no impediments to my working in the UK. I would use the time to explore, and hopefully find, the energy and direction to start again.

I invested my share of the assets and arranged to fly via Hong Kong to the UK. In Hong Kong I would call on friends for a few days before flying on. It was a strange feeling. I had divested myself of almost everything other than my tools, books and surplus clothes. It was as if I had died, I felt like the executor of my own estate.

CHAPTER 23
TIME OUT

The flight to Hong Kong was uneventful but the emotional toll of leaving weighed heavily. I had not been anywhere without the family before and to be alone after having had such intense family involvement was upsetting. I understood the logic. The boys were largely self sufficient and preoccupied with their studies and Glenys was on hand to provide additional support. I no longer had a role. The questions went around in my head. Have I no intrinsic value beyond the material support I provide? Am I so arrogant I can't accept I have character flaws that prevent me being emotionally co-dependent and indispensible to my family? I'm emotionally dependent on the family, but they no longer need me. I am alone. I have been here before. It was familiar, and frightening. I must toughen up and make a life for myself.

After landing in the old Hong Kong airport where there was barely a few metres to spare before crashing into the terminal, I crossed to the island and found the accommodation I had booked. The view of the harbour was excellent. When settled, I placed a call to the Hong Kong family of my Chinese friends in Australia and in no time I was picked up and given a valuable insight into the lifestyle of wealthy influential local people. My new friends were senior journalists who wrote for the daily newspapers. After an enthusiastic exchange of greetings we went to dinner in exclusive clubs reserved for members. When my guides were obliged to leave me, I explored the back streets and sights of Hong Kong. My ramblings during the day took me all over the island and even on a train journey into the new territories on the mainland.

I felt sorry for the thousands of Filipinos, mostly women, who congregated on Sundays along the low walls of the old Admiralty Building on the harbour foreshore. The meeting provided their only contact with family or friends as most were employed as house servants to wealthy Chinese. They stood or sat while grooming hair or doing their nails. Chattering quietly, they were alienated by fate, race and poverty.

After four days, I flew out in the evening bound for London. The flight path was a semi circle over Russia so I peered through the window and saw the lights of Russian villages and towns below me. The immensity reminded me of how insignificant an individual can be. My family was in Australia while I was at 35,000ft above Russia and heading for London where I didn't know a soul.

The flight landed around 5.30 a.m. on a Tuesday early in February 1993. I caught the bus into Victoria Station and bought an AKZ Street Directory to find the address of a Miss Betty Philpot who ran a small business placing locum dentists and selling insurance in Piccadilly. I arrived at her office about 9.30 a.m. to be greeted by this extraordinary lady who welcomed me and dispensed the advice I needed. She was tall, beautifully dressed and possessed a regal crisply efficient English manner. She spoke with great deliberation. 'You will have to have a psychiatric evaluation before registering with the British Dental Board. I have arranged for you to have that at 11 a.m. with a specialist I know In Harley Street,' she said. I left my bags with her and walked up to Harley Street where

I was relieved to find an Australian psychiatrist eager to meet me. Over a cup of tea and a discussion on life for an ex pat in London, it was established I was indeed sane and fit to begin work as a dentist. This was reassuring for throughout the journey I had reflected on recent events and seriously wondered -- was I mad? We had avoided the obvious question of why a sane person would want to practice dentistry in the first place. With my certification of sanity in hand, I visited the British Dental Board where, after duly verifying all my qualifications and experience to their satisfaction, I was entered on the register.

By 1.30 p.m., I was back in Miss Philpot's office. She revived me with another cup of tea and went on to say that in my absence she had made some phone calls and could place me in a practice in Aldershot, the home of the British Army, some 30-40 miles from London. The practice, she said, was owned by two Australians, one of whom I had graduated with in Adelaide.

I agreed to the arrangement. Miss Philpot called the practice and I was invited to stay for a few days with my former student colleague and his wife. I was to start work on Thursday. I found my way to Waterloo Station and caught the train to Frimley Gardens, where I was met and welcomed. The following day I visited the practice and went through the process of formally accepting the responsibility for the management of 2,500 patients and their dental problems. I had no idea of how the National Health system operated up until then and was surprised at the complexity of what I had agreed to do. I learned the people on my register had an obligation to see me and I had a reciprocal obligation to see them. They could request to see another dentist, but the other dentist would need to agree to have them assigned to his or her register. Similarly, I had the right not to accept others into my care. In addition to this, I was expected to treat private patients.

Somewhat sobered by the weight of the responsibilities I had accepted, I was pleased to meet my new nurse. Joanne was an attractive young woman of 22, who proved to be a bright and efficient nurse. She proved quick, capable and thankfully, able to manage the paperwork of the health system.

The following day I started work. I was instantly inundated by demands for every aspect of dental care. This was familiar, except I noticed with alarm, the little regard given for careful conservative dentistry I was used to. Both patients and dentists had become conditioned within the British health care system to placing crowns and bridges without first exhausting the routine conservative alternatives. Dentistry, by 1993, had a range of superior tooth coloured filling materials that in many cases, if placed with care by conscientious operators, could adequately prolong dental function without recourse to more radical solutions.

Relieved and tired after such a confronting week, I began looking for a place to live. A search of the local newspapers netted a number of alternatives. I found myself following a lead on accommodation to Number 2 Beech Court, Wimble Hill, an old hospital converted to self contained units on the top of a hill near beautiful castle town of Farnham. The room I accepted was modest and attached to a kitchen I was to share with two other younger people.

The next problem, because I was walking so far, was the need for a car. Over the next week I searched high and low before finding a Ford Fiesta for private sale at an address in the village of Liphooke. With wheels at last, life began to resemble that of a working dentist living with a sense of independence. Was it prophetic? Farnham had been the resting place of Charles 1st on his way back from the Isle of Wight just prior to his execution on Tuesday, January 30th, 1649.

My companions at Wimble Hill proved to be good friends. Felicity Azavedo was from Wales, in her early 30s, a graduate of Cardiff University and a practicing accountant. Andrew Port was a similar age and a physiotherapist at the Basingstoke Hospital. He was making a new life after a failed marriage and now courting his new friend Susan Lucy-Smith, also a physiotherapist. In no time we became a mutually supportive group of close friends. However, the owner of the complex was a pushy egotist who tried to gouge my friends for more money. Not wishing a confrontation and following a discussion between us, we agreed to jointly rent a house in Fleet, a town nearby on the rail line to Winchester, through which passed the Basingstoke Canal.

From Wimble Hill, the prospect of walking across the fields to visit these delightful pubs and their fascinating patrons was something I looked forward to after a grueling day of dentistry. I had been accepted readily by the locals and had only minor misgivings about the impending move to Fleet, feelings outweighed by the prospect of sharing the large modern home with my new found friends. I would miss the colourful hot air balloons that drifted low over Wimble Hill every weekend when the weather was calm.

The move to Fleet was accomplished painlessly. In no time I discovered an equally rewarding route from the new home to the Fox and Hounds Pub which nestled in a copse of trees on the far side of the Basingstoke Canal on the southern outskirts of Fleet. I became aware a group of people interested in folk music met there every Thursday in the back room of the pub. All were welcome. It was free with no formalities, just participate in any way you feel inclined. I was made welcome despite being unable to play an instrument and was quickly absorbed into a sizable group of talented people.

Part of my commitment to the National Health dental scheme was to be on call occasionally -- making house calls where necessary on a weekend. Clearly, any service offered in the home would be limited without adequate lighting and equipment. Despite this, I did make many visits to older people with a variety of dental problems, most of which concerned poor fitting dentures. Some were in respite care or hostels, but most were in their own homes. It was sad to see how so many old people were obliged to spend their final days confined to a bed or a chair in tiny rooms, either too hot or freezing cold to reduce expense. In England in 1993, facilities for the disabled were few and in many cases their absence caused the premature confinement of even partially disabled people. Confined as I was to providing the most basic of care for so many people in need of much more saddened me. It reminded me how fortunate we are in Australia that older citizens and the disabled are better served by the climate and the design features now an essential part of civic planning.

I worked most Saturday mornings. Once free I aimed to keep active and explore all I could to avoid the depression that would insinuate into my consciousness whenever I was off guard. The separation from family and friends was an ever present source of sadness. Apart from letters to and from my mother, I received little news from home. Thankfully, my house friends were supportive and we went as a group on a wide variety of excursions to historical sites, family visits or occasionally to the indoor heated swimming pool at Guildford.

I had read Edward Rutherfurd's books, 'Sarum', and 'Russka,' also a historical novel about Poland, combined with the others and the 1991 collapse of communism in Poland and East Germany. The combination propelled me into a travel agent to take a tour of those countries. The borders of East Germany, Poland and Hungary had only been open for a short time, the tour was new. I was excited and eager to see and compare the images I had formed long ago of the oppressed countries with the reality I was about to see. The tour group met in London before being conveyed first by bus to Dover and then via ferry to Calais where a guide met us. The drive from Calais to Brussels completed the first day. Then we travelled to Berlin for a two-day stopover.

While the tour group eagerly visited the usual Berlin tourist sites, I headed off alone on a train to visit Potsdam, some distance to the south west of the city. I was amazed at the immensity of the palaces and the gardens. The Sanssouci Palace, built in 1745-7 from sketches by Frederick II, was a long building with a domed hall in the centre. Round pavilions were built into the narrow sides. The grounds had extensive unique terraces that complement the extensive landscape around the palace. Without a guide and isolated by my inability to speak the language, I walked miles through the enormous gardens where other palaces too numerous and architecturally arresting for me to take in were seen. The combined effect of the beauty, the history and the immensity of what I saw was breathtaking.

The vista of the Unter den linden is beautiful, tree lined and spacious, justly serving the classical architecture of the many fine buildings facing it. I found by exploring the back streets that many buildings still bore the scars of a tumultuous past. With little time, I walked briskly toward the Brandenburg Gate that, until November 1989, had the wall of separation built in front of it. On arrival, I found the space occupied by food vendors with many tourists walking about trying to reconstruct, as I was, a mental image of what had been until 1989 the cruel separation of this magnificent city by a wall in an effort to maintain and expand the communist ideology imposed by East Germany.

A little to the north west of the Brandenburg Gate, in a loop of the river Spree, stands the Reichstag, the building in which Hitler wrested the destiny of Germany from the people by imposing martial law. By way of relief that evening, my tour group attended the famous revue theatre to experience the 'La Vie en Rose,' which, accompanied by a stein or two of Berlin beer, was a fitting salute to this beautiful city I hope someday to revisit. Next day it was on to Warsaw.

As we approached the border of Poland I thought we were going to have an enormous problem because there were miles of vehicles lined up in single file on the side of the narrow road. Lorry drivers were standing about or sitting in chairs patiently waiting. Our driver simply overtook the entire line and on arrival at the checkpoint we were all required to leave the bus while they checked our visas. Apparently, being tourists, we were accorded priority. We then resumed our way across the flat plains of Poland, all under cultivation in small lots.

On the bus, the Polish guide explained that many older people who had received money from the government during communist times had no concept of providing service. More than a few pined for 'the good old days'. We were to experience many examples of this indifference. As for the lack of reinforcement in concrete I had seen being laid, there was no money or material available - it was a symptom of the country's problems.

In the historic city square a huge effort had been made to restore damaged facades and to recreate a semblance of what had been for hundreds of years. The guide explained that when the German army was retreating after the uprising in 1945, they had systematically destroyed what was left of the city. During the early urban combat of the war in the city, 25 percent had been lost. A further 35 percent loss occurred in 1943 as a result of the Warsaw ghetto uprising and then on the orders of Heinrich Himmler, the remainder was systematically bombed and burnt. In all, 85 percent of the city was destroyed as part of a policy to reduce it to a transit camp before the arrival of the Russians in 1945. The intention to destroy the city had been formed in 1939 by Adolf Hitler as part of the plan for the Germanisation of the East.

Our bus moved on through rich farmland on which I could see small plots of intense agriculture. I marveled at how small the plots were and how primitive the equipment being used was. I was even pleasantly surprised to see horses at work but the inefficiency bothered me. The roads were mostly tree lined and the traffic light. Suddenly we arrived at Auschwitz, on the outskirts of the small town of Oswiecim, roughly due west of Krakow.

We descended from the bus with a trepidation imitating what the victims might have felt - aware this was the site of man's greatest inhumanity to man. An ominous silence belied the rush of thought in my mind. 'Arbeit Macht Frei' (Work Brings Freedom) was the imposing sign over the gate at K L

Auschwitz I, able at the height of its infamy to house 20,000 prisoners. This was the first part of a highly efficient machine where individuals strong enough to work were employed in the war effort while the young, old and infirm were exterminated. A map in the main building illustrated with simple clarity how the railway lines of Europe were conveniently utilised, because they converged on this place, allowing forced labour to be used in the essential industries supporting the war effort while the unwanted majority were exterminated with detached efficiency.

As the daily train loads of people arrived, additional camps were needed. KL Aushwitz II-- Birkenau was created 3km away. It held 100,000 people at its maximum in 1944 and required four crematoria with gas chambers to dispose of the unwanted humanity. In 1942 KL Aushwitz III was created close to the chemical plant of Farbenindustrie. It spawned other smaller camps to form a complex of 40 camps to serve steelworks, mines and factories, all using slave labour.

Like other shocked visitors, I walked in silence around the remains of the complex. Some facilities had been removed by the Nazis in an attempt to avoid their capture as the war came to an end. Fortunately, enough was preserved to remind future generations of man's capacity for evil. In the light of world history and subsequent events, we know such depravity is not confined to any one ethnic group -- it is a capacity within us all. We left in sober silence.

Our next stop was the Wieliczka salt mine. It had been worked for 900 years, reminding us that salt was once an important commodity for trade, the medieval equivalent of oil we were told. We descended to 135m and were amazed to find a huge space lit by candelabras and used today for orchestral recitals. In the caverns were sculptures of many Christian Icons cut from the black rock salt which sparkled as the light reflected from the crystals within it. In all, the guide told us, there were 200km of passages and more than 2040 caverns in the mine.

We pressed on through the Polish farmland still divided into medieval size plots farmed with ancient machinery. Then we were in the Slovak Republic, almost indistinguishable and passed without note until we entered Hungary, headed for Budapest.

Unfortunately, I experienced a serious disturbance to my vision and balance which caused me to vomit in Budapest. It was a frightening sensation that could be bought on by even minor movement. Scenes seemed to roll on through my head even after I had stopped moving. The condition plagued me off and on as we toured via Vienna, Salzsburg and Munich back over the romantic route through Germany into Belgium to the UK. There were many great moments but I was anxious to have medical treatment for my worsening undiagnosed condition.

Back in Fleet, my doctor, who had seen the condition before, confidently diagnosed viral labyrinthitis. He said it would last a few weeks before disappearing and might return some time later for another period of a week or two. The symptoms slowly abate – an enormous relief. It would be irresponsible for a dentist to be working with visual and balance problems. I was so far from family support.

Life in Fleet was pleasant, especially because my house friends were cooperative and functioned as an extended family. The weekly sessions of music with my new friends at the pub were also supportive. I continued my trips into London most

Saturdays to visit everything I could find of interest and on dusk would find a show in one of the many theatres. Often I would visit the National Theatre complex on the Thames a few hundred metres from Waterloo Station, convenient for the return home on the train.

Apparently the boys were managing, Stephen with his matriculation and David exploiting every diversion possible while attending university, ostensibly, to obtain his degree in Agricultural Resource Management. I felt terrible and powerless to assist in any way. The year rolled by and I decided to go home. The break away and the UK experience had been invaluable but I was Australian. I felt the need to go home and start a new life.

Back on the farm I had been a member of Rotary and host to a number of young adults who had come to Australia for vocational experience. One young woman who had stayed with us was Mary Zelli, an orthodontist from Virginia in the US who had insisted if I was ever in the country she would like me to stay with her. I contacted her and yes, she would be pleased to see me. I arranged my flight home from London to New York, then to visit Mary in Virginia and finally to take the train from Washington to San Francisco and fly home from Los Angeles.

My UK friends had been wonderful. I was going to miss them. Andy, Sue and Felicity arranged a surprise house party for my leaving and about 25 of my musical friends arrived to provide a happy farewell. Now I was faced again with the realization I was leaving this wonderful and interesting group of supportive friends to begin a new life, albeit in Australia where the remnants of my former life were scattered. I had enjoyed the opportunity these people had given me to sample their rich culture. They valued their history, their customs, literature and musical inheritance. I miss them and their warm embrace of me. Felicity drove me to the airport and for the second time in twelve months I flew away to a new life, after a sojourn in America.

The previous visit to the States had been with my family in 1986. This had raised my interest in American history. In the meantime I had read a number of books which heightened that interest. Now I would have a better look at this fascinating, enormous country. I landed in New York and found a hotel up town before heading off to visit the Metropolitan Museum, that is, after a walk through Central Park, noting with pleasure the city seemed a lot cleaner and safer than in 1986. The museum is an architecturally beautiful building designed to showcase American art and culture. I meandered for hours, attempting to slow my mindset to be receptive to the vibes and impressions the precious collection created.

Next morning it was a visit to Ellis Island, a short ferry ride across the bay close to the Statue of Liberty soaring above. This was where millions of refugees had come ashore to begin a new life in a free country. They were escaping oppression, famine and prejudice in all its forms and combinations. They gambled everything for this opportunity.

I saw the huge sheds in which the emigrants had sat waiting to be sorted and examined for entry. I had no trouble empathising with the hopes and anxieties they must have experienced. What, I wondered, was the fate of those who were rejected? The medical tests were basic but adequate to detect the lame and those with overt symptoms of disease like tuberculosis or syphilis. Were they returned to their country of origin? Were families split up if one member failed the tests? Perhaps I was told, but now I cannot remember.

I caught the train to Fredericksburg, Virginia. It was about a two hour journey via Philadelphia, Baltimore, Washington DC, over the Potomac River to Fredericksburg. I was greeted by Mary Zeli waiting patiently in this quintessential small university town, enhanced by the beautiful spectacle of its tree lined streets in a blaze of autumn colour. As we walked toward Mary's home she pointed out the stump in the main street where the slaves had stood for inspection while being auctioned a short 130 years before. There were many signs and reminders of the Civil war of 1862-65. This was the site of General Lee's stand against the Yankees led by General Burnside. We walked beside the low stone wall marveling at the full view the Confederates had of their enemy as they climbed the long open slope rising from the river toward them. It was a turkey shoot, simply a massacre. The trenches beyond the wall are still visible and remain as a reminder of the bitter savagery of this civil war.

A contradiction of terms -- there was nothing civil about this war. The Rappahannock River can easily be seen in the distance. In December 1862, after a dithering delay that allowed the Confederates to consolidate and prepare on the high ground, General Burnside ordered his 130,000 men across the river to face the 72,000 opponents. The men charged across open ground to be cut down like grain. One wave after another rushed forward over the dead and dying, only to be ripped apart by concentrated artillery and musketry. When nightfall came, nearly 13,000 Federal soldiers lay sprawled on the plain, in places three deep. General Lee's ironic observation is recalled. 'It is well war is so terrible, otherwise we should grow too fond of it.'

In Fredericksburg, I went sightseeing and sampled the local cuisine. In one restaurant I noted a sign, *'Firings will continue until staff morale picks up'*. My stay had been pleasant but I moved back to Washington where I visited the new Holocaust Museum to ensure they had not betrayed the memory of the millions killed. They had not. It was a faithful and chillingly accurate memorial, fitting for the large American Jewish Diaspora and the world at large to visit.

I decided to take the train from Washington to San Francisco with a short break in the journey in Winter Falls, high in the Rocky Mountains. The Amtrak train had seating arranged high in the coaches above the utility areas below. The view was excellent. We headed west toward Chicago where the train was delayed for some time. I took this opportunity for a brief exploration of the city, feeling it was familiar because of the many films I have seen that were made there. The impressive concourse had been the scene of many cops and robbers shows but that aside, it has a grand significant architectural merit of its own.

On leaving, we turned south west toward Denver. We travelled across the State of Milwaukee and Nebraska in daylight. I gained a feeling for the country and noted it was largely under cultivation. The train found the terrain easy and moved quickly before it gently rose again as we approached Denver. The Rocky Mountains of Colorado rise steeply on the western perimeter of Denver and the views glided past slowly as the train worked hard to climb to an altitude of almost 11,000 feet, where the air was noticeably thinner. At Winter Falls the train stopped to allow me to get off. I was met by a man in a large vehicle who drove me into town where I walked the length of the main street looking for accommodation to suit my needs and pocket. My time there allowed me to walk some trails in the region and to marvel at the way of life these people enjoy but it had little appeal for me --- I like to be where agriculture thrives.

On reaching Oakland the train terminated. Along with fellow travelers from the train, I caught the bus into San Francisco and was immediately surprised at the steepness of the hills. I left the bus near Fisherman's Wharf and began to appreciate that finding a hotel could be difficult if I had to scale these hills dragging my luggage. Luckily, a friend I had made on the train directed me to the San Remo Hotel near the lower end of the tram route. It proved satisfactory and I spent three days exploring the city with an afternoon visit to the island of Alcatraz where I wondered why it had been closed down by Robert Kennedy. I don't condone the excesses of how the prisoners were treated but for the incorrigible, who elect to behave like animals, it seemed a suitable place to keep them.

I decided to fly to Seattle and return to Los Angeles on the train with stop offs as it suited for I wanted to see the giant Californian Redwoods. A friend of Felicity who lived in that region had indicated I was welcome to stay a night with her. In Seattle I found accommodation readily and began walking to explore the city. Surprise, surprise. A renovated W class ex-Melbourne tram rolled into sight - now a valued tourist attraction on the Seattle water front. The walk continued until I came across a museum dedicated to the Klondike gold strike of 1896. Like gold fever in Australia, the strike fired the imaginations of the desperate, the brave and the plain foolish who staked their lives on finding the elusive, addictive material. I boarded the train for Portland Oregon where I stayed two nights. Barely enough time to explore this city of half a million people on the shores of the Willamette River, close to its confluence with the Columbia River which opens to the sea. Portland had many parks and the rose gardens for which it is widely known were beautiful.

After rejoining the train, I hopped off again just over the border in California and found my way to the home of Felicity's friend who had offered to accommodate me for a few days while I explored the giant Redwood forests. In fact, there are many species of tree growing in the region beside the Douglas fir. The family proudly took me on a tour of the stunningly beautiful region. Redwoods belong to the genus sequoia which can reach a height of 110m and can survive for 2000 years. Most live 500 to 700 years, making them one of the longest living organisms in the world. They prefer the slopes near water away from the ocean. To stand alongside a living thing of such immense age is humbling -- a reminder of one's fragile mortality.

While in America, I had one last call to make. Jan and Ossie Gontang in San Diego had insisted I call when passing through. Jan was the sister of my good friend Lyn Bellamy in Warragul. Lyn would be disappointed if I failed to see her sister and family. The call was made and yes I should hurry on down to San Diego on the train. I had to stay with them she insisted. The train wound through the southern suburbs of Los Angeles and over the sand dunes alongside the ocean all the way to San Diego. I saw little of the fertile country I had heard about so often. My farming instincts are strong and I'm always reassured by the sight of arable country.

San Diego proved to be the break I needed from the constant travel. My hosts were charming. Ossie, Jan and their two daughters made me welcome despite their having to work. One day the youngest daughter, only 13, took me on a conducted tour of the world famous San Diego Zoo and on Jan's first day off she announced we were going over the border into Mexico.

As we approached the Mexican border, we were confronted with a barrage of signs warning that under no circumstances were we to pick up or to aid people attempting to escape to California. The border check was thorough but accomplished easily with Jan able to explain I was a visiting Australian. On entering the city of Tijuana, it was immediately obvious we should take care. The streets were teeming with people, the shop keepers inviting us to buy or at least enter their shop and the strollers exhibiting the anxious watchful behavior of a desperate but dignified poor. Persistent vendors invited us to be photographed with deformed and decorated animals.

After a Mexican lunch washed down with tequila, we retraced our path to San Diego. For us it had been a pleasant and interesting day out. For the desperate Mexican poor it was another day of grinding poverty. I'm left with the stark imagery of the closely policed border crossing with its fences, surveillance equipment and signs holding back a people desperate to access the endless chances for success we have in the West.

I was missing the boys badly. I had travelled widely, discovered many friends and maintained my integrity. I had even saved money and endured the heart rending separation from my family. Now it was time to see the boys and start a new life in Australia.

CHAPTER 24
A NEW LIFE

The surge of excitement I felt as the plane entered Australian airspace removed any doubt about my decision to return. I had not notified anyone so there was no reception committee. I recovered my car from storage and drove to my mother and stepfather's house in San Remo, where I was met with a warm welcome.

I visited Glenys and caught up with the boys, who were pleased to see me. That stirred my feelings of guilt. Had I been right to leave them almost a year before? I had tried to maintain contact but the replies were few. There was no sign of any resentment at my leaving and it was clear they were glad to have me home. However, to continue being supportive of them in the future, I had to stabilise my own life. I needed to find work and a place to live.

I accepted a position with the Churchill Community Health Centre which required a dentist to provide both public and private dental care for the students and staff of the Churchill branch of Monash University. The centre provided the whole range of medical, psychological, dental and welfare support needed and the collegiality for the providers was attractive to me. I rented a two bedroom unit and began assembling the few possessions I had entrusted to others to care for while I was away. The task now was to rebuild a social life, but now I was alone, the silences longer and harder to fill than they had been in England.

I was invited to a dinner by Polly Winterton, the practice manager for my friend Richard Edwards, the orthodontist. His business had grown enormously to include a number of branches throughout Gippsland. The dinner was at Polly's family farm at Nilma, near Warragul, and she had invited her lifelong friend Pamela, youngest of three daughters of fellow members of the Rotary Club of Warragul. Evidently I had met Pamela at a previous dinner before leaving for England. The meeting had gone unnoticed by me. This time there was a strong mutual attraction. She had three children, Caroline Sally and Timothy, all attending St Paul's Grammar School and contemporaries of my boys. She had been divorced for many years and was working for a local travel centre. The dinner was a great success and a relationship blossomed quickly.

Pamela and I enjoyed a whirlwind romance that renewed our optimism. I was actively canvassing options with regard to buying a new practice. A number of years had passed since I had sold the former Warragul practice and I was aware that if I could buy a practice in the locality I could benefit from previous goodwill. My long standing colleague in Drouin, Bruce Drysdale, offered to sell his practice. He had started it in the 1950s and now, following other misfortune, his marriage had failed.

I bought the practice assuming it to be as busy as it had been when my family were patients in the 1960s. Unfortunately it was not. It needed urgent refurbishment, new equipment and a change of direction. I relocated from Churchill to a unit in Warragul and threw myself into the alteration of the Drouin practice, invigorated by the new and purposeful direction my life was taking. Pam was supportive and her family readily aligned itself with mine. It was more than I had dared to hope.

While Pam and I continued to enjoy our lives, her parents were beginning to fail with age. I was often called upon to do maintenance chores around their home and garden. We had dinner together weekly and reciprocated visits with Pam's older sister, Jill, and her husband Mick on their beef farm near Lang Lang.

Pam and I planned a holiday. We would visit her other sister, Anne, and her husband David in Oklahoma and then travel on to London where Pam's oldest daughter, Caroline, had been working for some time. It seemed a great opportunity to meet Pam's sister and her family while affording us some time to share the experience of a travelling holiday using the money I had left invested in the UK.

In Oklahoma we had a happy time with Anne and David, who was a journalist sports writer. It was a culture shock to find they went out for most meals, including breakfast. Pam and I thought it a real hoot to drive up town for a huge breakfast, routine for Anne and David who were unconcerned about the cost or the excess food consumed. We had a good look around the city and enjoyed a drive to an Indian reservation that featured their traditional life and the artifacts they made. We were surprised to find that In Oklahoma City the current craze of some of Anne's friends was to adopt a monkey which was then treated like a child and given nappies, birthday parties and toys.

In New York we rode around Central Park and enjoyed the tourist delights of the city. It was a romantic and enjoyable two days. In London we caught up with Caroline. This led to a breezy happy visit to the Cotswolds where we hired a rowing boat for a turn on the Avon River. We visited Anne

Hathaway's house, made a detour to Lower Slaughter and had an idyllic overnight stay in Bourton on the Water, where we enjoyed a great dinner. The weather was fine and we saw these stunningly beautiful icons of Britain at their best.

My boys had also been sowing their wild oats. David had partied through his time at university while still working part time. He had such a good time he missed most of his assignments. Although passing the exams, he failed because both are required. He repeated some subjects before finally completing a Diploma of Marketing. He had begun employment in the Post Office and had worked his way up to the position of market manager for Australia Post in Victoria and Tasmania. Partying with his friends however, enjoyed high priority.

Stephen had completed his Matriculation and entered Monash University where he had chosen Science. This was clearly failing to motivate him. Like David, having left the busy disciplined life of the farm, the new found freedoms proved irresistible. The mates, grog and girls were simply far too enticing. What could I say without being a hypocrite?

I was busy renovating my dental practice. I knocked out walls, painted, redecorated and bought new equipment which modernized and revitalized the business. Old patients from the region found me and I was pleased with the steady growth of the practice.

Pam too was pleased with the progress Sally and Tim were making. Sally had been an outstanding student at St Paul's and had started her physiotherapy course at Melbourne University. She was a highly capable student whose success was assured. I always enjoyed talking to Sally. Her quick methodical mind led to a logical solution to most problems. Caroline too had taken work in real estate and was fast gaining a reputation for managing the letting department of a large office.

Tim, the youngest, had had little exposure to males in his life since his father had remarried and made a life in Melbourne. I suspect Tim felt the change in the dynamics of the home with me around for my presence redressed the feminine bias that had become the norm. Tim was a capable student with an aptitude for mechanics. He began as an apprentice at a local machinery and car franchise. Besotted with cars, he acquired a number of them and, like many boys, systematically destroyed them.

By 1997 Pam and I had decided we would like to buy a small property. In her previous married life she had lived on a 1000 acre property her father had bought for her and her husband at Shady Creek. They built an extensive new home with all the features and equipment necessary to run the farm. This was her children's first home. With the freedom afforded by affluence, Pam had acquired a license to fly. In fact the flying was something both she and the former husband enjoyed prior to the breakdown of their marriage only a few years later.

The developed properties we saw proved unsuitable for various reasons. They either needed a lot of money spent on them or were on small acreages. Many small properties were under or near power lines that pass through the region from the Latrobe Valley power stations. We revisited a block we had seen in Drouin West. The sign on the gate said '*40 Acres for Sale.*' It was just the ticket. The agreed plan was that I would buy the land and Pam would sell her house and use the proceeds to build the house.

Everyone was thrilled. Her parents were pleased and began coming out to see and enjoy the preliminary work we were doing to clean up the property. In fact, Pam and I were taking her parents out almost every week for dinner, driving and or a picnic. I admired her mother the more I knew her because in my opinion, although smart, she had been denied any knowledge of or access to the family's business dealings. Her husband's habitual lateness for dinner after drinking with friends after work and his inability to confide with her over the affairs of their business emerged increasingly as a divisive issue between them.

Plans for the house were drawn on our instruction by Bill Hezeltine of Neerim South. The builder's quotation to build the house was accepted and so the process began. Meanwhile, I bought a tractor and some implements, prepared the site for the large sheds we wanted and had the principal workshop erected on it. The rest, including a large second shed, the dam, cattle yards, animal shelters, watering system, fences and landscaping, I built myself.

Pam's house was sold and the proceeds put toward the cost of the new home. About this time Pam ceased working for the travel agency and began working part time in the surgery as a receptionist. This flexible arrangement allowed her time to help her parents and to share time with friends because she was free to come and go in the practice as it suited her.

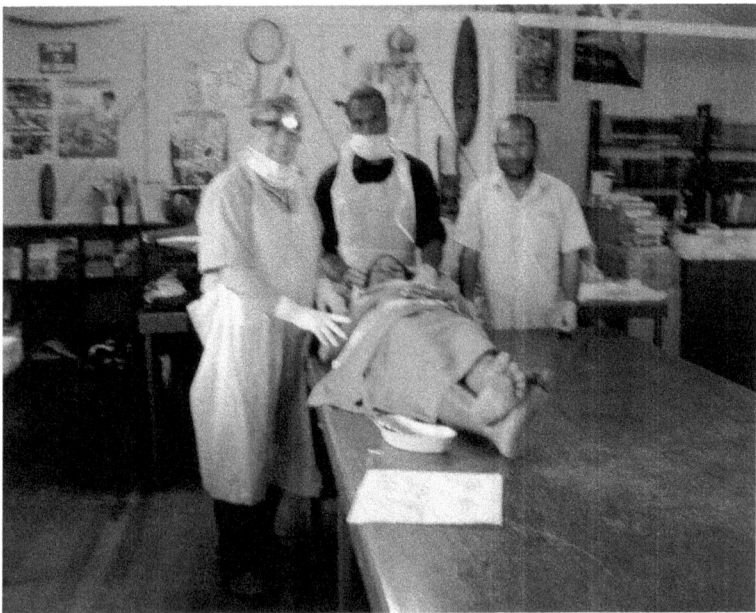
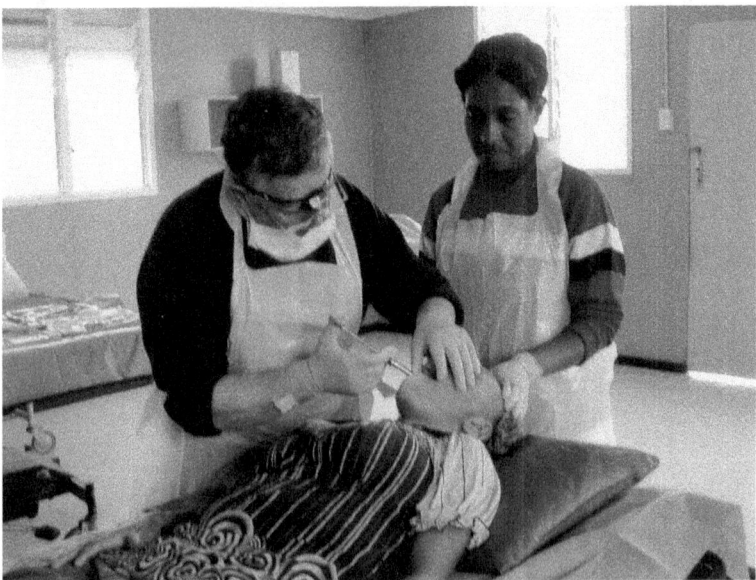

CHAPTER 25
THE LAVENDER FARM

We wished to create some income from the farm and knew from experience we would be unable to claim a tax deduction from cattle rearing on such a small property. To obtain a deduction for the creation of farm assets we needed a viable farm income. We considered growing a number of crops and then heard of a lavender grower's conference to be held in Lilydale. Pam and I attended and were seduced by the commercial lavender buyers who urged us to grow and produce lavender oil. They promised 'We will buy all you can produce.'

We met and made friends with a number of other lavender growers including Dawn Baudinette, an organiser of The Australian Lavender Growers Association (TALGA) and owner of a thriving lavender farm near Portland in the Western District. After a number of meetings with her and other producers, Pam and I decided we would produce lavender oil. I submitted a detailed plan to the Taxation Department and was granted tax deductibility for the farm improvements, including the cost of establishing the crop and equipment. In addition, I bought cattle to control the balance of the farm.

To explain the basis of plant selection used to produce lavender oils it is necessary to describe in brief the botanical background of the plants.

The lavender genus *Lavandula* (family *Lamiaceae syn. Labiatae*) spans 20-odd species, mostly of Mediterranean origin. There are three main species within the genus producing lavender. True 'lavender' oil is derived from *Lavandula angustifolia (syn. L. officionalis),'* Lavendin oil' is derived from a hybrid of *L. angustifolia x L. latifolia*. Finally, spike lavender oil is derived from *L. latifolia (syn. L. Spicae)*. Lavender is the most highly prized of these three oils.

The difference between the oils is that broadly speaking, lavender oil is sweeter smelling and contains no camphor and therefore is the higher grade whereas lavendin oil has a strong aromatic smell and contains up to 6% camphor by analysis. The yield of oil from the varieties is roughly in the proportion of Lavender 1 to Lavendin 4.

After fencing off a four acre paddock, I ploughed and then rotary hoed before forming the hilled rows with a machine I made. The rows were 2m apart with a 1m space between them. We planted our first 2000 plants of Lavendin, L. *Angustifolia x Latifolia*, a hybrid strain called Grosso, commonly used for oil production. We also planted 500 plants of Lavender (L. *angustifolia*) Varieties collectively called English Lavender.

Perennials like lavender present a further difficulty in that weeds grow within the plants making their control a special difficulty. At a meeting of lavender enthusiasts Dawn Baudinette observed that the lavender industry would remain a cottage industry unless it was mechanised. I thought about that for weeks before borrowing an idea I had seen for weed control in market gardens. From that I developed and made an implement for weed control that attached to the tractor.

Following the initial Lavender plantings, in 1999 the building of the house took place and we were able to occupy it in early 2000. The house had a wide, generous deck in front of the large double glazed windows which overlooked most all the property with a glimpse of the Baw Baw Mountains in the background. With help from the family, I landscaped the gardens after building the retaining walls on both sides and across the back. David and Stephen helped me build stockyards, a cattle crush and a shelter shed to keep the young and the sick out of the weather.

Following the development of the weeding machine, plans for a lavender harvester evolved and I settled on the conversion of a second hand forage harvester. At a clearing sale of a Gippsland machinery agent, I bought a new but superseded forage harvester that was easily demountable from the tractor. Rather than just cut grass at or near ground level as designed, I had to devise a way of lifting lavender stems and holding them vertical while the machine harvested the flower. In addition, the cutting height needed to be independent of the flower lifting mechanism which worked at ground level. The cutter-bar was a horizontal flail type that created an updraft that would blow the cut flower into the still on a trailer behind the tractor. When full, the still would be detached from the tractor and harvester and taken to the shed for processing.

By trial and error, and many hours at night in the shed, the harvester took shape. Then I needed a boiler large enough to provide the volume of steam necessary to pass through the lavender. I studied the only available notes on the subject written by Tim Denny, engineer and founder of the Bridestowe lavender farm in Tasmania.

Most modern boilers are electric or diesel fired. This makes them a poor choice from an environmental or cost of running point of view. I had plenty of fallen wood on the farm so I went looking for a wood fired boiler and found a few. The one I bought had been in use by a dry cleaner and was in a scrap merchant's yard in Moama NSW. I had it taken to a boiler specialist in Wangaratta who checked it over and certified it for use with a new safety valve set at 100psi and a new a multi-stage water feed pump. I hired a tandem trailer and took it home to the farm. It was about 3.2m long, 1.3m wide, stood 2m high and weighed about two tons.

A Warragul sheet metal factory made the condenser and separator to my specifications. The condenser was 2.5m long and consisted of 16 x 15mm pipes through which the steam passed, all contained in a water filled jacket that was fed constantly by cold recycled cold water.

The oil separator was designed to receive the oil water mixture from the condenser and allow oil to float on the water. The separated oil and water were run off in a continuous process.

Of necessity this development took place over the first two years. In the meantime, we built a plastic hothouse and began propagating new lavender plants from our early stock. We planted three other varieties of the true *Angustifolia*. After three years we had a mix of over 20,000 plants, including 600 *Rosemary officionalis* planted in about six acres.

The house was completed and we moved in the summer of 2000. It was so gratifying. We were thrilled. Our builder had done a fine job and the inspired design complemented the location to perfection. The huge deck along the northern face afforded a view of not only a broad expanse of our property but the distant mountains as well. The double glazing of the living rooms allowed the moonlight to stream in, a phenomenon usually denied those in most homes.

I reduced my dentistry working week to four days, a welcome relief because with five young people between us, one or other of them was moving for various reasons through different living arrangements. We were called upon to move them from one place to another using the horse float because it had a drop down door which enabled refrigerators and washing machines to be moved more easily.

Visits to my father Stan and his wife Dora had gradually become an annual event for reasons I hardly understood. As a father myself, it was with strange clinical detachment that I observed how he could maintain his buoyancy of spirit despite the near estrangement of his children. He exhibited no remorse and had clearly forgotten the children he had abused and failed to support. His manner was one of blissful unconcern. His life with Dora and her family was comfortable although both were living on a pension. He played bowls and made sinkers out of scrap lead. It might have been this hobby that led to his admittance to hospital for kidney failure in early April 2000.

On receiving the call, I visited him in the hospital to find him in a state of progressive organ failure, able to speak clearly and even a little euphoric -- despite awareness of his impending death. His sister Marjorie was present also. I had not seen her since my grandfather's death in 1980. As my father was wheeled to an intensive care ward he was peacefully singing hymns from the rituals of the masonic lodge with a clear voice and a smile on his face. Mercifully, helped by morphine to reduce pain, he maintained his speech and clarity of mind before passing into unconsciousness on his last day. On the evening of 14th April, his sister Marjorie, my brother Bruce and I maintained a vigil over him through the night into the morning. He died peacefully at 10 a.m. Saturday 15th April, 2000, aged 88.

My sister Pamela and brothers Ross and Geoffrey refused to go to the funeral. Bruce gave the eulogy and I wondered why I had gone. It was surreal to hear that in his second life, although impecunious, he had somehow managed to gain the regard of his adopted family. I worried, had I been fair to him? I wanted to be. I can remember fragments of smiling happy times, but in truth, they were momentary, his dark side always ready to crush feelings of paternal love or concern. He was unreachable and unable to accept responsibility for his actions. He died without remorse - which was a pity. I wanted to love and respect him, but without recognition of his actions I am unable. Stanley Emmanuel Cliff, rest in peace.

Pam and I were active members of The Australian Lavender Growers Association. We had seen lavender growers leave the industry because of the impasse between being big enough to be worthwhile financially while being still able to cope with the work required to maintain a clean crop. During those years TALGA become a large organisation with some growers content to harvest and produce dry lavender flower while a few distilled small quantities of hand cut produce. Some of the oils produced in this way were of a high quality but in time, the expense of the equipment and the intense labor required wore them down. The promises of the oil buyers were not fulfilled. They were not interested in the relatively small quantities produced in this way regardless of quality. It was easier and cheaper for them to buy dumped oil from France or other middle European countries.

Undaunted, and hopeful of overcoming the emerging difficulties, Pam and I prepared for our first oil harvest. I had enjoyed the help of the extended family who had rallied to the cause for the planting of seedlings and the previous hand cut harvest of former years. This time I was depending on the harvester and the distillation plant to work. Our still was designed to hold 4 - 500kg of cut flower and providing the components of the plant worked as planned, distillation would take about 50 minutes.

An additional problem for the inexperienced was when to harvest while working four days a week in a dental practice. The optimal time to harvest the flowers for oil is when half the flowers open. In our locality this occurs in early December. Luckily, my sons were keen to participate in the harvest. There was shared anticipation as the day arrived for the first harvest using the as yet untried equipment.

The harvester was attached to the tractor, then the trailer with the removable 'still' hitched behind and the whole outfit driven into the crop. To begin there were minor problems with the arms lifting the stems and minor modifications were necessary to maintain the cutting height. We were relieved to see the machine was a success. We were amazed to find we could harvest a full still of 400kg of flower in 16 to 20 minutes, depending on the maturity of the plants.

In the first years of production, the machinery was so efficient the harvest was completed in few loads. The initial glitches had to be identified quickly and resolved for subsequent harvests. This meant many hours tweaking the design features of the harvester and other components during the winter downtime.

The real success of an enterprise is measured by the profitability of the operation. Considerable time and work was devoted to the presentation and the sale of the oils. The assurances given by the commercial oil buyers that there would be a ready market for our oil proved to be hot air. Despite the superior quality of our oils, neither I nor my other fellow Australian producers were afforded the courtesy or cooperation with intention to buy by those who had enticed us into the industry just a few years before. Naturally, as a member of TALGA we tried to resolve the problem but ultimately, we learned to develop our own market opportunities.

I sent regular samples of our oil for analysis by mass spectrometry to the Charles Sturt University which also conducted extensive trials of the oils to test the veracity of the claims made for their therapeutic benefits. In short, almost all the common claims for the efficacy of lavender oil were endorsed as described in the summary of the trials given at a TALGA conference by Professor Heather Urwin.

Sale of our oil was slow to begin. My family agreed we would market the produce under the label of "Bellbird Lavender Farm" because the familiar ring of the bellbirds could be heard daily on our farm. We felt it added an easily identifiable Australian icon to the image of our product. With family participation, I had the label designed and printed with the appropriate signage and, after procuring the bottles, spent many hours decanting and labeling our finished product.

I was still working part time in my dental practice and, because my interest in lavender was essentially technical, I was not a highly motivated oil seller. Despite this reservation, enquiry increased and steady sales were made. Over time, enquiry came from buyers all over Australia requesting quantities ranging up to 20 litres or more that they bottled for sale in their own name.

David, my elder son, had become a marketing manager

for Dairy Australia during this time and his research revealed Australia imported about 75 tons of lavender oil each year, most for commercial use in soaps and detergents. It was also known a substantial financial incentive was given to the French producers, the result of which was that the oil imported to Australia was sold under the cost of production, or ;dumped' to use the international term. This explained the reticence of our importers, who could bring in large quantities of the oil cheaper than we could produce it, albeit of a lesser quality. Some Australian oil was bought, but it was exchanged for a lesser price because of the distorted price of the dumped imported oil.

Ultimately, recognition of this fact caused me to leave the industry. The financial return for the effort required to produce the oil was too small an incentive to enlarge the enterprise, even though I had the means to manage a large crop and harvest it efficiently.

In 2002 Pam and I visited France to see her son and his wife Sondrine, the only daughter of a successful importer and exporter of machinery. The family business was in a village close to Besoncon, a large town near the eastern border of France with Switzerland. After a few days with the family we headed off for a tour of the Auvergne region of France.

One reason for wanting to visit Auvergne was I had read the biography of Nancy Wake, the Australian woman known as the 'White Mouse'. Auvergne was the region into which she was dropped by parachute during the Second World War to arm and co-ordinate the French Resistance to distract the German Army when the Allies launched their new 'Overlord' plan. The large town at the head of the valley running south is Clermont-Ferrand, itself only a little south of Vichy, the centre from which the collaborating southern part of France was run.

We entered the Provence region, famous for centuries for the production of dried lavender and lavender oil. I was anxious to learn anything that would increase the efficiency of the growing, harvesting and distillation of lavender in Australia. In this regard we were going to be assisted by a man our hosts in Besoncon had contacted on our behalf because he had bought and sold machinery throughout Provence. We met and spent a day with this congenial Frenchman. Our first visit was to the distillation plant owned by the Reynard family.

It was April and their harvesting time lay ahead which allowed farmers time to talk with us. We knew the folly of interrupting at harvest time. After our introduction to this principal producer and his family, we were greeted warmly and with the help of our new friend acting as interpreter were given a conducted tour of the whole operation. First, we inspected their extensive machinery collection. They planted their new stock with a potato planter with minor alterations. The lavender harvester was as I mentioned earlier, a large machine that could only be detached from a big tractor with a lot of work. Consequently it was a dedicated machine with the one purpose. It had additional driven components to my basic machine but produced the same result. I was informed the harvester alone cost 35 to 40,000 Euros, I quietly rejoiced at my good fortune in creating such an efficient machine with so little money.

In their home we were shown a video of their farm and the whole operation in production. We shared a beautiful French Provence lunch, accompanied by a magnificent wine made from the Grenache grape, often wrongly considered the poor cousin of grapes in Australia. Over the lunch it was explained the French Government did indeed pay an incentive to farmers to grow lavender - 3 to 4,000 Euros a hectare, as near as language difficulties allowed.

We bid fond farewell to these wonderfully generous people and toured on to see other variants of the same machinery and growing techniques. We learned that essentially the difference was scale. The financial incentives for these people ensured a profitable return for their investment of time and energy.

The lavender growing region seemed to be a roughly triangular region with the northern village of Sault at its apex. As we moved north, the country became steeper and the unoccupied land was scattered with native varieties of lavender that in the beginning had been harvested by hand and later distilled in homemade systems. Arrangements I suspect that in many cases did double duty for spirits. The scenery and hospitality we enjoyed in our few days left us with genuine warmth for the people.

I rationalised that perhaps the French Government took the wider view when giving an incentive to produce lavender oils. In that scenario they keep a community viable while maintaining useful management of the land which in turn provides the basis for a lucrative tourist industry. If this is true, the net return to the government may well be justified.

After a pleasant lunch on the deck of a restaurant overlooking the lavender covered slopes of Sault that fell away to the south, we headed north into the mountains along the border between France and Switzerland. The road was torturous but vantage points high in the Alps afforded breathtaking views. Our new destination was a holiday chateau owned by our family friends in le Grande Bornard.

At the chateau we were greeted by Pam's son Tim, his wife Sandrine and their twin sons Jules and Noah. It was a happy reunion and an occasion to enjoy their company, free for the time being of their usual work commitments. The home, built in typical French Alps style, was located on a high vantage point west above the village with a view to the east of Mont Blanc. In the following days we visited the breathtakingly beautiful town of Aix and then Chamonix where we walked through the glacier. It was a happy time with the children. I took them for a walk up the road beyond the house to a tiny dairy farm that had about 10 cows. The owners made a special cheese from the milk in a parlor that was spotlessly clean. The boys, like me 50 years before, were overcome with the sight, smell and sound of the cows.

The drive back to Besancon and in turn to the village of Scey Sue Sao'ne, where the family lived, completed a textbook holiday in France. It had been a happy time with Tim, Sondrine, the children and her family. We returned by train to Zurich where we enjoyed a further two days before returning to Australia.

We arrived home at our Drouin West farm on a Saturday morning early May 2002.

CHAPTER 26
ABOUT TURN

As I was preparing for work on the Monday morning, Pam announced she was leaving me and moving to Melbourne. I was so shocked and had difficulty believing her. I knew Pam was deeply troubled by the behavior of her ageing parents, in particular her father who had developed a fawning childish dependence on his wife. As a result he was calling Pam many times a day in regard to the administration of his estate. The tragic death of Jill, their eldest daughter had been a terrible blow to the family. Consequently, Pam was the executor of the family estate. Without prior business experience, she struggled with the responsibilities thrust upon her.

Overnight Pam changed from her cheerful self to being overwrought and unapproachable. Any attempt to discuss our problems was met with anguished insistence she was unable to talk. There were no major issues past or present in dispute. Our closest friends had not seen the breakup coming and indeed seemed to be almost as concerned as I was for her changed behavior.

I still had a busy dental practice to run. Together with the farm it meant I was working under considerable strain although sustained by family and friends. I was 61 and realised if I was obliged to buy Pam's half of the farm there was no option but to sell the freehold of the dental practice in Drouin. After consideration and consultation, I offered the practice and freehold to my colleagues in Warragul. They declined to buy the freehold but offered to buy the practice. The irony was that the purchaser was the same dentist who had bought my previous practice in Warragul in 1986. I accepted the offer and agreed to continue working for an indeterminate time. I put the freehold on the open market and sold it readily. It was a valuable site in the main street of Drouin.

I was offered the position of senior dentist at the Bairnsdale Regional Hospital working four days a week. I would be well paid and provided with a car and accommodation near the hospital. My duties would include providing support to the dental therapists working there.

My mother had been diagnosed and treated for breast cancer in 1998 with a good prognosis. In late 2002 the disease struck again -- this time a cancer of the left lung. David, her husband, was also having difficulties and becoming increasingly dependent on Mum for the management of their affairs. Time was limited for Mum and Dad was going to be bereft without her.

My son David and his partner Claire decided to marry in May 2003 so that his grandmother could participate in the happy day -- they knew it was her dearest wish. Everyone was excited and assisted in planning the big day. It would be held in a marquee on the lawn in front of the farm house. A dance floor was installed and a band from Melbourne hired. Brother Bruce would be the Anglican Minister who married them after which 150 guests would be serenaded by a string quartet playing in the garden until dinner was served.

The weather on the day was perfect. All went as planned. After the dinner the guests danced and partied until the carefully prepared speeches had us all in convulsive laughter.

The evening was an outstanding success, all the better for the presence of not only mum but Claire's large family who had come down from Cairns for the occasion.

Two months later, while working at the Bairnsdale Regional Hospital, I was visiting Mum and Dad at their home in San Remo. It was obvious Mum was extremely ill. After dinner, she attempted to stand but could only do so with help from Dad. I watched with anguish as they shuffled from the room together and then saw them fall to the floor as one in the passage. I was able to get dad to his feet with difficulty; he was a large man and a dead weight. With great difficulty I managed to lift Mum and put her into bed.

Days later, I was visiting again with my sister Pam who lived nearby. Throughout the whole period of their failing health, Pam had taken Mum and Dad shopping, to appointments and cleaned their home. On this day, Mum was unable to stand. She had lost her sense of balance and had fallen heavily from bed a number of times. We called for an ambulance. Pam and I followed her to the Wonthaggi and District Hospital where she was admitted with the instruction 'Do not resuscitate'. As mum was wheeled to the ward she said, 'I hope this doesn't take long.' Mum's mental state was as clear as ever. She knew she was near death but, as in every other crisis in her life, she dealt with it without self pity or recourse to drama.

Mum was placed in the ward reserved for the terminally ill. I sat in a chair next to her as she lay quietly. It was a communion of spirits, mother and son reflecting on a lifetime of open and honest communication in loving silence. Then she said, 'Peter, why do we have to die?' I hesitated, my mind reeling as I struggled to find an appropriate response. My answer had to be something figuratively beautiful – a recognisable truth that would be a comfort to her in eternity.

'Mum…' I began hesitantly. 'Plants and animals come into the world with beauty and vigour, vibrantly alive and strive upward to the light. They mature and flower, attain beauty, colour and form. The fortunate bear young, or flower. The strong and the fortunate grow tall and strive to withstand the vicissitudes of weather and time. In time, the parents whose task is complete, enter a period of senescence before ultimately dying. The life force of the living is common to all species. It is an unexplained continuum passed from one generation to another across all forms of life. Death is a natural part of the life cycle - an impersonal and nonjudgmental phenomenon. The elements of the earth are finite.'

She said, 'That's lovely. That will do.' I kissed her, told her I loved her and said goodbye.

Jean Stuart Graham Dawson died peacefully on Thursday, 17th July, 2003, almost 82.

I was troubled for a long time after Mum's death. I spent hours questioning what being alive really means and what happens in death. My life experience, first as a farmer and then as a perennial student, had taught me much. The excitement and wonder on viewing a living specimen through a microscope for the first time in biology, the study of physiology, physics, chemistry, psychology and philosophy. The appreciation of literature, art and music. I reflected upon my life as a husband, father and dentist. How could I not be in awe of all that is in nature? I am comfortable with the idea that in death my elements may morph into other life forms. I find beauty in all I see. The union of spirits is another thing and hopefully persists as a pleasurable memory in the mind of those in the generations to follow.

Back on the farm, Pam's solicitor was furiously fanning the flames of our burning relationship. The paper war had begun. After eighteen months of legal extravagance we were finally able to attend the Family Court for a hearing and signing of a settlement. The emotional toll sapped me as did the settlement. At 61, I had little working life left to rebuild my superannuation fund. The inexplicable breakdown of our relationship was accompanied by a terrible feeling of loss. It plunged me into deep self doubt.

David and Stephen offered to buy a one fifth interest in the farm. As a result, although financially drained, I was debt free and able to work and manage the farm. It was a generous gesture by the boys who had both secured a sound education and attained responsible professional positions in the workforce.

In my capacity as a representative of dentists in Gippsland, aided by Doctor Nola Maxsfield representing the general medical practitioners, we petitioned the State Health Minister, the Hon Bronwyn Pike requesting the fluoridation of the water in all towns in Gippsland not having it. A minority of the Gippsland population had been beneficiaries of fluoride to the water but the vast majority had not. We were received well and a successful outcome the result. It can be safely asserted there will be a greater than 60 percent reduction in the decay rate of teeth in children born subsequently in those areas fluoridated. We were very pleased that a significant positive health measure was achieved with minimum cost

After much disagreement and disappointment with management, I resigned as senior dentist at the Bairnsdale Hospital and headed for Vietnam.

On return, my former associate and friend Dr Peter

Kingsbury, asked me to work in the Morwell practice he had now relocated and modernised. I accepted. Thus began my gradual wind down from the ownership and principal responsible for others in dentistry. I had time to enjoy patients again. Believe it or not they exchange a lot of information and appreciate gentle, painless, high quality dentistry.

I was still working four days a week besides having the cattle, lavender and general maintenance of the farm so it was also a strain trying to keep up with friends and family. In winter I had to feed hay each day to the cattle and horses consequently the days were long and the work repetitive. The prospect of retirement as planned with a partner had dimmed -- it was time to sell. Surely there was life beyond work and what about all those other interests I had pushed to the back of my mind while making an income? How much money is enough?

Clouds of depression and grief continued to drift into my reality. I could not work to the point of distraction indefinitely. Was I fatally flawed? How would I know? I spoke to my friend, Dr Bruce Osborne and explained I had this locked box of the past in my head. Perhaps the cause or solution lay within it. I was reluctant to open the box if it would serve no purpose. Although Bruce was training to be a psychiatrist at the time, he referred me to an experienced specialist that he held in high regard.

According to the psychiatrist, I was a victim of post traumatic stress syndrome, the result of stress in my early life and the recent relationship breakup. My coping mechanisms, he said, were appropriate but I should make an effort to meet other single women. Indeed, for the second time in my life I was declared sane, without major character flaws. I would just have to accept that 'shit happens'.

A representative of the Northern Institute of Tertiary and Further Education in Preston asked me to sell the lavender harvesting equipment and the distillation plant. I sold and it was promptly removed. With no equipment to work the lavender, the crop was redundant and I put the Farm on the market.

CHAPTER 27
CITY LIFE

The farm was sold in November 2007. The purchaser agreed to buy almost all the remaining equipment, including the tractor. Although the imminence of my retirement had been carefully considered for some time I was nevertheless undecided as to where to live next. My thoughts about art classes, writing and time for research into subjects of interest, like family genealogy, added to my growing interest in moving to Melbourne. I considered buying a home closer to the city.

To buy time, I chose to rent a house in Mount Waverley and started part time work with the Southern Health Government Dental Service whose offices were in Prahran and South Melbourne. I travelled by train or tram as required finding that Mount Waverley had been a good choice.

A dentist I had become acquainted with years before offered me a part time position in his practice in Lilydale. This was a welcome return to general dentistry so I restricted my work in the government clinics to occasional sessions.

Meanwhile, I made friends with my new Mount Waverley neighbour, Richard Peterson, who shared my interests in history and red wine. Richard was a history teacher at Presbyterian Ladies College. A thorough professional, he was dedicated to the students he taught. As the year rolled on he asked me whether I would care to join a party of teachers and students planning a 'Revolutions Tour' to France and Russia in

October 2008. The school had done it before and the organiser would travel with us.

The aim was to enlarge the students' knowledge of the French and Russian Revolutions as part of their modern history course. We would spend seven days in Paris, fly to Saint Petersburg for a further six days, take the train to Moscow for five days and then return to Australia. I jumped at the opportunity but planned to further my stay by flying from Moscow to London to spend a night before flying to Edinburgh the next day. In Edinburgh, I would hire a car to retrace the history of my wayward ancestors in Dundee. From there I intended to drive south via Liverpool to visit remnants of the family before calling on my ex-housemates now living in Mortimer, a village just south of Reading Berkshire. I allowed a fortnight for this excursion with an additional week in France to revisit World War One sites and the beaches of Normandy.

In late September 2008 we assembled to leave. There were fifteen Year 11 girls and twelve adults made up of six teachers, one staff member, two grandparents and three friends. The girls were a credit to themselves and their families. There was not one negative incident and all participated with interest and attention to the details of the different revolutions. The program was packed with visits to the museums in the respective cities and bus trips to the principal palaces, such as Fontainbleu and Versailles in France and the Winter and Catherine Palaces in Russia. The history of the Revolutions is a complex and compelling story, beyond the scope of my autobiography. I recount only a little of our experience, since for me it was the culmination of a lifetime of reading and speculation about the origins and consequences of the respective Revolutions.

My impressions of Russia were tempered by a feeling the populace was frightened. We had heard of the millions Stalin killed and caused to die and the systematic removal of the educated and the brave for generations. Families today were reluctant to be noticed. It was unhealthy to ask questions or challenge decision making. It would be the well dressed emerging middleclass of young people who I hoped would resist any attempt to revive the extreme communist ideology and they were more noticeable and numerous in St. Petersburg than in Moscow. Overall, we discovered a great and interesting country that possessed enormous resources. It is embarrassing that we know so little about Russia, a country that straddles almost a third of the earth's surface.

In Dundee, I found the courthouse where I hoped to retrieve details of my ancestor's crimes and their circumstances. There were many people waiting about because the court house was busy processing the latest wave of miscreants, a steady harvest of people unable to survive in this still tough town where unemployment was rife and opportunities fewer. I wondered, had anything changed?

My enquiries led to meeting an officer of the court, a keen historian who apologised saying he was unable to help me as all records had been archived in Edinburgh. To salvage my day, I determined to have a good look at the town to gain a feel of how things might have been for my forebears in 1848. Dundee is a substantial town, the fourth largest in Scotland and had a population in 1848 of about 64,000. This was the time the Graham of my origin committed her crime, aided by her younger sister. The town was noted then for producing linen, canvas and rope from flax and jute imported from India. Later it was also known for making marmalade jam and, from the early 1900s, for its journalism and printing. The city emblem now lists jute, jam and journalism as the prime sources of local employment.

In Edinburgh, after finding a guest house, I took the bus into town. The city was in a state of near gridlock because tram lines were being laid in the main street. This obliged the enormous number of buses to be rerouted through back streets. I headed for the Registry of Births Deaths and marriages where I found the trial of sisters Robinnie, alias Robina Kerr, aged 25, and Janet Graham (nee Kerr), aged 30.

It was exciting to untie a ribbon possibly untouched since the trial of 1848. I spread the documents out and read of the desperate petty crime that resulted for the sisters in a sentence of seven years transportation to Van Diemen's Land. Prior to committing the crime, the notes said Janet had spent the evening in a hotel with a man who had been drinking. The hotel keeper said Janet had not been drinking at all. The couple left around 11pm and Janet returned to her home in a nearby street, A little later, neighbours were woken by the sound of a man crying out as two women set upon him in the street outside. In the process, he was assaulted and robbed of his cane and 14 shillings and 6 pence. No weapons were used and the man was not seriously hurt.

I read and reread the whole of the material, marveling at the insensitivity of a legal system that would deal so harshly with two women for a crime that invites us to consider there may have been provocation. Nevertheless, it happened and I look forward to researching further what happened to these women from that point on including an account of their time in Tasmania. I made notes and left amazed at what I had found.

I soon headed for Dover to take the ferry to Calais. From there I hired a car and drove to Ypres where Australians were sent to fight in the First World War of 1914—1918. I wanted to see the land on which my grandfather had fought and where he had been wounded by machinegun fire. His brother was gassed while working with the Ambulance Corps and died soon after. My knowledge of the region had recently been expanded by reading Roland Percy's biography of Sir John Monash. However, the Australian general's principal campaign was fought further south on the plains through which the River Somme flowed.

In Belgium, I visited the Tyne Cot Memorial, the largest British and Commonwealth war cemetery in the world. Initially much smaller, it was enlarged to commemorate those names too numerous to be recorded at the Menin Gate. There are 11,953 headstones of men killed in what was known as the Flanders Offensive. Behind the headstones is the long wall on which are the names of 34,863 British men who have no known grave. I tried to imagine the sight of so many healthy young men slain mercilessly by a war in which they were simply taking orders – men obliged to fight and die in defense of freedom.

Only a few kilometres away in the Polygonwood Cemetery, are the graves of the 5th Australian Division. Having read extensively of the First World War, I was deeply touched by the magnitude of the slaughter here. The gently rolling open country is fertile farmland fought over for four years. It fittingly embraces the bodies of those who fell. The windswept silence belies what must have resounded with the abominable grinding cacophony of relentless war.

I visited the Thiepval Memorial, built on the peak of the

low hills a few kilometres west of Pozieres. It too was a large memorial with thousands of graves. A total of 1,357,000 French soldiers had died in the war while the British and Commonwealth dead numbered 1,115,000. In all, about 2.5 million Allies, plus countless civilians. German military deaths were almost 2 million.

The next day I visited the village of Albert. Albert, ironically, is the name of the Williamstown street in which I grew up. Set in the hollows are tiny villages, such as Le Hamel, a few kilometres northeast of Villers Bretonneux. Just outside Villers Bretonneux on hill 104 stands a high tower with a wing wall either side, this being the Australian National Memorial built in 1938. From this tower is a clear view over the country Australians and New Zealanders fought so decisively for. To the west, across the open fields, Amiens is clearly visible. From the valley of the Somme in the west Sir John Monash heroically led our forces including Americans, to a decisive victory in Peronne in the east.

My tour of the Normandy Beaches in October 2008 began the next morning with a slow drive westwards. The eastern end of the assault had been by the British 3rd Infantry Division on Sword Beach and the next, Juno Beach, by the Canadian 3rd Infantry Division. The remnants of the smashed fortifications are still littered along the coast, a reminder of the bitter fighting here. Then there was Gold Beach, just north of the township of Arromanches, where the British 50th Infantry Division came ashore, its western end marked by the town of Port-en-Bessin. On a bluff a little further west overlooking the broad expanse of Gold Beach is a small theatre in which visitors can see films of the invasion. Standing on the hill the remains of the Mulberry harbour can be seen offshore.

Huge pontoons that were towed into place and sunk to form an artificial harbor within which ships could discharge the weapons fuel and food required to sustain the huge army. The magnitude of it is breathtaking, the more so because it was put in place so quickly.

In Port-en-Bessin, I had a leisurely stroll and a beer to settle my imagination, stimulated as it was by all I saw and read of this historically amazing feat. To rest, I sat at a small table outside the hotel overlooking the loch and attempted to take my own photo. A man came out of the hotel and offered to take my photo after watching my attempt to take my own. That small welcome spontaneous gesture of civility bought me back to earth.

Steadied, I resumed my exploration. Next beach west was Omaha, where the American 1st Infantry Division came ashore. On the western extremity of this beach is a high bluff, a small, short peninsula standing perhaps 200 feet above the water, Pointe-Du Hoc. Because of its command of the beaches, this site was especially heavily fortified by the Germans with a number of huge gun emplacements. Today a car park and memorial building commemorate what took place.

I walked out skirting the huge craters still scattered on the bluff. Some are 10 to 15 metres across and up to four metres deep. The remains of huge concrete emplacements and block houses blown open lie about like broken Lego, a grim and terrible reminder of the horrendous force needed to destroy them.

A guide described his understanding of what took place on Pointe-Du Hoc. He said the Allies had been bombing the site before D-Day but had not realised on the eventful day that the guns had been removed inland by the Germans. The weather was poor and the seas rough. The ships from which the landing craft left stood well out, he said up to 8km. The intention of the American soldiers was to scale the vertical cliff and expel the Germans. To achieve this, they had rockets attached to grapnels, in turn attached to long ropes coiled on the floor of the landing craft. Because the sea was rough, water came aboard and wet the ropes making them too heavy for the rockets to carry to the top of the cliff when fired. The result was a terrible loss of life as the men bravely fought their way up despite their defective equipment, trying to displace the German soldiers who were firing down on them with small arms. The noise and terror created on the point that day by the combined bombardment of the ships, the bombing by air and the frontal assault was too terrible to imagine.

I returned the car and toured Bordeaux by tram before boarding the GTV train to Paris. My brief visit to this second largest city in France did not allow enough time to appreciate its beauty or history. I left with the hope I can visit again. Like everything wonderful, I was left wanting more.

CHAPTER 28
BERWICK

On return to Australia I saw a doctor about my painful and swollen knee, an injury sustained in Paris that would not heal. I was promptly referred for an arthroscopy. Unable to work post surgery, my friend Bruce Osborne urged me to take up golf. He knew I had never played sport before but insisted I would enjoy playing with a group of his friends who played early on Saturday mornings. How right he was. I only wish I had taken time to learn when younger.

I bought a house in Berwick, 35km from the city. It was well situated close to the original village on a large block with access at the rear to a recreation reserve. The interior of the house had become dated so I busied myself replacing the kitchen and painting through. I received help from friends of my youth, Clem and Thelma Thompson who had resided in Berwick for the past 30 years. The Thompsons, in turn, introduced me to their friends in the region so I was privileged to be quickly included in a wide group of accomplished people who were all managing issues of retirement.

I discovered I had a serious problem with my neck. The discs at two levels had collapsed and I would need surgery to fuse the cervical spine at these points as I was at risk of becoming a paraplegic from something as minor as whip lash injury. The decision to operate was readily made given the obvious truth of what the doctor showed me. In February

2010 the offending discs were removed.

Unable to work, I continued with the writing, art and English Literature while contemplating the sad realisation that while at the peak of my competence as a dentist, I was about to walk away. It seemed sad and must be a similar thought for many retirees. Whilst in recovery it occurred to me that I no longer had the need or the drive to continue work so my hobbies and interests expanded to occupy the space. The habit of attending night school, which began of necessity in early years, was now one I would turn for interest and pleasure.

Three months after surgery I was feeling better. Retirement had been a process, not a single event. For many years I had contemplated volunteer work in third world countries so I made tentative enquiries with a number of different charity bodies and let the matter rest over the Christmas period of 2010. In January 2011, I turned 70 and celebrated with 91 members of my family and friends at home. As I gazed over the assembly I was moved by the speeches and the effort made by so many to be present. I was humbled and grateful to them all for it was with their support I had achieved anything in life.

In February 2011, I was contacted by the Salvation Army. They could use me in Papua New Guinea but I would have to provide my own instruments. The administration of aid to Papua New Guinea by the Salvation Army was located in Sydney. Slowly a picture of what and where I would work evolved as I learned the control of medical services in Papua New Guinea was managed by a National, Charlie Clement, operating out of the Salvation Army office in Port Moresby.

The proposal was that I would work and train their medical officers to perform basic dental procedures in the Salvation Army first aid stations dotted throughout Papua New Guinea.

I was told the stations had sterilisation equipment and that my accommodation, food and travel needs would be provided. With this assurance, I set about raising money to buy the necessary dental equipment.

Friends sprang to support the program. The Lions Club of Berwick donated the initial $1,300 and a further $7,000 was raised following talks to past Rotary Clubs of Warragul and Drouin. The Friends of Wilson Botanic Park in Berwick organised a dinner and raised a further $1,200 which bought the fund to $9,500. The exercise had unleashed a surprising reserve of community goodwill for the project. A genuine concern for the people of Papua New Guinea emerged which was encouraging.

A colleague and friend in dentistry oral surgeon, Mr. Steven Hookey, was also supportive offering advice, materials and equipment. Another friend and past associate, Dr. Peter Kingsbury, generously donated the stock of local anaesthetic that we estimated would be necessary. Thus supported, I ordered the balance of instruments and surgical equipment. When assembled I had three complete surgical kits, a rechargeable vacuum unit, surgical hand-pieces, an electrical drive system and a selection of forceps, and basic dental instruments. In addition were the disposables such as sutures, anaesthetic, gloves, masks, aprons, and needles.

Meanwhile, I applied for a visa and registration with the Medical Board of Papua New Guinea which was sent to Dr Mathias Sapuri, Chairman of the Papua New Guinea Medical Board, in the last week of June 2011.

I was to leave on Sunday 7th August, and return on the 30st October. Arrangements had been made for my excess luggage to be carried free by both Qantas and Air Nui Guinea. A standard sixty day visiting visa arrived the week before leaving and I was authorized to take five bags - four with dental equipment and a fifth with my clothes and personal belongings. Major Lorraine Hart, a senior representative of the Salvation Army in Melbourne, would meet me at the airport to facilitate the departure process and Charlie Clement would meet me on arrival in Port Moresby.

CHAPTER 29
ARRIVING IN PAPUA NEW GUINEA

We landed in Port Moresby 4.15 p.m. Sunday 7th August 2012. Only four of my five bags arrived and there was no one to meet me. I waited in the foyer under the watchful gaze of the security guards who periodically asked why I was there. I was unable to contact Charlie because I did not have his phone number. It was hot and I was foolishly aware I had no idea where I was intended to go. The constant attention of the guards as I stood waiting became embarrassing because at 5.30 p.m., the airport began closing down for the day. A few minutes before six o'clock, two young people who worked for the Holiday Inn in Port Moresby offered to give me a ride into town. With the terminal almost empty and feeling desperate, I accepted. The only address I had was 'Marpang'. They had not heard of it but assured me their bus driver would know. At 6.15 p.m. I was delivered to Marpang, a missionary hostel in the suburb of Boroko.

'Yes,' the manager said, 'We are expecting you, but not for dinner, which has been served.' I explained I had not eaten and that I was supposed to have been met at the airport at 4.15 p.m. She said she would find something for me to eat and would make enquiries with the Salvation Army. Later, about 7 p.m. as I ate the food provided she returned saying

Charlie had arrived and was sitting in the lounge.

I entered the lounge to meet Charlie Clement, Medical Services Director for the Salvation Army Papua New Guinea, a national with a beaming face devoid of guile. 'I'm sorry,' he said, 'I was watching the football and forgot!'

That was my introduction to the work and business etiquette practiced in Papua New Guinea. Colloquially known as Papua New Guinea time, you accept that even when you are assured they will do as proposed they most probably have no intention of doing so.

Charlie was unconcerned about the missing bag, 'We will look for it in the morning before you fly to Goroka at nine o'clock.' Exhausted, I retired to examine which of the cases was missing because they were all similar to look at. It was my bag of clothes, toiletries, shoes and books that were missing. I had a shower and went to bed resigned to another day in the clothes I had arrived in and with little confidence that my luggage would be found.

The airport was busy because all major towns in Papua New Guinea are only accessible by air or sea. There are no main roads connecting Port Moresby to any other provincial centre. Although early, it was hot. Hampered by the four cases I pushed back and forth between the domestic and international terminal, I tried in vain to find the lost luggage. The leisurely manner of looking and the indifferent attitude of the staff amazed me. On my second visit to the international terminal I was assured they had found my case. On examination, the case held construction workers gear. With time running out and still needing to exchange money and check in for my flight at 9.15 a.m., I was worried, but Charlie wasn't. Air Nui Guinea demanded another 150 Kina for the flight. I boarded

DARE TO DREAM

the plane conscious I was already a sticky mess with no change of clothes, shoes or toiletries. But Charlie was unconcerned.

As the plane took off, clouds prevented me seeing anything but a few glimpses of the mountains until we landed in Goroka. On disembarking our luggage was thrown onto a large table. I retrieved my cases while glancing at the large wire exit gate against which a crowd of black faces watched us intently. With four large pieces of luggage I was concerned for their security. A small man identified himself as my appointed welcome committee and promptly stowed me and my bags aboard his Toyota utility. His name was Deeson.

As we negotiated our way through the teeming crowds, I was struck by the sight of so many people with apparently nothing to do. They were wandering about, sitting in parks and apparently oblivious to the rubbish strewn about. In minutes we turned into a gate marked Salvation Army Offices and Hostel Accommodation and I was introduced to Andrew. A tall young man who quickly grasped the gravity of my predicament and took me shopping, instructing me as we approached a huge second hand clothing store to keep behind him and be careful he said, it could be very dangerous.

I bought two shirts, some underclothes, two pairs of shorts, some socks and, on Andrew's advice, a warm jacket. We found a pharmacy where I persuaded the chemist to sell me anti malarial medication, tooth-paste and a brush. I then rushed back to the hostel passing crowded market places and broken rubbish strewn roads. At this stage I had no idea what was planned for me other than we were going out into the provinces of the eastern highlands. It was midday by now. With a sense the shopping trip had delayed some unspoken agenda, we loaded some new faces into the utility, bid Andrew

283

goodbye and Deeson began a two hour drive to Kainantu.

The condition of the roads had to be seen to be believed. Vehicles swerved all over the road as we negotiated huge pot holes, some more than a foot or more deep with torn edges and entire segments ripped up. Deeson explained that since the Australian administration of Papua New Guinea had ceased in 1975, no maintenance had been done. There were many people walking on the side of the road and it seemed the walking was aimless but Deeson reassured me, there were many villages hidden in the bush, along with coffee plantations and occasional schools.

On reaching Kainantu, I was immediately surprised by the huge crowd of mainly men standing idly about in the wide main street that extended for about a kilometre. Asian owned stores were one side and a jumble of others run by Nationals on the other. The atmosphere was heavy with watchful anticipation as so many people loitered with intent to gain if someone was careless. Our truck swung into the impressive wrought iron gates of the Salvation Army Medical Training School. A large and impressive building, it was here that young graduates of schools throughout the country, year seven for most, year nine or ten for a few, came to receive three years of basic medical training.

With a sense of urgency we transferred to the ambulance, a diesel Toyota troopy into which an ever growing throng of fellow passengers squeezed. After a push start in reverse, we were back on an even worse road to Onomuga along which were many traditional houses and small parcels of land growing cane, bananas and coffee. Many people were on the road. I asked about the children freely roaming around and was told that although school instruction is cheap, many are unable to afford the cost. The journey took more than two hours and ended as we climbed a steep drive to arrive in front of a long rectangular building, the hospital.

On the grass covered lower slope on the long side of the hospital were dispersed about eight well spaced cottages. I was shown to the nearest. Designed for guests, it consisted of three small sparsely furnished rooms and a kitchenette with a balcony overlooking a valley. The officer in charge, Andrew, asked me what food I had bought to eat. Surprised, I explained that the Salvation Army had assured me I would be fully accommodated including food. He said he had not been told and that there were no provisions for me. There was not even a towel or utensils to eat or drink from. After some thought, he said he could manage to feed me that night and would send for supplies the next day. Then we took Geoff, a fellow traveler and aid worker, to the outpost clinic he ran an hour away over a mountain. It was the worst road I have ever seen. There were people moving about and large audiences watched minor earthworks along the way. Andrew explained the ambulance also served as the hearse and the loud rattle in the front left suspension had been there for ages. There was no budget for its repair, as was the reason for it having to be push started.

On our return to Onomuga, I had dinner in darkness with Andrew and Lyell. Rice and noodles into which was added a small tin of processed meat. No tea or coffee and no refrigeration. The power generator, required mainly to charge mobile phones, came on at 7 p.m. and ran to 9 p.m., its use limited by the cost and availability of fuel.

The aid centre Geoff managed was a bungalow about twelve feet square with a waste basket in the corner full of blood stained dressings. The rear half of the cabin was entered by a door in the centre of the dividing wall. The back room had a short wooden bed with a thin vinyl covered pad for a mattress. Geoff explained this was where he conducted his ante natal examinations and delivered babies. He showed me a pair of rusty molar forceps he used to extract teeth. Because his understanding of anatomy was poor he was unable to do nerve blocks and observed that his extractions seem to cause a lot of pain.

At dinner the conversation was about tooth fillings. I was obliged to show them my old amalgam fillings. They have never heard of amalgam, composite resin or glass ionomer filling materials. The next day promised to be interesting. My arrival had been unexpected. Charlie had only notified the hospital of my presence by phone that morning. Consequently, the news of my free service could only begin to be broadcast to the surrounding villages which meant the people were not given time to walk in. I was told many people would walk 40km or more, sometimes taking days, so the later part of the week could be busy.

On Tuesday morning 9th August 2011 I walked to the hospital. A number of people were already waiting. Bare footed with mud socks they stood quietly near the front door. Others with children sat on the grass of the steep bank along the top side of the approach. One of the two men standing near the door was carrying a large bush knife. We waited without talking until eventually the door was unlocked. I was due to start work at 9 a.m. but it was now 9.30 -- I reminded myself, it is Papua New Guinea time.

The hospital was a rectangular building about 8m wide and 30m long. The front third was divided into segments for assessment, counseling and medicine distribution. The centre third was for in-patients and had eight low narrow wooden beds, four each side with a thin upholstered vinyl pad, but no blankets. Two beds were occupied, one with a woman of about 35 suffering from inflammatory pelvic disease for which was receiving an intravenous solution of chloramphenicol. The other woman, a little older, had typhoid and was also on an intravenous chloramphenicol drip. Patient's families were responsible for the general comfort and management of the sick and there was a side door through which they could come and go at all hours to use the crude and neglected facilities behind the building. The rear third of the building had a small anti-room, ostensibly for sterilization, but empty and unused. The rear space was the operating room. It had two operating tables with wheels and adjustment for the head to be raised, a trolley on which to place instruments and empty benches along the side. I set out my instruments and waited.

The patients began to arrive. They were a cross section of the people all with bare feet and wearing simple coloured clothes. All had a shy reticent but cooperative manner. Their English was poor. The spoken language was pidgin. They presented with a range of common dental problems, mostly molar teeth that had decayed since youth and progressively become worse to the point where they were aching or were infected. I placed anaesthetic and extracted the offending tooth/teeth, sometimes as many as four or five. My fifth patient was a man who placed a large axe under the table before climbing up. I enquired why he was carrying it. Was it in some way a warning to me? The nurse explained that many men and women carry a bush knife or axe for protection

At lunch on my second day I was invited to join Major

Mais Kihi and his wife Paula, who lived in a Salvation Army house about 300m away within the compound. They were a gentle retired couple who provided sweet potato chips, pasta and tinned mince meat. The home was clean and simply furnished for they had travelled in the past to Australia for training. I was impressed with their generous hospitality. They began to relax and share details of the culture.

Mais explained that while not so bad this year, tribal warfare around the compound had raged for years, gradually decreasing over the past one or two years. People of bickering Wontoks had occupied the valley continuously in that time with the death of one or two, sometimes five or more people a week. Women were also killed -- collateral damage because they accompany the fighting men. The main weapons used were bow and arrows, bush knives, spears and guns. The increasing use of high power military style weapons became a theme in many subsequent explanations about tribal warfare

Mais explained to me that a Wontok was a family or tribal group, largely related but able to adopt others into it who occupy, at least in this region of the Eastern Highlands, a piece of land about 14 miles diameter but this varied greatly. Tribal leaders were the administrators of the land and maintained the social order. There were no titles to the land which was parceled out for use by all in the Wontok. Those earning more by working harder or who were thrifty were obliged to provide the basics for everyone regardless of their input. Those who obtained a job or who enjoyed good fortune were also obligated to provide for others in the Wontok.

My day was completed at four o'clock, having seen 14 patients and extracted 19 teeth. I was helped by Diane, a nurse who had received training in the Goroka Hospital and who proved to have natural aptitude. She was pleasant and helpful especially in providing interpretation of the spoken pidgin. I was shocked to learn that the sterilisation of my instruments throughout the day consisted of a swish in water followed by a wipe with alcohol soaked paper as used in skin preps for an injection. I insisted that the next day everything would be boiled. There was no autoclave so we found an ancient disused pan and a partly filled gas bottle and burner in preparation for the next day.

Andrew told me he would be cooking that tonight. He proudly displayed a large cabbage under his arm and added he has been able to contact Charlie for more food which he hoped would arrive the next day. There was still no news of my missing suit case.

The indolence of so many people seemed to be of concern to only a few vital people in the region. Good programs lapsed for want of willing workers, there seemed to be no vision of a better way. I observed that it was little wonder, given so few had even the most basic education. Most patients were illiterate.

The country had been extensively cleared of trees. An obvious thing to do would be to replant the forest that had retreated so far. The soil was fertile. Beds of sweet potato, onion, cauliflower and yams were flourishing, along with avocado trees growing wild along with many other varieties of fruit.

The week was passing quickly. After work one evening, I walked down to the marketplace which occupied a corner of a large river flat. This was the ground over which the recent wars were fought. The crowd of kids thought it was a hoot that I was a white man. They called out to each other to come and see me and on doing so, fell about laughing. The craft work in progress and the food on display for sale was provided by the women. A large number of men stood around doing nothing at all. There were no appointments. The people just rolled up and either stood around the front door or sat quietly on the grass without complaint or impatience. I tried to see them in the order they arrived until none were left. An old man came in with large yellow rubber boots he removed to climb on the table. His legs were wrapped in a mess of muddy wet plastic bags to provide a better fit. It all had to be replaced for him to leave. Each day I saw between 20 and 30 people, always extracting a slightly greater number of teeth. There was no option, the teeth were grossly decayed, broken down, infected and causing pain. All submitted for treatment without fuss and openly expressed their gratitude on leaving.

On the Friday morning I saw 11 people and extracted 17 teeth before packing for the trip back to Kainantu. We loaded my gear and the patient who had not responded to the antibiotic drip during the week into the ambulance parked ready for a rolling start in front of the hospital. She was being transferred to the hospital in Kainantu where we, Andrew and I, had to find accommodation before moving on to Kamila the next week. An assortment of unknown men and women squeezed in to the last remaining space. With a lurch, the truck started. The heavy persistent rain had turned the road into an endless bog hole and it required four wheel drive all the way. The 38km to Kainantu took two and a half hours.

After discharging our patient at the hospital we went looking for somewhere to stay. Charlie, true to form, had failed to arrange our accommodation. We stopped at the Salvation Army medical training school thinking we might elicit some sympathy for our plight. I asked if I could use the toilet and was directed to private quarters where I was shocked to find a dirty grime covered toilet that could only be flushed with water from a bucket. It occurred to me that if this was the best the medical school could manage, it was no wonder there was no appreciation of basic hygiene or sterilisation in the clinics.

Andrew reluctantly booked us into the Gateway Motel where a shared room cost 200 Kina a night, without cooking facilities. This was a worry for Andrew because we were there for two nights and he had no authority to spend such a large sum of money without meals for the weekend. The motel was surrounded by a twelve foot high stone wall topped with razor wire. A guard controlled the front gate. This was a comfort for the atmosphere in this town was simmering with danger. An estimated thousand or more people, mainly men, stood around the few large shops on either side of the wide open street, ready to pounce without mercy on the smallest indiscretion. The waterways and drains across the street were crammed with rubbish which was piled and strewn everywhere

Andrew made many phone calls. One of which resulted in an obscure branch of the medical health system allowing us to eat at their expense at the Kainantu Lodge Hotel for the weekend. At this point I had to give him money to top up his phone. The offer to pay for our meals was welcome news. We were fortunate to enjoy two days of near normal food by walking rapidly back and forth between the motel and the hotel, a distance of about a 1km.

I asked Andrew why the Toyota ambulance was not maintained since it had only covered 100,000km and was running well apart from the starter motor and the front shock absorber. The starter motor required new brushes and the left hand front shock absorber had come away from the body, which caused the vehicle to slump badly when cornering. He explained there was no money in the budget for repairs. But not to worry, a new vehicle has been ordered. I mention this because it illustrates the expectations of these people who have no appreciation of the need to maintain buildings, vehicles or infrastructure generally. When something breaks, a new one will be provided.

Monday morning came and Deeson arrived to take us to Kamila, a drive he said, of up to four hours. Before leaving, we stocked up with a food supply for the week and refueled the truck. On the food list was a large bag of rice, six to eight packets of dry biscuits, the same number of Maggi noodles, five small tins of processed meat, a bottle of orange cordial, three bottles of water and a large pack of toilet rolls. As was the custom, a collection of new faces filled the truck and we left the hostile town of Kainantu.

The trip was interesting apart from the constant violent lurching of the truck as we negotiated the track that became worse the further we went. We passed through hilly terrain in which were scattered small villages, many with coffee beans spread to dry on sheets of plastic. The flourishing small vegetable crops we saw dotted about were indicative of good soil. Children waved with great excitement when they saw me, 'White man, white man!' and collapsed in giggles. If we stopped, the children became shy and hid behind adults while staring through legs at me.

Finally, as we descended a steep incline off the crest of a small mountain, the Kamila health centre could be seen on the high side of the road within fenced, grass covered grounds.

CHAPTER 30
VILLAGE LIFE

We were greeted by a group of curious people at the medical centre who helped us unload the truck. They had only learned of our visit that morning so there was consternation as to where I would be accommodated and what we had bought to eat. They had a vague idea we would be coming but not the when or how we were to be provided for.

I was taken to a group of huts on the lower side of the road. One was on stilts. The upper level was divided into three. Underneath were two small pig sties and a space stacked with building materials. I was assigned to a small room upstairs in which was a bed over which my helpers hung a mosquito net. Two similar rooms with closed doors opened from the common entry in which were a collection of building tools, a box that served as a table and one chair. My 'helpers' this week were Andrew, Iso and Holive, the brother of Joite the regional manager of the Salvation Army.

The intention to teach the assistants how to perform extractions was in jeopardy because my efforts to teach basic oral anatomy using diagrams held no interest for any of them. They preferred to simply watch, believing that was all that was necessary. They would simply copy what was done. Learning by reading from books or thinking in the abstract was not something they are used to. My attempts to teach them about structures beneath the surface and how they were to be avoided were in vain. Reluctantly, I concluded it was better that they do nothing than causing greater pain than already existed.

As usual, it was raining in late afternoon. The owner of my hut was Major Kenoti. He unlocked the door of the large round cook house to allow preparation of the evening meal. I was surprised that the doors were locked but learnt this was to prevent theft. The round thatched cooking hut was about eight metres in diameter. The one entry opened onto a narrow rectangle of bare earth which served as the fireplace, each side of which inside the doorway were shelves where basic cooking utensils were kept. Surrounding the fire place was a raised thatched bamboo floor on which the occupants sat while piled in the rear was a supply of drying wood.

The fire was lit and women prepared the food. Vegetables were cut up and peeled as required on the floor. Rice was boiled in one container, pumpkin greens in another, yams and sweet potato in a third. Maggi noodles were added for taste but I was unsure whether this was for my benefit or used anyway. The one source of protein I saw used was the small tin of processed meat added to every mix. The rate of cooking was managed by pushing in or withdrawing larger pieces of wood from the fire. While cooking was under way, people continued to join the group and sit about watching. Children darted in and about with total freedom. Dogs hung about too, small emaciated curs that unlike our dogs, avoided humans, perhaps because, as I was frequently assured by the nationals, they were the best and tastiest source of meat.

I had received no briefing about the culture and was learning by trial and error. I had noticed that once my meal was handed to me I was expected to leave the cooking house. I would take the food back to my room and eat alone. This seemed to be accepted practice in many villages. In my hut I could hear the family chatting as they ate but they rarely lingered much beyond an hour or two before dispersing to their sleeping huts. There were about three or four cook huts in this Wontok. Others were a little further down the road in another part of the village around the corner of the valley.

The common toilet, with which I was becoming increasingly familiar, consisted of a slot over a large deep pit over which was a thatched roof. I had recurring visions of how Billy Connelly would describe my antics as in near panic I struggled to disrobe and take aim without touching anything that was already wet while thanking God for having the foresight to bring toilet paper. In a version of the Papua New Guinea barn dance conducted to the tune of my loudly protesting gut, my movements were to say the least fluid. It was even worse during the day while working in the aide station because I had to run through a crowd of waiting patients and scramble up the steep hill to the toilet perched in full view of all. It had been especially constructed for the staff. I was glad I could not speak pidgin for I'm sure the locals had their own version of my 'panic' attacks.

Only the children of families who could afford to pay for schooling sent their kids to school. In this village they were the majority. The others simply played about and did nothing. Those who attended the primary school of Kamila had to walk to the school, a journey of two hours each way. I had seen the school miles back down the almost impossible road on our way in. I marveled at the fortitude of a people who would accept this as normal and necessary. When I asked why a more direct path across the valley was taken, instead of the long way round the rim of the valley, I was told the forest abounded with voodoo and other superstitions that made it far too dangerous to enter.

I was humbled by all I saw and only hope that my little dental service was of some relief. The alternative otherwise for those with toothache meant they would have had to walk to where the Public Motor Vehicles (PMVs) terminate on their road, pay about seven or more Kina each way for the three hour trip each way and go to the Goroka Hospital where they would be charged at least ten Kina per tooth extracted. For a people who have hardly a kina to their name it just doesn't happen. Consequently, the patients make it clear they are grateful for gentle, painless, free treatment.

At the end of the working day the women returned from their garden plots. Those with pigs returned them to the sties beneath my hut. Each pig had a rope made from the vines attached to a back foot. When on the garden plot it was tethered to a stump left in the ground so that the pig roots up the soil, In effect, ploughing and fertilizing the soil at the same time.

Alfred and Usula, the aid workers assigned to the centre were a husband and wife team who extended an invitation for me to join them for dinner. While eating the customary fare, they explained that the people going to market would set out from their homes at three or four o'clock in the morning, often walking more than 20km before returning later the same day.

A small crowd of people hovered around the front gate waiting to see if the first patient survived treatment before committing themselves for dental relief. Eventually a brave soul pushed through the crowd of kids hanging around the door and submitted to two extractions. Then the stampede started.

Alfred had a busy day. Many women attended for pre natal checks and other general ailments for which he prescribed and dispensed medicines and care without washing hands or sterilizing the instruments. The waste bin overflowed with dirty dressings. The tap over the sink had not worked for years and there were no towels for drying. There was a concerted effort being made to vaccinate people for a variety of diseases. Apart from cold packs, there was no refrigeration available for the vaccines and heat renders them worthless.

I insisted on having a bucket of water available to wash my hands between patients. Even that required a long walk to the communal tap. The dental work was difficult because the high and wide desk top my patients lay on made it hard for me to operate, exacerbated by having untrained assistants who hover around regarding the process as a game. I felt isolated and frustrated by the mindless, primitive dirty conditions that could so easily be improved.

The long cold night passed. Morning light revealed the village surrounded in mist and drizzle. Incongruously, I awoke to loud strains of the song 'I Don't Know What Love Is,' coming from a hut where I was told a sound enthusiast lived. Breakfast was two large dry biscuits and a glass of cordial as I contemplated my isolation and the idleness the locals seem to relish. I could detect no sense of future planning or a will to change anything. I washed in a bucket of cold water drawn from the communal tap but was unaware of others washing at all. The steady stream of men women and children moving along the road all had mud caked to their legs because their bare feet provided better grip on the wet mud that I found so dangerous. The natives made no complaint and exuded an air of carefree happiness. The previous day, a group of five women and a number of kids had sat happily chatting on the side of the road in the rain all afternoon. While the kids played, the women offered their wares for sale, a hand full of beetle nuts.

At the aid centre gate, I saw a boy of about eight whose eyes were streaming with a mass of yellow infected matter. Predictably, he had ear problems as well. He was barely able to see and obviously in pain. I asked what treatment was intended. Alfred said they had tried antibiotics but since they failed to cure the eyes, he had decided it must be a congenital problem. There was no eye wash or eye drops and as we spoke the father wiped the bulk of the yellow mass from the boy's eyes with his thumb. The blissful demonstrated ignorance of it all was frightening. I made a note to ensure the boy was transferred to the Goroka Hospital because, without treatment, he would surely go blind.

I was introduced to the village warden, Jack Asi. Being the warden made him responsible for the maintenance of the aid station and the position carried considerable status. I was pleased to be asked to dine with him that night. Jack was fluent in English having been educated and worked for years in Raboul as a policeman. He told me that until recently, boys up to age eighteen were taken to the men's house for instruction on their role as a man and the behavior expected of them. Similarly, girls were taken at puberty to the merri's house and the woman's role taught to them.

The bride price of a woman in this region was 3 – 5000 Kina. Ursula had cost Alfred 4000 Kina. The price could be supplemented with coffee, pigs and other tradable items. Jack Asi's wife had only cost 2000 Kina in Raboul and because her features where finer, he considered he had a bargain.

I asked about the process of payback. Jack and Alfred

explained that if a person in one Wontok is killed by another, the aggrieved elders of the first Wontok will demand up to 50,000 Kina from the other payable in 21 days. This money will be a burden on everyone in the Wontok. If default occurs, payback will result in the death of someone in that Wontok. Alfred said it works because everyone knew the price of payback. I was concerned so little was done to make the perpetrator accountable. Alfred argued that the perpetrator would be dealt with by his own Wontok.

Men, I learn, plan for retirement age 40 but the women work on. The men present laughed but agree readily, women do most of the work.

The rain stopped. I went for a walk through our part of the village. There were a number of families, each with its own cookhouse. Between the huts were the garden plots and a women was hoeing the ground and planting yams. Nearby an old lady was drying peanuts. She sat patiently on the side of a large canvas square on which the nuts were spread, turning them slowly to dry before moving to another side.

The rain began each day around four o'clock. When it started I put up the borrowed umbrella and walked back to the hut to prepare for the evening meal; I would be a guest of Jack Asi for dinner.

There were 14 people gathered in the cook house. Girls prepared the meal while the men talked among themselves. The elementary school teacher in Kamila was there and he explained he was only one of three teachers who managed about 20 kids in each of the years 7, 8 and 9. I put the question to him that since the Salvation Army would ask me what it was that the people of the village needed most; he might put it to the assembled people. This resulted in an animated exchange and he informed me that they would discuss it after dinner and let me know their decision the next day.

I noticed the girls were cutting up an enormous African yam. It was almost a metre long and 150mm round. The meal consisted of rice, chicken boiled with pumpkin tops, pumpkin, yam and Maggi noodles. The food was cut up on the dirt floor and rinsed in old fuel containers containing water. I was feeling a little embarrassed for I was uncertain when to leave for so far while in the cooking huts I had not eaten with anyone. Jack arrived and livened up the proceeding with his open, direct manner of communication. We discussed how Danny, Major Kenoti's son, would raise his bride price which apart from cash would require many pigs. I suggested they breed more which met with unexpected interest for they said they had no experience at breeding pigs. They were used to buying individual pigs from others, but not joining them and I explained how it might be managed.

As the guest of honour I was presented with a can of Fanta. When consumed, the meal was handed to me and I was told by Jack it was time for me to leave.

While on the walk with Joe he told me hunting in the jungle was common but the only animals he knew was the cuscus and small deer which were generally shot with a bow and arrow. There seemed to be no attempt to conserve animals, timber or birds. The degree of ignorance in the face of the wanton destruction and clearance of land was deeply disturbing to me.

Gibsy, the teacher I had met the previous night, told me that after an animated chat, the people decided what they need most was a factory in the region to process their coffee and a lumber mill to let them value add their own timber. I am told this village was in ward five which contains eleven Wontoks, each with its border in the forest. A representative councilor was elected by each Wontok to the ward management.

Further talks with Jack and Gibsy revealed there had been a number of attempt over the years to have coffee processing plants but after establishment, all failed in time due to lack of interest and poor management. The timber situation was similar. The people of Kamila had once jointly owned an Australian built Lucas timber mill that they used for some time but another party simply took it away and no-one knew where or why it went? This was a common story, suspicious given the propensity for stealing in Papua New Guinea.

I found the week taxing as the family I was staying with were unfriendly and kept me at arm's length. I was told Major Kenotai intended to charge the health department for my accommodation and yet we had donated a liberal excess of food including ten pounds of rice and charged nothing for the dental service. Working alone in such primitive conditions, without my clothes, phone or even a book to read was confronting. To compensate I maintained my diary.

Friday came at last and I packed my three plastic bags of personal stuff and transferred them to the aid station. It was cold and wet but an assembly of about 50 people had gathered for the departure. I had anticipated seeing patients but Joe had told them we were not working. I packed my four cases and circulated among my grateful, curious, recently made friends. Eventually, Joite and Deeson arrived with a large load of huge cardboard boxes of AusAid medicines, half destined for another village while on our return to Goroka. After greetings all around and a brief inspection of the centre by Joite who evidently approved of what he saw, we loaded my equipment onto the truck with the boxes of medicines. Then, after an entreaty to Joite, 3 x 65kg bags of coffee beans were added followed by Andrew, Joe, his second wife and their baby who were piled on top for a bone shaking return to Goroka. This loading process had taken some time. I was surprised when I was about to take my seat in the truck by a presentation Ursula made to me of a beautiful billum bag she had made from natural fibre. The assembled people clapped as we parted. My mind was plunged into a mixture of love and concern for such a resilient people, trapped as they are within a culture unable to evolve because its structure was rigidly fixed.

On arrival in Goroka we dispersed our passengers. Joite and I bought rice, some sausages, Maggi noodles and biscuits in preparation for the next week before returning to the hostel about one kilometre from the town centre. Great news -- my missing case was at the airport. Relieved to be reunited with my clothes I was returned to the hostel where, with a wave, I was left to cook my sausages, rice and noodles and spend the weekend -- this time with a book.

The Salvation Army hostel was on a large block high above a fast running river. There was an office block, a church, the manager's home and numerous small bungalows for staff clustered to the rear of the two storied hostel. In my room there were two single beds, a kitchenette with a bottle gas stove and a shower-toilet. There was no hot water. Having not had a shower for a week, I asked if I could use the shower in the office unit the Major used. With reluctance, he agreed.

So began the first of three weekends in exile within a church run hostel designed to teach and accommodate people, mainly men, wishing to be pastors in the Salvation Army. I was advised not to venture beyond the compound because it was too dangerous. Showered and wearing clothes that fitted, I persuaded different male visitors to accompany me up town where I was able to buy a pile of books in the second hand store. There were no book shops or newsagents as we know them in Australia. Apart from newspapers that only a few can afford or read, there was a total absence of reading matter everywhere I visited. I read in the Nation paper on Friday the 2nd September that Dr Mathias Sapuri, former president of the Papua New Guinea Medical Society, was now under investigation for the misuse of society funds totaling 1 million Kina.

CHAPTER 31
THE CHURCH

The Salvation Army staff, while pleasant if asked a question, kept me at arm's length. Seemingly, their preoccupation was with the religious agenda of the church. Each weekend of my stay, a large number of people would attend for religious training or to celebrate some aspect of Christian life. One Saturday there were more than 90 men from the region listening to a sermon by Major Mathias where he explained the role of women from a biblical point of view. His literal interpretation involved God fashioning a women from the rib of man which he emphasised, was the authority for asserting that women were created to serve men. In view of what I had seen so far in Papua New Guinea and my experience in the wider world, I thought this teaching to be ridiculous and inappropriate. Quite apart from being logically unsound and consequently wrong, it was the women of Papua New Guinea who maintained almost all daily existence.

In my opinion, the teaching of dogma generally, given the need instead for basic education aimed at improving the reasoning capacity of the people, served only to retard the process while reinforcing the view that God would provide, which quite clearly, he did not.

Despite the safety warnings about walking into the town I decided to do so because I wanted to buy local phone cards because my Optus phone had given up. My excursion was strategically planned with the need for a suitable toilet such as that provided by the Bird of Paradise pub. Shopping and toilet over, I enjoyed a gentle rehydration before tackling the hazardous streets to return. Walking briskly back, I was picked up by the police who said it was too dangerous for me to be at large. They were a jovial lot who were happy to return me to the hostel, but in general, they were distrusted by the public for corruption and the frequent violent bashings that sometimes were fatal.

On Monday morning I was picked up and transported to another village, which for my third week was Omkolai in the Simbu province north west of Goroka. We would leave the highway to Mount Hagen at Kundiawa and travel west high into the mountains. Our Toyota Utility was loaded with a large plastic water tank and my gear. The road was busy with endless huge trucks laden with containers and building materials, destined for use on the country's biggest industrial adventure, the Liquid Natural Gas project in the North West. We weaved around huge deep potholes, traversed waterways and one way lanes where the road had fallen away, all the time rising higher. Despite the presence of heavily armed police, we encountered two small groups of locals who demanded payment for them to remove obstacles they had placed to stop us. I don't know what Deeson said to them but we were allowed to continue without payment, possibly, because he had no money to give.

At Kundiawa, we stopped for a break. It was as squalid, crowded and dangerous as any village I had seen. On leaving we turned west from the main road and climbed for an hour and a half before reaching the aid station which was perched on a corner of the road overlooking a large secondary school and a flat that served as a meeting place for daily markets. Willing hands picked up the water tank and carried it away. As I began to unpack my gear I realised the space I was meant to occupy in the aide station was too small to work in. I approached the school principal who was eager to help, saying many of his 700 students had dental problems and we were welcome to set up in the school library. The next day we saw 30 patients and extracted 36 teeth. The large number of patients obliged me to examine them in batches of three or four, injecting local anaesthetic and then recalling them later. The following day I set my record of 33 patients and 36 teeth extracted. Totals for subsequent days were only slightly less. The extent of dental neglect was disturbing and although my service was a help, I had no way of providing a preventive dental program. Almost all the extracted teeth were in an advanced state of breakdown, many with associated infections. One young woman had her front teeth missing. I asked her how she had lost them. She explained via my helpers that she had been in a fight with another woman over a man and her opponent had knocked them out to deliberately disadvantage her.

Max, the aid station worker had two wives, one of whom took him to task one night for perceived neglect. It was a noisy public affair that we found amusing, but Max didn't as she set him straight with wildly waving arms. I thought he was either brave or mad to have two wives living together with numerous children in and around the one small cooking hut. Assisting Max was Michael, the pastor who proved to be a big help to me. He was a pleasant fellow who spoke English well. He was worried because he had been advised by the Salvation Army that he must vacate the house he lived in with his wife and children. The house had been reassigned to someone else. Michael had nowhere to go and was deeply concerned for his family. He served me well, speaking to the patients in many languages and enlightening me on many aspects of the culture.

Early morning at Omkolai was especially beautiful. To the west, behind the school was a high mountain, lit by the rising sun and providing views through the mist from the valley floor far below to its cloud covered peak. As the fog slowly cleared, isolated huts and walking trails could be seen snaking into the untouched country beyond. I was told this land was occupied by a primitive and dignified people who were untouched by western culture and only reachable by walking - there were no roads into the region. One old man from the mountain walked in to us for treatment and, despite the presence of people versed in many languages, they were unable to understand him. Assisted by Michael pointing and the use of signs, I was able to extract the cause of his distress.

I was impressed with the school that catered for hundreds of boarding students. They were the children of the villages we had passed on the way in and to the north. James lamented it was a difficult task to run the school and worse, harder because he had not received the Government money allocated for paying the staff and feeding the kids for the first quarter of the year. It was now August. Again, the issues of lack of maintenance and hygiene were obvious and disturbing. In any case there was no-one with practical knowledge or money to repair basic infrastructure like toilets. I was obliged to use the staff toilet and found it to be a blocked disgrace, impossible to flush so one can only imagine the condition of the student facilities. On Thursday I received the message that Joite was unable to arrange our transport to return on Friday. The prospect of being marooned in Omkolai for a weekend was unacceptable so I spoke to James who agreed we could return to Goroka on the school truck which was scheduled to leave Friday morning.

On Friday morning I carried my baggage down to the school and watched the truck being loaded with oil drums, tyres, bags of coffee, numerous people including Michael and the luggage. At 10.30 a.m. we left. Our driver was Collins, a wizened character who was enjoying his supremacy over all. With me beside him and a man nursing a small child next to the door, the truck departed. We hurtled down the mountain with Collins at the wheel, casually chewing beetle nut and pointing out where only the week before another vehicle had gone over into the valley with the loss of all aboard. The day was hot and on arrival in Kundiawa we stopped and all but the man with the child and me dispersed leaving us to sit in the shade of the tray, anxious for the security of my equipment. The delay of an hour and a half in Kundiawa was due to the teachers on board who earlier in the year had worked on a census taking, now attempting to get paid for their efforts at the regional Government office.

The road was unbelievably bad, the common wash-ways and holes over a foot deep, some requiring the truck to stop and negotiate in first gear. Again, I heard the lament that Papua New Guinea became independent in 1975. The Australian Administration, they recalled, had been highly efficient and had it remained in place might only now mean Papua New Guinea was ready for independence. Instead, the country had gone backwards. We dropped off and picked up people until in Goroka, I departed. It had taken five and a half hours of driving time to cover the estimated 160km. I felt guilty. How and where were the other men and women of the party to obtain food, wash and find a warm bed? My diary records that all I had to eat and drink that night in the hostel was two small cans of meat, dry biscuits and cordial - but the bed was clean.

On Saturday, I was woken early by David Temeny, an educated national normally based in the Salvation Army office in Port Moresby. He told me he had been instrumental in my coming to Papua New Guinea. Deeson arrived and together they drove me up town to buy food for the coming week using the 150 Kina he had been given by Joite. While in town I had a haircut by a lady who knew with certainty that she could fix me up with female company. She was insistent, seeming to regard my single status as an un-natural state that she could remedy easily. I declined her help and left 30 Kina lighter and almost bald.

Michael had come with us to be part of a rally for pastors being run the next weekend. He was hopeful of learning what the church had in mind for him and his family. He had no luggage or money so I gave him the warm coat and the shirts I no longer needed plus money for his return to Omkolai on the public motor vehicle. He told me he was a friend of Mathias and together they were hopeful of publishing the result of their research into the voodoo and tribal superstitions of the people in the region. I was concerned for Michael. He was 36, had four children, no money and untrained for anything but the church. Being from a Wontok near Kainantu, he was unable to obtain employment in Goroka because positions were only available to those who belonged to local Wontoks.

On Sunday peace was broken at 7 a.m. by amateur musicians using the electronic organ and guitars in the church. Joined later by a large congregation they sang a repetitive chant, 'This is the way we cope.' My diary reads, 'It's no bloody wonder when there is so little prospect of improvement in their living conditions.' I was saddened by it all and noted that because the pastors know so little of the world beyond religious teachings, their leadership, of necessity, must be ineffectual.

Mathias explained that the Wontok system, together with the 860 independent languages results in a distrust and suspicion bordering on hostility that made it difficult to teach or obtain cooperation. I heard him warning the budding pastors not to get big heads when they obtain positions of power and influence.

The latest report of murder and mayhem in Papua New Guinea was a weekend massacre in Kainantu where 23 bodies were found hacked to pieces and left scattered in the surrounds of the town. It was a payback war complicated by drugs and drug lord involvement. Police were flown in to restore order. Just after we had left weeks before, a policeman had been shot in the back and another man killed.

I invited Michael to use the spare bed in my room rather than sleeping rough because on Monday he was to return to Omkolai while I was to be picked up and taken to a village called Kwongi. That evening Michael found a large rat hiding behind my stove and said that people often ate them. He was grateful for the coat, shirts and money I gave him.

For myself, I was annoyed that I was dumped in the hostel each week seeing it as a waste of time. I had gone to Papua New Guinea to work and did not want to be left alone in a hostel each weekend. Then I received a message from Major Heather Gill, a visiting Salvation Army officer there to audit the books. Joite, she said, would pick me up at 10 o'clock Monday morning.

Monday 1.10 p.m., I was still waiting and stewing over the lack of efficiency that was seriously detracting from the number of people I might see. Joite arrived unrepentant at 1.40 p.m. without the additional needles and anaesthetic I had asked for. This could mean that I might be limited if the demand for service was high in Kwongi. Further, Joite had no assistant for me. Instead, Deeson and I drove alone to Kwongi. It was first gear all the way following the valleys through well developed coffee plantations and occasional villages until we reached the medical centre, perched on a projection of the mountain overlooking a deep valley.

Like the offices I had seen before, it was grubby. Instruments lay uncovered on a bench. There was no means of sterilization and used medical refuse spilled from the wastepaper basket. I was shown to where I was to sleep in the new larger building next door, but there was no linen or blankets. James, the aid worker, explained his wife was away until the next day and registered his surprise that I had no cooking facilities. I had bought an ample supply of food because I knew by now the food left behind was regarded as compensation for cooking my food. I was introduced to John, an intelligent upstanding man of 70 who had visited Australia and America during the 1960s. John assisted James to cook our evening meal using the standard formula. Instead of the bed I was shown at first in the incomplete new aid building, I was offered a bed in the small room at the rear of the hut occupied by James, Hanna and their young child because he said, it was the only place with a light.

I explained to James that I would like to boil my instruments as we used them. Reluctantly, he lit a fire in the cook house. For a time I was able to boil the instruments, but he begrudged the use of the firewood used and gradually withdrew cooperation. The table I worked on was high and designed for giving birth.

My long standing back problems began to play up due to the difficulties of having to stand on my toes in order to access the patient's mouth when working. James consulted in the opposite end of the same small room.

His patients presented with the usual variety of illnesses including a dislocated finger and a girl of not more than 15 who had already delivered a dead child and who was six months pregnant again. She weighed 45kg. James rightly decided she was too small to deliver safely and referred her to the Goroka Hospital.

A man approached me and asked me to read a letter written in English. The writer claimed to have found a mountain of huge wealth gold and diamonds. I passed it back but he pressed me saying it was real and that I should go with him to see it. I told him I was not interested and he became annoyed and insistent, unable to comprehend my lack of interest.

There was an elementary school just behind the centre and Jenny, a teacher there, came down for a chat. She told me the most difficult aspect of teaching for her was the lack of student motivation, in particular, of males.

A new aid building had been erected next to the old aid station but as yet was unused for reasons difficult to understand but involved superstition. The construction cost had been more than 100,000 Kina. The building had been plumbed for water to the sink, but was yet to be supplied. A pipeline had been laid running back through three villages to the supply point about 2km further up the mountain. It had only been part laid and supply had not reached Kwongi. After work the next day, because of the pleasant weather, I invited John and Pastor Dominic to take me on a walk to the source of the water. James and his wife Hanna joined us. As we climbed, we came to a sequence of well run, small orderly villages along the ridge. They had an air of pride about them. The 35mm poly water pipe ran through the centre of each village, but the lower sections were yet to be joined and covered. At the highest village the children were playing with the feed pipe which was gushing water and unconnected; a source of great amusement and excitement. I did not see the waterfall which I was told runs all year.

As we meandered back enjoying the scenery, we skirted a valley below in which another village could be seen. My guides pointed out that a year earlier, the pastor there had been brutally murdered, first by disablement by a slash to the legs with a bush knife, then shot. On investigation, the culprit was a cousin who was covetous of the pastor's wife together with a bizarre story involving superstition.

Sadly, as we passed through the villages the men in each were playing cards in the open. In conversation with Dominic I learned that he was the local court reporter because in early life he had travelled Papua New Guinea as a Government parole officer. He explained that next day his brother Bill, the region magistrate, would hear five charges at the small office outside the medical centre gates. Where possible the magistrate would issue orders to those found guilty to do community work. For instance, this might involve burying the last sections of water pipe. Dominic told me of a local boy who had been beaten by police who was later awarded 2500 Kina for crippling damage to his lumbar spine.

My diary notes read, 'I don't know if it is ignorance or not but Hanna cooked fish for everyone but me, despite my bringing loads of food for the week.' At 6.55p.m., long after they had all eaten, James asked me what would I like Hanna to cook. I suggested some noodles. Feeling a little peeved by such thoughtlessness I record that although some show gratitude for help, others are so used to handouts they don't appreciate anything.

James was called to a woman who had fainted on the Public Motor Vehicle while returning from Goroka. He placed a drip and left her unattended for an hour. When I asked what her blood pressure was, he said he didn't know so decided to go back and check it. Diagnosis, and consequently treatment, was often misplaced, but the people accept without question whatever is offered,

A man fell and cut his hand while drinking that evening. No attempt was made to wash the wound or clean it out before it was injected with local anaesthetic and sewn up. It took one and a half hours with no less than four people in the tiny room all talking at once. The instruments used were not sterilised and when used were left on a bare wooden bench until required next.

I had noodles for breakfast and then extracted a tooth before packing for my return to Goroka. James told me the truck was on its way and expected at 9.30 a.m.. At 10.45 a.m, Joite and Deeson arrived. We loaded my bags and then a large long load of sawn timber belonging to James for transport to his other home near Kainantu.

Jenny the teacher, Dominic and John came down to join the crowd assembled for me to leave. I was moved and record how strange it was to be able to get so close to some people in such a short time. I took photos of the children and we left at 11 a.m.. The leaving moved me deeply. There was so much that could be done. Fortunately, because the truck was heavily loaded, our trip out was more comfortable than on the way in because we travelled much slower. I would not miss the toilet or the cooking.

My 'straight talk' with Joite about inadequate food, lost time and the inability to sterilise equipment brought about a welcome change of attitude and he organized a lunch on our return to Goroka. The party included Joite, Deeson, John, myself and a man who accompanied us in. The meal was a Papua New Guinea version of Kentucky Fried Chicken and the best meal I had eaten since our pub meal in Kainantu. At the hostel I extracted some teeth for a gardener before boiling all the equipment and packing for my return to Port Moresby the next day. Joite presented me with a lovely card and a tea set. I was moved because from my point of view I seemed to have done so little to alleviate such a huge problem. The gift was unexpected and renewed my mixed feelings about such wonderful people.

Henry, whose wife Cathy was the housekeeper of the hostel, volunteered to take me to the airport at 9am next day to allow plenty of time to book in for the 10.40 am departure. After push starting the Toyota Dyna truck, we set off accompanied by a group of children in the back. When checking in I was allowed 16kg of excess luggage and charged 430 Kina for the balance. Eventually the plane arrived and after loading quickly, we left at 11.40 a.m. to arrive in Port Moresby at 12.45 p.m.

CHAPTER 32

PORT MORESBY

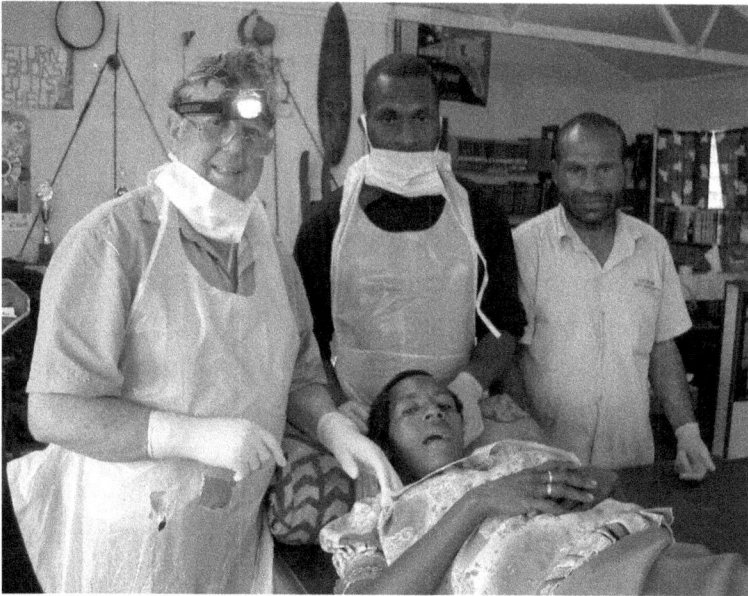

Charlie met me and we drove to the Salvation Army headquarters in Angou Drive, Boroka, a suburb of Port Moresby. It was Saturday so the headquarters was closed. Behind the multistoried office building was a large school and some living quarters, to which I was taken. While the school buildings looked modern and well kept the old building into which he took me was third world standard. Having realised I was to be left here alone until Monday I protested and made it clear this was not what I had been promised by the

Salvation Army in Australia. Charlie deflected my complaint by deciding to take me shopping explaining as he did so that visitors usually provided for themselves. I told him I would call Rita Brown in Australia on Monday. Charlie became agreeable and offered to take me on a drive around the city.

Port Moresby was not as I had imagined. The port was a small harbour nestled below a steep hill on which the principal commercial buildings of the old town are built. The waterfront to the east is called Ella Beach which is overlooked by many large homes set well back on the low hills overlooking the water. The rest of the city lies a kilometre or more to the north behind the hills and is accessed by roads that complete a broad circle from the sea to the suburbs. There were many large markets operating and all looked more crowded and dangerous than those in the provinces.

The Boroka shopping centre was literally over the road from the Salvation Army headquarters but I was warned not to walk the streets or enter the shopping centre without an escort. Confined like this, there was little to do but cook rice and noodles and read, incongruously, the biography of Patrick White by David Marr.

I had not anticipated being confined to a site by security guards or living in dilapidated third world conditions alone with inadequate food. Sunday began with a glass of water and two dry biscuits before a woman came to the door and explained that the toilet was blocked and the water turned off. Luckily, I had just had a cold shower. I went for a walk around the Salvation Army complex. An attendee of the church invited me to the service which was in full voice next to the main building. I declined. Too dangerous to leave the compound; unable to contact my family and let down by the

Salvation Army, I was angry. Charlie called to say he would pick me up at 8.30 a.m. on Monday morning.

Charlie arrived at 9.20 a.m. and informed me I was expected to attend a morning-prayer meeting in the headquarters building. While in the office I phoned Sydney and voiced disapproval of my treatment in Papua New Guinea. Rita Brown agreed it was not what had been agreed to and assured me she would take the matter up with management. In the prayer meeting I was welcomed and a thank you offered for my services by Colonel Webb, who then had photos taken of all present because the staff had new uniforms. I thought someone in the management of the Salvation Army in Papua New Guinea might be interested in what I was doing and the problems I was having, but they evidently preferred to remain ignorant of the medical service run in their name. Of course, they knew there were difficulties but it was plain the focus of management was with the religious agenda; Charlie was the manager of the medical division, he would deal with the problems.

My new driver for the weekly visits out of Port Moresby was David who took me down to the commercial business centre to buy two additional boxes of local anaesthetic and a box of needles. The seven boxes I had taken were almost gone. The usual food supplies were bought at a supermarket and we left for Kokorogoro. David estimated it would take three to four hours. On the way we passed a number of villages, including Borogaina, where I was scheduled to stay the following week. The road was so bad beyond Borogaina that the Public Motor Vehicles terminated there. This meant that for supplies all people to the north, including the aid workers of Kokorogora, had to walk the steep 30km of slippery, impossible to pass when wet track. I was fortunate, the track was partly dry and our four wheel drive vehicle was able to pass – just.

Surprisingly, the aid station at Kokorogora was the biggest and best equipped of all I had seen. It had been built with money supplied by Australia and displayed a plaque to say so. Michael and his wife Anna were the station officers, assisted by a young man, Elvis. This village of about 1300 people was built around a small level plateau which provided the only playground for the children who attended the combined primary and secondary schools built on one side with the hall and aid station opposite. Fran, the primary school teacher, was a charming lady who was attempting to provide a meaningful education to the poorly motivated children. The school had no windows and a beaten earth floor. A short shelf in one room held the school book collection. Fran was trying to teach a combined grade class of about 40 children. She had two children of her own and lived alone because her husband worked in Port Moresby and disliked Kokorogora.

The aid station had one inpatient, a baby about 12 months old who was adopted after being abandoned by the mother. The new parents were caring and deeply concerned for the child who had bacterial meningitis, a common secondary event to malaria infection. The child was responding well on a chloramphenicol drip despite appearing to be underweight and undersize.

The rain started at 5.15 p.m.. Anna enthusiastically prepared a meal with the rice, tinned meat and sausages we had bought with us. At 6.30 p.m. Michael started the generator, which ran until 10 p.m. to provide the family in the centre light.

The next morning Elvis was ill with a headache and fever

that he thought was malaria contracted in Port Moresby weeks before. I began to see patients until later in the morning when I was asked to speak to the children of the school in an attempt to improve their motivation. I tried to explain the importance of obtaining an education but felt silly because the children speak mainly pidgin. Despite the language difficulties, some did ask questions I found encouraging. I discussed the issue of language in the school with Fran who said that although they tried to speak only English at school, it depended mainly on what was spoken at home.

The centre was almost out of water. They found a little for me to wash in. Apparently a pipe on the roof had been broken some months before and there were no tools or materials to repair the problem. I discussed this with Charlie, who made it clear he had no intention of having it fixed.

Demand for my services was slow and I saw about 12 patients each day. Boredom set in for me, as it had for the other staff. They wished to be relocated because they had so little to do. They were obliged to laze about with nothing to do - no radio, tools, books or curiosity. The five hour walk to Borogainer for supplies was a further disincentive, especially when raining. The road was little more than a track and the earth like ice when wet. To meet the Public Motor Vehicle in Borogaina it was necessary for the nationals to leave Kokorogoro at three in the morning. After a day in Port Moresby the return trip was in the dark, carrying all their food and supplies. A constant flow of people carrying a large load and accompanied by children passed the centre while making this journey.

Elvis and Michael shared harrowing stories with me about the delivery of babies. They had to deal with a wide range of medical problems and seemed to cope well. I was amazed by the lack of infection control or even attention to basic hygiene. This station was the best equipped yet, but like the others, it had no water supply or equipment to sterilise instruments.

The rain, although desperately needed after a long dry spell, added significantly to the sense of isolation. Without books, radio, TV or water, perhaps living for these people becomes a process of endurance that fosters boredom, lethargy and perhaps, belief in voodoo and superstition.

Anna had a phone call from Charlie to tell us David would come and stay the night and take us out the next morning. Meanwhile, Michael had to circulate the news that the malaria control people would arrive soon to educate people on the latest methods of mosquito control. I was told the new regime of preventive medication would include a combination of chloroquin, quinine and something new that would improve treatment significantly. It began raining heavily. We feared David would be unable to get through, but he arrived at 7.20 p.m.

We left next morning at 4.30 a.m. in darkness, having already packed the vehicle with goods and people; Anna and child, Flora, a male teacher, David and me. The road was greasy and mainly downhill. It took an hour and a half to reach Borogaina, where we left my dental gear in preparation for the next week. In all, it took more than three and a half hours for us to reach Port Moresby where we let off passengers before going to Charlie's home. This house was the property of the Salvation Army. The large house owned by Charlie and his wife Anna had been let for an astronomical rent in the region of Port Moresby occupied by various embassies and the university.

Charlie said we were going to visit the Kokoda Trail site the following day. I spent the remainder of the day shopping for more second hand books before being returned to the quarters in Boroka that I had occupied the previous week.

With Charlie's family aboard the Toyota utility, we drove to Owens Corner to visit the Australian memorial commemorating the southern end of the Kakoda Trail over which our soldiers had fought the Japanese in World War Two.

Owen's Corner was a grassy knoll furnished with picnic facilities and overlooked the jungle covered mountains through which the trail ran to the north. On the rim of the knoll, astride the start of the trail was the Australian memorial to the heroic deeds of the Allies. Designed as a symbolic gateway, it consists of six poles that at ground level display a plaque for each Australian State, topped by a horizontal beam connecting the six states. This fitting memorial was designed by Dr Ross Bastion, a dental colleague in Melbourne, Australia.

From July 1942 to January 1943, the destiny of Australia was in dire peril from a Japanese invasion force that intended first to occupy Papua New Guinea, and then mainland Australia. In that seven month period there was a vicious struggle as the Japanese Army thrust south from the northern coast of Papua New Guinea to meet the determined resistance of the Australian and American forces who met them head on. The casualties listed on the memorial record the death of 1,200 Australians, 900 Americans and 12,000 Japanese. Quiet contemplation of the hell that reigned at that time is almost certainly what those who fought would recommend before entering into another war.

Sunday 11th September; I had dry biscuits and peanut butter for breakfast. There is nothing to do for the day but read. The site was empty apart from security staff and they insisted, it was too dangerous to leave. By 9.30 a.m. on Monday I had not seen or heard from anyone so I ventured to the Salvation Army office where I was briefly interviewed by a young girl asking superficial questions about what I had come to do after which my photo was taken. When David arrived we completed the now routine weekly shopping and left at 12.30 p.m. for Borogaina with Anna and her child in the back of the truck. On arrival, I was introduced to the health workers George, Geoffrey and Mathew. They eagerly told me they were paid about 400 Kina per fortnight out of which 60 Kina was subtracted for rent, 3 Kina tax and 40 Kina to savings. George, more senior, received 540 Kina a fortnight which left him with about 400 Kina on which he and his wife lived with three children. Like all other health workers, their own home was far away. To work, they live in the centre they were assigned to. They complained strongly about paying 60 Kina per fortnight for accommodation such as that we were living in. There were no cooking facilities, running water or refrigeration. The walls of every room were covered in black mould. They cooked on an open fire on the ground beneath the raised rooms we slept in. While cooking we sat on rocks around the fire attempting to keep warm and dry, for it rained every night and the wind was cold.

On Tuesday it was raining heavily. I met Rita, the senior and better trained health worker. She lived alone with her two children in the hut adjacent to ours. She was unhappy with the lack of maintenance and the poor condition of everything. Like Anna, who had had to walk on with her child to Kokorogoro the previous day, she felt outraged that they were paid by a cheque they had to pick up in person at the Boroka office.

This obliged them to spend money and time they could ill afford aboard the Public Motor Vehicle. They told me it takes the Salvation Army office at least an hour to pay them after which they have to go to their own bank which can easily take another hour to serve them. On receiving their money they then have to complete the weeks shopping before returning on the Public Motor Vehicle to their workplace.

The indifference of bank staff and other officialdom to fellow nationals is a practice I can confirm from personal experience. It was hard to believe the lack of courtesy I saw extended to customers. On one occasion I was in mid discussion with an officer in the Goroka post office when he left to have a smoke outside. When he finished smoking he returned to complete our conversation.

Many patients were expected on Wednesday because the centre served a collection of villages, including some further along the river. The villagers traveled in by canoe or outboard boats. The staff aimed to deal with vaccinations and an instructor coming to teach the health workers how to insert intra uterine devices. In addition, there were the patients with dental problems I would see.

I heard David Temeny, who I had met in Goroka, was fortunate to survive an attack by rascals in Port Moresby a week earlier. Almost over the road from the Marpang hostel, he had been driving a car in to a compound and while waiting for the gates to open, he and his fellow occupants were held up by rascals armed with bush knives, axes and a hand gun. With presence of mind, he had been able to barge through the gate without injury. Reports of this kind were heard almost every day.

I note the absence of filters and covers on the water tanks

which would prevent mosquito's breeding in the water tanks attached to the huts. However, the significance was lost because there were so many like issues and so little prospect of fixing them. Rita told me that her requests over the past four years for oxygen for the revival of sick people have never been answered.

The demand for dental service was high. I saw many patients who presented with familiar problems. Although chewing beetle nut is unsightly and corrosive of tooth enamel the damage done did not seem significantly greater than what I saw in the general periodontal condition of people who did not chew beetle nut. I had been warned there was a high incidence of oral cancer in Papua New Guinea but so far I had not detected any.

After work one afternoon in Borogainer I went for a walk to the river about 2.5km away and saw people from villages up the river jockeying their small craft on the fast running wide river. To disembark they had to paddle in against the three metre high mud bank and using a few irregularities in the face of the bank, clamber up. It was a dangerous but routine process for these people who seem incapable of complaint about such trifles. What bothered me was the rubbish strewn about the rubber trees dotted along the river bank.

We planned to return to Port Moresby on Thursday because the Friday was a public holiday to celebrate Independence Day. On the Wednesday evening the staff made their position clear to me. They were unhappy with the way the Salvation Army medical system was run. Management was poor and many questions went unanswered. They felt taken for granted and ignored. Maintenance was simply not done and Charlie refused without explanation their wish to be paid by direct transfer of their salary to their bank accounts. They all considered the living conditions unsatisfactory and the requirement to visit Boroko to be paid every fortnight put them under great strain and involved significant unnecessary expense.

At 10 p.m. a woman was admitted in labor. Her family and friends sat quietly on the grass outside. I noticed the generator was left on and the staff were worried. I went to bed but because my little room was next to another occupied by three of the men, I was aware of them talking and taking turns to be with the woman. I joined them at 4 a.m. and asked how the birth was progressing. The baby was in a transverse position. There was antenatal bleeding and the presentation was placenta previa. The staff was concerned for the patient and the baby's life. At 7am the staff was trying to make phone calls on their mobiles to the hospital in Port Moresby, a process limited by the amount of credit left on their phone cards. The short wave radio was not responding and from one phone call a story circulated to say the ambulance from Port Moresby would cost more than 400 Kina which the patient would have to pay. Finally, a call was made to the health centre 30km away in the next village closer to Port Moresby and their ambulance was dispatched. An open Toyota utility arrived a little after 8 a.m.

The woman was transferred to the utility and placed on a blanket in the open tray before departing with Rita and Geoff from our medical staff. Three or four other men joined the party for the ride. I wondered how many times a day someone in need of medical help was subjected to such pain and suffering for the same or similar reasons.

A little later my transport arrived. Accompanied by an assortment of passengers, I was returned this time to the

Marpang Missionary Hostel which was a welcome relief. At last I was able to shower, rest and read before having a meal of spaghetti bolognaise.

To celebrate Saturday 16th September 1975, Papua New Guinea's Independence Day, it seemed everyone was going to become involved. Masses of people assembled on the recreation reserves across the country, many in traditional costumes. Charlie and his family picked me up and we drove to the grounds of the Port Moresby University which was packed with a huge number of people there to see a gathering of tribes dressed in traditional dress, some performing dances and other customs. The heat was oppressive and the dust swirled. But nothing was allowed to interrupt the dancers. The celebration was only sobered by the admission by many older people that their independence had been premature and inopportune.

CHAPTER 33
FINISHING UP'

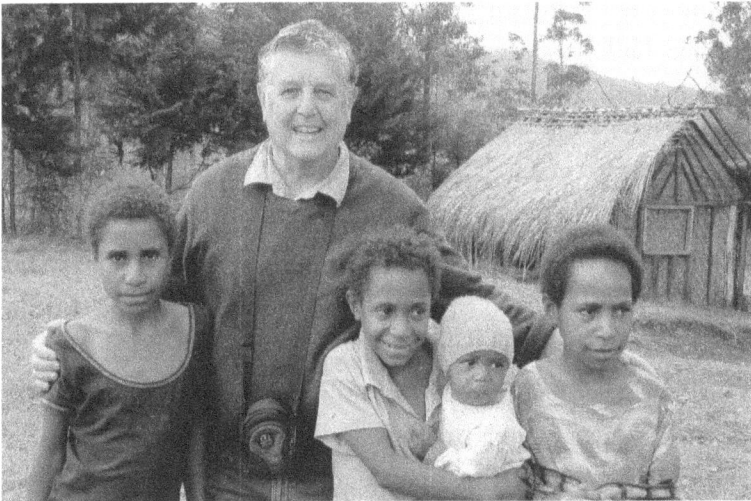

The plan for me was to live in Marpang for the rest of my stay. The next week I would travel back and forth each day to Papa, a village along the coast. For the final week I would work in the beach front suburb of Koki in the Salvation Army medical centre. This was welcome news because the accommodation at Marpang was clean, the meals good and varied and the centre always occupied by interesting people either coming or going to projects somewhere in Papua New Guinea.

The drive around the coast to Papa west of the city, took us past villages suspended over water while others clung to the shore line. All were depressingly alike with people living in dire poverty. The sanitary arrangements did not bear thinking about and people needing water drew from communal taps dotted at different points throughout. We passed huge compounds inside which the huge infrastructure required for the National Liquid Gas Project was being constructed and noted the elaborate measures taken to provide security.

The medical centre at Papa was large and almost new. Again, they were surprised when I arrived as advice of my service had not been sent. As the oppressively hot sticky days passed, trucks arrived and threw off large loads of sawn timber. We were told it was for a house to be built in the space between the back of the medical centre and the medical officer's house. The space was small and the intended result a bad choice given that the buildings would be so close. The site had been selected by Charlie who apparently ignored the extensive land available elsewhere on the block. That Charlie would be responsible for the building or location of a house or medical centre I thought amounted to negligence. The design and finish of the existing medical centre, finished only months before, was a deplorable example of what can be expected if untrained people are made responsible for spending so much money. The opportunities for graft and corruption that such decision making presented was a further issue only the naïve would condone.

The week passed slowly, with at most nine patients a day. The centre was barely above tide level half a kilometre from the coast in a wide open space. The main village of Papa lay a little further to the west. Without adequate forecasting of the free dental service, only a trickle of patients was seen. I enquired about the outcome for the woman in labor who had been transferred the previous week and was relieved to learn both mother and child had survived after a safe delivery in Port Moresby.

A boy had a small sore on the sole of his foot. George decided to open the wound and clean it although it was minor and not infected. The child, about seven, was held down by his burly father and mother while George injected the local anaesthetic into the sole of the foot. The child's screaming was utterly unforgettable. George was unmoved. He ineptly proceeded to open the wound with a scalpel and probe deeply. The child became utterly hysterical and his father slapped him hard many times before holding him down again. The process took more than half an hour and was totally unproductive. I will never forget or forgive the brutality.

I met many people while living in Marpang, most of whom were professionals working in some capacity or other. Quite a number were connected to Christian churches and passed through on pastoral work or church associated educational programs. Dr Duncan Mc Kinnon, a doctor from Bega in NSW, Australia, was returning from a week working as an anaesthetist in the hospital at Mount Hagen. He told me they had run out of halothane this visit. On his previous visit it had been oxygen. We discussed the probable incidence of HIV and he stated that he had no doubt at least 2 percent of the population was infected. Many women he had seen with HIV also had variants of the new resistant forms of TB now prevalent in Papua New Guinea. The new TB strains were of particular concern because treatment for the disease is prolonged and complex and exacerbated by the poor patient compliance with the medication regime.

I arranged a meeting with the Dr Mahood Siddiqi, the senior lecturer in dentistry at the University of Port Moresby.

He told me he was severely hampered by a lack of funding and a health department that did not accept responsibility for the sad state the department was in. He said he lacked dental chairs, laboratory equipment and materials which frustrated his wish to teach a wide range of dental techniques to a high standard. There was also a public dental practice component of the hospital run by about six dentists. They saw Port Moresby patients who presented with dental problems. A sign in the waiting area said 'We treat only the first 30 people to arrive each day.' I noticed while visiting at 1.30 p.m. only one dentist was working despite a large number of people in the waiting area.

My week at the clinic in Koki proved disappointing because, as with every other site I had visited, no prior advice had been given to the staff or local community. There was a list of names of people who wanted dentistry but despite Charlie knowing I was not equipped to do fillings, he failed to make this clear and further confounded the problem by insisting the department would charge 10 Kina for each extraction. To charge such a fortune when I donated all that was needed underlined the lack of compassion that seemed to exist between Nationals.

At breakfast in Marpang I met Tony Hall-Mathews, from Yungaburra, Queensland. His church had donated a banana boat and 40hp outboard motor to serve as an ambulance to carry patients between Pompondetta and Alitou on the North Eastern coastline. Tony was on his way to check out whether it had arrived and to arbitrate some civil rights groups claim they were owed Australian citizenship by virtue of Papua New Guinea once having been an Australian Territory.

I met Max and Meredith Moore during my stay in Marpang. They had visited a large school they had established in Lae six years before and were pleased to have found it thriving. With their skills, Meredith was a teacher, and Max with his knowledge of building and related practical matters a motivator and experienced manager of people. The Moore's typified the sort of people Papua New Guinea needed. He and Meredith had a deep understanding of the Papua New Guinea culture and I was fortunate to discuss and clarify issues I had experienced during my time there.

My daily patient tallies in Koki increased but I was unhappy that Charlie imposed the 10 Kina charge. The manager of Marpang asked if I would see a group from her church. I agreed and they came for treatment in a bus and were relieved when I waived the fees. They had no money. I was not allowed to do more, which irked me because I had gone to Papua New Guinea to relieve pain, not make money for the medical centre. I wondered - was it coincidence that the acting secretary was Charlie's wife?

My time in Papua New Guinea was coming to an end. Issues like extending my visa and my disappointment with the management of the Salvation Army in Papua New Guinea would remain unresolved. I tried instead to foster a relationship with a dental colleague in Port Moresby. Dr Richard Pickworth and his wife Sandra had gone to Papua New Guinea from Queensland many years before and now conducted a medical supply business in conjunction with his dental practice in the city centre. Richard had a history of providing a benevolent dental service while he and Sandra were sailing their large motor cruiser from port to port around the coast. I was taken to dinner by Richard and Sandra and was pleased to learn one of his regular patients was Sir Julius Chan, former Prime Minister and incumbent Governor of New Ireland, North East of New Britain. Sir Julius had expressed a wish for Richard to upgrade the old practice on the island. Richard further suggested to me that if this were done, I might like to contribute time and help with its establishment. If this were to proceed I was keen to assist because with Sir Julius in control the Island was reputably a safe place to work and could eventually allow us to take dental nurses to assist. I agreed and arranged to leave the bulk of my dental equipment with Richard on completion of my visit. My hope was that a colleague in Australia may welcome the use of the equipment in the near future or at least be available should I return because the expense and difficulty of taking dental equipment to Papua New Guinea was a disincentive to bringing it home. I had hoped on leaving Australia to find an opportunity to establish a clinic or to support an existing one in Papua New Guinea, but I was confounded by graft and corruption and now despaired apart from the slim chance of helping on New Ireland. I was only able to keep my kit together on this visit by insisting I knew exactly what was in it and if anything went missing I would be unable to complete my brief. I had seen covetous glances and fended off many requests for different items in the collection.

The next night Charlie insisted we go to dinner together to celebrate the completion of my time in Papua New Guinea. It was a subdued gathering; Charlie, Anna his wife and children, the finance officer Dessie and me dined at the Chinese restaurant in Boroko. I was genuinely sorry for Charlie. I was told later while in Sydney that The Salvation Army of Papua New Guinea had advertised for someone to run the medical division and Charlie was the only applicant. He was a graduate of the medical training school in Kainantu and an experienced medical officer. However, he had poor people skills, no administrative experience or practical aptitude with regard to maintenance of vehicles or buildings, nor an appreciation of hygiene or sterilisation. These deficiencies, together with the lack of informed supervision, offered little resistance to the reigning ethos of graft and corruption in Papua New Guinea, no matter how well intentioned the person in charge might be.

The facts were that while I was working under the umbrella of the Papua New Guinea branch of the Salvation Army, not one officer elected to talk to me about what I had seen or to discuss the problems I encountered. Nor did anyone in the system show any interest or concern for the deficiencies and grievances voiced by the health care workers. I could only conclude they had no interest in the problems or conduct of the medical department run in their name. I acknowledge I was thanked for my services and treated in a cordial manner by the senior management of the Salvation Army, but I was dismayed by their reluctance to engage in a meaningful dialogue over medical matters. Their preoccupation was religion.

In Papua New Guinea I was reliably informed that 80 percent of medical care was provided by church run organizations of all denominations. Funding for this was primarily provided by the Papua New Guinea Government which lacked the skills to provide the care directly. If what I experienced was any guide, the skill base and priority settings of people there because of their religious training and convictions was inappropriate for the delivery of a sound medical system founded on good medicine.

I had seen AusAid boxes of medicine worth a huge amount of money torn open and left part empty and unsupervised in almost every aid station. Was there an inventory or drug list? Who signs for the drugs and who are accountable for their use? The aid workers provide an account of what they have seen and the drugs used, but, who read and acts on the information provided? Prescription drugs are sold openly on the streets of Port Moresby.

I had seen more than 450 patients and extracted more than 500 teeth. In doing so I know I relieved pain. I returned to Australia with mixed feelings about what had happened. Was it the best and most efficient use of my time and resources? These questions remain unanswered. The conflicting elements of the culture that prevent a significant shift toward the modernization of living standards are an even deeper and more complex issue to comprehend. Random reported facts within Papua New Guinea have an overwhelming effect on the visitor. It is difficult to accept the alarming deaths and morbidity statistics and the fact that five women die every day in childbirth. Along with this is the emerging incidence of TB, HIV and hepatitis, the 860 separate languages, rampant superstition, polygamy and bride price, a primitive race of indolent uneducated men and women, extreme violence, endemic sexual predation, the plight of women, failed infrastructure, corruption and nepotism.

In mid November 2011, I attended a debriefing with the people with whom I had communicated prior to going to Papua New Guinea. We met in the Salvation Army headquarters in Sydney where Major's Rita Brown and Edith Cordell listened with patience to my verbal account before offering their apology for the breakdown of understanding that had occurred after I left Australia. Neither had anticipated I would be treated with such indifference and poor support by the management of the Salvation Army in Papua New Guinea. During the interview, I expressed my concern for the possible misuse of AusAid saying that I intended to contact the responsible people in Australia. The unexpected response was that they had such a person in the building. A short call was made and the AusAid liaison lady joined us.

I stated my concerns about the way I had seen aid handled and was taken aback when she countered that I was applying western standards and thinking to conditions prevailing in a third world country. The obvious response to that was made and endorsed by the other woman present. What other standards would or should be applied if ever improvement in the delivery of health care is to occur? I doubt the AusAid officer had ever been to Papua New Guinea, and if so, not into the provinces I had been. The point was, my visit to Papua New Guinea, despite the added difficulties and frustrations, was a unique and marvelous experience that obliges me to record and report to the people of Australia. The facts are, our nearest neighbor with a population of 6.7 million people, is a failed state and we are told almost nothing of its plight by the Australian media.

For the opportunity to serve, I thank the Salvation Army of Australia.

CHAPTER 34

IN CONCLUSION

The Papua New Guinea experience left me with deep concerns about the endemic corruption and the vulnerability of its people in a changing world. I had been unable to identify an opportunity to improve the delivery of a meaningful dental program in the face of barriers such as traditional land ownership, nepotism and corruption. All I could do was keep a watching brief and attempt to build on the few contacts I had made while in that country. Meanwhile, I would do my best to respond to the curiosity my visit created at home.

I was invited to talk about my Papua New Guinea experience by a number of Rotary Clubs and other organisations who all responded with interest and concern by asking a wide range of questions. The description of my time in Papua New Guinea accorded well with the scant political news of that country that features from time to time in the Australian media.

The February saw the resumption of my classes in Art, English Literature and Writing as well as my social life with family and friends. In April I met Jill Holmes – a widow of eleven years. This life changing event led to coffee then dinner and outings which led to the realization that we had much in common, including that we each had two sons. Jill had graduated with a Bachelor of Education majoring in Fine Arts to become a teacher of primary school children. The lonely spaces in our lives gave way to warm and loving companionship. As we planned a six week tour of the United States of America in September and October we agreed on return, to be married. It would align our affairs for this exciting final chapter of our lives while giving direction to our respective families.

Jill and I were married on November the 23rd 2012 at the 'Old Cheese Factory', Berwick. No pun intended. Our cup was overflowing. The weather had moderated for the ceremony and the formalities of the day concluded with generous speeches by our respective sons. All four congratulated us on our marriage and assured us of their best wishes for a long and happy future together. Witnessed by more than 92 family and friends, we were deliriously happy and optimistic for our future together.

In early 2014, Jill and I bought a new home in Mount Eliza. It was almost new, modern and spacious, with a nice outlook near the beach and close to the village centre of Mount Eliza and health services. An additional feature is that we have ready access via the freeways to the rest of the family.

As my story comes to conclusion I am conscious that many anecdotes and experiences have been overlooked in the interests of brevity and relevance to the story. Nevertheless, I see that my life experience accords with an observation made by the philosopher Frederick Nietzsche whose work was included in a book by Alain de Botton titled, 'The Consolations of Philosophy'.

Under the heading Consolation of Difficulties, Nietzsche wrote that difficulties of all kind are to be welcomed by those seeking to find fulfillment. Although sincere in sending his best wishes to friends, Nietzsche knew in his heart what was they needed. He wrote: 'To those human beings of importance to me, I wish suffering, desolation, sickness, ill-treatment, indignities, the torture of self-mistrust, the wretchedness of the vanquished'. These were some of the elements Nietzsche believed humans naturally need for a fulfilled life. He added an important detail: it was impossible to attain happiness without feeling miserable some of the time. The most fulfilling human projects are inseparable from a degree of torment, the source of our joys lying awkwardly close to those of our greatest pains.

And that has been my experience. I have been in many dark places which by perseverance and maintaining contact with friends were replaced by unimaginable better times. I have heard it said that we make our own luck but - I think that is only partly true. Bad luck is the wild card of life that can negate our best effort. We simply have to live with the possibility of its intervention and insure where possible against it.

Throughout my life, I have admired my Mother for her resilience and stoicism, qualities counterbalanced by her humour and courage. She had no time for petty drama nor did she dwell unduly on the past. Her pragmatism, love and commitment to family, selflessly drove her forward.

Sadly, too many people do not feel fulfilled, or find peace, love or companionship. For the first time in history the seriously disturbed and evil can possess guns, computers, fast cars, mobile telephones and collectively pose the threat of anarchy on fragile democracies.

Despite these concerns, I remain an incurable optimist. I revel in the daily growth of my grandchildren's vocabulary, the company of family and friends, a good book, delicious dinner or a beautiful rose. The generalizations above overlook the wonderful accomplishments of the vast majority who do find fulfillment and who hopefully, will learn to identify and veto those who are evil. My stepfather, David Dawson once said, when people are lost they should return to the land. I now understand and heartily agree. The closer one is to nature, I believe, the better the perspective and more real the life experience. It is the antidote for the human tendency to hubris.

A recurring disappointment on my farm in Drouin was that every year one or more of my finest trees would blow over revealing shallow roots inadequate to withstand storms. The explanation given was that with plenty of water in the soil there was no need to put down substantial roots. I suspect there is analogy to be recognized by parents raising children.

I cannot be prescriptive about how to live because although we can speculate what may happen in the future, events and circumstances will be infinitely varied. However, the virtue of valuing ones integrity, being courageous and persisting in adversity can be seen, I hope, in this story of my life's journey. And so the wheel goes around, difficult times being replaced by unimaginable better ones – such as I am living now.

I turned 74 in January 2015 and give thanks for my good health. I have lived a rich and varied life at the heart of which was always a commitment to family and friends for it was their love and support that sustained me.

ACKNOWLEDGEMENTS

The principle motivation for writing my story came from my friend of the late 1950s, Ed Featherston. Ed, who became a senior journalist, observed that my life story was a little different to most and urged me to put it in print. Once started, I thought it might be interesting to my family but he insisted, and I am hoping he was right, that it might help others to rise above their difficulties. For Ed's guidance throughout the writing, I am very grateful.

I am also grateful to the men who encouraged me, and who, by example, provided the blueprint necessary for a man to be regarded well for his integrity and wisdom. Men like my teacher Trevor McEvoy (dec), Bob Graham (dec), Tom Hobbs (dec), Dr. Don Hopkins (dec), George Nash (dec), Rudi Himmer (dec) and Jeff Wilkinson.

I would also like to acknowledge my brothers and sister who, despite the difficulties of our youth, have always put the family first, cooperating wherever possible for the common good. Similarly, to recognise my friends and associates who were ever ready to provide generous willing support when our lives and needs intersected, their contribution was invaluable.

In 1967 I married Glenys who gave me unwavering support for the next twenty-five years. Our two sons, David and Stephen, are integral to our mutual success. The boys grew up happy children who progressed to invaluable help on the farm and then became successful husbands, fathers and businessmen. There can be no greater reward.

After ten years alone, in 2011, I met Jill Holmes, a widow of ten years. Jill became the centre of my life and we married in 2013. Jill's sons, Adam and Tim, their wives and children, united with mine to become a family happily committed to mutual support. With love restored to the home, our present is a time of unimagined joy that exceeds all expectations. We regard ourselves as boundlessly fortunate while enjoying family and friends in retirement.

I would also like to thank the Editor of Brolga Publishing, Ms Tara Wyllie, who assisted in bringing this story to you.

DARE TO DREAM
PETER CLIFF

ISBN 9781925367041   Qty

                              RRP   AU$24.99   .....

Postage within Australia   AU$5.00   .....

                              TOTAL* $_____

                              * All prices include GST

Name:...

Address: ....

....

Phone:..

Email: ....

Payment: ❑ Money Order ❑ Cheque ❑ MasterCard ❑ Visa

Cardholder's Name:...

Credit Card Number: ....

Signature:...

Expiry Date: ....

Allow 7 days for delivery.

Payment to: Marzocco Consultancy (ABN 14 067 257 390)
                 PO Box 12544
                 A'Beckett Street, Melbourne, 8006
                 Victoria, Australia
                 admin@brolgapublishing.com.au

Be Published

Publish through a successful publisher.
Brolga Publishing is represented through:
• **National** book trade distribution, including sales,
marketing & distribution through **Macmillan Australia.**
• **International** book trade distribution to
    • The United Kingdom
    • North America
    • Sales representation in South East Asia
• **Worldwide e-Book distribution**

For details and inquiries, contact:
Brolga Publishing Pty Ltd
PO Box 12544
A'Beckett St VIC 8006

Phone: 0414 608 494
markzocchi@brolgapublishing.com.au
ABN: 46 063 962 443
(Email for a catalogue request)

www.ingramcontent.com/pod-product-compliance
Lightning Source LLC
Chambersburg PA
CBHW071404090426
42737CB00011B/1343